ELM

Ulmus americana, U. rubra, and others

IMPORTANCE: Ancient, historic tree of soaring beauty. An urban street classic. Battered by disease, the lofty American elm has been replaced largely by more compact, crossbred (hybrid) street elms. Handsome and hardy new varieties show promise.

FAMILY: Ulmaceae (Elm). GENUS: *Ulmus* (elm).

COMMON URBAN SPECIES: ❀ American elm (*Ulmus americana*) or white elm. ❀ Slippery elm (*U. rubra*) or red elm. ❀ Siberian elm (*U. pumila*). ❀ Chinese elm (*U. parvifolia*) or lacebark elm.

CLOSE RELATIVES: ❀ Japanese zelkova (*Zelkova serrata*).

TYPICAL CITY LOCATION: Arching over boulevards or dominating residential streets. Big elms in town squares and older park areas.

KEY FEATURES: *American elm and larger hybrids:* Massive tree with tall, straight trunk and wide fountain of branches forming a vase or wineglass shape. Heavy, rough bark.

Leaf 4–6″, shaped like spear tip, lopsided at base and edged with double teeth (large and small tooth together). Many slightly curving, parallel veins. Yellow in fall.

Small reddish flower in spring. Seeds enclosed in coin-sized papery oval, like tiny wafer. American elm seed clearly notched at tip.

Popular *Chinese elm* has thumb-length leaf and peeling bark with smooth flakes, orange patches.

AVERAGE MATURE SIZE IN CITY: 40–80′ high, 40–80′ wide, 3–4′ thick.

RECENT CHAMPION: *American:* 112′ height, 115′ spread, 24′ circumf., Grand Traverse County, Mich. *Slippery:* 100′ height, 119′ spread, 20′ circumf., Village Park, Sugar Grove, Ohio.

❧ FOUNTAIN IN SEARCH OF SURVIVAL

Most trees find life an ongoing struggle, but elms have been through a singular hell. Since 1930, they have been infested by an imported beetle (later a local one, too) and strangled by the fungus the beetles carry. In cities they have been choked by pollution particles, burned by road salt, stressed by traffic. Branches fall in ice storms and sometimes drop as if by their own will. Yet the elm family hangs on and we refuse to let it go; because in town as in countryside, we adore our elms.

A healthy American elm has a look and feel all its own. It rises high and straight before its trunk divides and the branches fan out and fall gracefully at the outer edges. Its distinctive shape—or "habit" of growth—provokes lyrical outbursts from tree lovers. Most liken it to a fountain or vase. Some call it a wineglass. A feather duster. One observer in need of a Rorschach test calls it a colonial woman standing on her head.

Given a chance, elms live three times longer than we do, grow 20 times taller, and work themselves into our hearts and folklore. Hardly a town is without its history of great elms or its Elm Street, the thirteenth most common street name in America.

Before Dutch elm disease—the real "Nightmare on Elm Street"— destroyed some 90 percent of the native species, American elms were the favorite tree of urban landscapers. They were massive, adaptable, tolerant of sea air, and resistant to city pollution. The tall trunk and spreading canopy of the elm made it ideal as a shade tree that cooled buildings and allowed trucks to pass beneath. A street blessed with rows of elms was like a cathedral. The reddish tint of the elm's small flowers perked up a town in early spring.

HUMBLED BY A FUNGUS

But bad things happen to good trees. In 1930, American cabinetmakers were importing elm logs from Europe, using their lumpy growths— "burls"—for the swirly grain you can still see on fancy furniture. However, a shipment of logs bound for Cleveland, Ohio, was found to be infested with European elm bark beetles, which spread to the American trees and still plague them today. The beetles carry a fungus whose nature, unfortunately, is to choke off the tree's food lines. This is Dutch elm disease—and don't blame the Dutch; they merely discovered the disease, in 1919.

The fungus—now carried by a domestic beetle as well—has killed some 100 million elms of varied species in America, a near wipeout. You will still see new victims in a city, an elm that wilts at the tips, turns yellow in early summer, and soon looks as if it were fried by radiation. In Sacramento, where the city is hard-pressed to care for its 1.7 million trees, a renowned stretch of 80-year-old elms is developing gaps like missing teeth.

The disease continues to spread—including to western and northwestern American cities that had long escaped it. But there is good news, too. A number of elms have resisted the fungus and lived into their hundreds. These "heritage" elms, including bicentennial elms of 200 years or more, are often protected by their caretakers and hand-treated against disease. In Minneapolis, about 87,000 (of 210,000) elms survived 20 years of blight into the mid-1990s, and the yearly loss was down to 2,500 thanks to attentive tree specialists. Technicians in Westmont Borough, N.H., clean, trim, and feed each tree to maintain one of the nation's last cathedral-arched boulevards of American elms. New

Typically pendant elm shoot. Background: the flat-topped, fountaining shape of older elm.

York City, for all its density and psychic stress, has managed to sustain a grove of American elms in Central Park as well as old elms scattered through the boroughs (though 1997 was a killer year for some 10 percent of the city's elms).

Resistant elms are used in creating tougher crossbred strains. The Morton Arboretum in Illinois has worked for a quarter century developing disease-resistant hybrids. Its 'Accolade' elm, a cross of Japanese and Chinese species, is a tough, handsome 60-footer. The 'Princeton' elm has done well since the 1920s. With fanfare on June 6, 1997, the National Arboretum planted its new American elm variety on the U.S. Capitol grounds. The results of long research, this 'Valley Forge' elm and a 'New Harmony' variety are expected to go toe-to-toe with Dutch elm disease. An official claimed they could "restore the American elm to Main Street USA."

GOOD DREAMS ON ELM STREET

Other agriculturists have been putting the elm back in Elm Street. Chemical insecticides have proved unsavory as a general approach to the disease, but constant crossbreeding of American elms with European elms, the small-leafed Chinese (lacebark) and Siberian elms, and other breeds are producing an American elm lite. Known by such nursery names as 'New Horizon', these hybrids may be less spectacular than the original, but they are street-tough—even in cold-weather industrial towns like Detroit—and elmish enough as wide-spreading shade trees.

But not everyone who loves elms wants them dominating the

streets again, especially not in rows that can fall like dominoes when disease hits. "Diversification" is the word in city landscaping these days, keeping the single-species epidemics at bay. Also, the elm's relatively shallow roots sometimes get rambunctious and push up sidewalks or reach into sewer lines. Elms share the bad reputation of so-called "hazard" trees, which occasionally and unpredictably drop heavy branches on people and parked cars. In England, where elm is the traditional wood for caskets, death by elm has a special irony.

HANDS-ON OBSERVATION

Seeing an elm from a distance yields the big drama; but the small parts of the tree give pleasure, too. The robust green and rugged texture of the leaf are the stuff of the great outdoors. The leaf's double-sawtooth edges are geometric marvels, as fine as if machine-tooled. The veins are like gently curving tracks. The leaf tip often ends in an elongated pennant. Even the leaf galls, when they appear, have character. Shaped like a cockscomb, each of these growths on a leaf's surface houses a mite. If you're not squeamish, open a gall and say hello.

Uneven base, double sawteeth, and long tip of the elm leaf. The American elm's seed-carrying samara has an open notch, as shown.

Leaf shape is one clue for identifying an elm, especially for species without fountainlike branches. At the base of the leafblade, one side begins higher up the leafstalk than the other, coming off the stalk at a different angle (see figure). This lopsided feature together with the double sawteeth says elm loud and clear.

But even before the leaves have sprouted, distinctive seed fruits mark the elm species. They take the form of a *samara,* a papery winged structure carried by the wind. The elm samaras, dime-size and round or tear-shaped, enclose a nutlike seed at the center. They cluster like blossoms on the elm branchlets and sail off like legions of flying saucers. The legions like to collect on windshield wipers and mix with curb trash in a flaky mush. But pick one seed up and examine it, and you'll have found new wonder in the city.

TREE WITH A PAST

Whatever its struggles with pests and abusers, the elm remains a cherished tree in Western culture. From its hard, cross-grained wood came posts, ties, and pilings in support of commerce; hubs and spokes that bore wheels across continents; hockey sticks that whacked opposing players.

In folklore the elm is known as a tree of sleep, of wisdom, of creation. Pregnant Swedish women hugged an elm to assure easy delivery. Like John Quincy Adams, the Clintons planted an American elm at the White House in the tradition of presidential families marking their tenure with trees. North Dakota honors the American elm as its state tree. So does Massachusetts, where this species played a role in the American Revolution: "The Liberty Tree" was a gathering place for the Sons of Liberty, a group of Boston colonists rebelling against British taxation. When the taxes were eased, the colonists hung lanterns on the elm branches.

Fame can have its price, though, even for trees. The angered British cut down the Liberty Tree in 1775. And in 1997 a troubled teen firebombed the champion (most voluminous) American elm, an eight-foot-thick, hundred-foot-high beauty near Louisville, Kans. It died, but an elm outside the federal building in Oklahoma City withstood the tragic bombing there in 1995. Named "The Survivor Tree," it lives on in a walled memorial.

SLIPPERY ELM

The bark of a mature American elm befits a power tree; it is thick and deeply ridged in interlacing diamond patterns. But it draws less attention than the inner bark of another urban elm: the slippery (or red, moose, or Indian) elm. The Iroquois called this tree "oo-hoosk-ah," for "it slips." And so it does, beneath the outer bark, where the new bark layer produces a mucilage famed as a medicinal.

Urban observers will find good sport in distinguishing slippery elms from other smaller city elms, but stripping the outer bark is against the rules. The tree would starve and the medicinal slime of the inner bark would be neither obvious to the amateur nor ready for medicinal use. Instead, seed and leaf give the two best clues in summer:

FROM A TO ZELKOVA

It may come last in alphabetical tree lists, but the *Zelkova serrata* (Japanese zelkova) has been a leading replacement for urban American elms. A member of the greater Elm family, it recalls the vase shape of the American elm, but hardly achieves the majesty of that species—perhaps an unfair standard. The zelkova and its varieties are relatively hardy, disease-resistant, and elegant in their own right. Growing to 40 to 60 feet in cities, the tree bears elmlike leaves, but with crisply cut single—not double—teeth. The fruit is like a malformed green pea. The smoothish gray bark sports subtle orange flecks and pinkish stripes and flakes as it ages.

■ The wings of the slippery elm samara are joined *without* a notch at the tip; the American elm seed has a definite open notch (see figure above, page 57).

■ The leaf of the slippery elm is sandpapery-rough on both top and bottom surfaces; the American elm is leathery-smooth on top, rough on bottom. The difference can be subtle, especially with so many elms of mixed breeding. Keep rubbing.

Processed from powdered bark, the various slippery elm medicinals—in teas, gruels, pastes, capsules, or liquid extracts—have been used to treat about every common malady and several exotic ones, including worms. One of the few ailments slippery elm does not address is its own—Dutch elm disease. The tree is highly susceptible. It is doubly at risk in America, with many healthy trees stripped to death for medicinal products. The righteous consumer must demand nonlethal harvesting of the bark—or stick with aspirin (once derived from willow bark, but no longer).

Sycamore (Planetree)

Platanus occidentalis, Platanus x *acerifolia,* and others

IMPORTANCE: The American sycamore is the nation's largest broadleaf tree, a forest giant that sometimes adapts to urban life. State tree of Indiana.

London planetree, the hybrid offspring of American and oriental sycamores, is the big shade tree of boulevards around the world. New York City's tallest street tree. Dominant street tree of Brooklyn, N.Y. Recognized by its distinctive peeling bark.

FAMILY: Platanaceae (Sycamore). GENUS: *Platanus* (planetree).

COMMON URBAN SPECIES: ❀ American sycamore (*Platanus occidentalis*) or western planetree, buttonwood, buttonball tree, whitewood, Virginia maple. ❀ London planetree (*Platanus* x *acerifolia*). ❀ Oriental planetree (*P. orientalis*) or eastern p. ❀ California sycamore (*P. racemosa*) or California planetree. ❧ Arizona sycamore (*P. wrightii*).

TYPICAL CITY LOCATION: *American sycamore:* Parks, large properties, wastelands. *London* and *oriental planetrees:* Plazas, squares, along streets. *California sycamore:* Streets, random locations.

KEY FEATURES: Large tree, wide-spreading branches. Outer bark peels away to create mottled shades, including tans, whites, grays, greens, and sometimes yellows. Parts of branches smooth and distinctively white or brightly dappled. Older trunk bark forms small squarish flakes.

Leaves are large, often 7–8″ long and wide; they resemble maple leaves but are duller green with woolly, possibly allergenic undersides. Leaf lobes number 3–5 on most planetrees, vary in shape by species; shallow on American sycamore, deeper for other planetrees. Leafstalk is hollow and fits over new bud.

Fruits, dangling from long, stringy stems, are 1″ thick, ball-shaped aggregates of feathery seed nutlets (*achenes*). *American sycamore:* 1 ball per string. *London planetree:* 2. *California sycamore:* 3–7.

AVERAGE MATURE SIZE IN CITY: *London planetree:* 40–80′ high, 1–3′ thick.

RECENT CHAMPION: *American sycamore:* 129′ height, 105′ spread, 49′ circumf., Jeromesville, Ohio.

❧ OLD SOLDIERS IN CHIC CAMOUFLAGE

When you spot a broad-leaved tree whose trunk or smooth branches wear mottled camouflage—shades of green, tan, and cream—you are looking at an American sycamore or one of its city-loving relatives in a group known as planetrees (genus *Platanus*). These sycamores wear the camouflage proudly, for it identifies them as one of the planet's oldest, largest, and most adaptable clan of trees.

Sycamores have been standing tall for some 100 million years, longer than most other forest giants. The hardiest individuals live for half

PLANETREE TALK

Sycamore nomenclature is anything but plain. Some people call sycamores planetrees, or planetrees sycamores. In Great Britain, the name "sycamore" (as in Shakespeare's "under the cool shade of a sycamore") has always meant a sycamore maple, not a planetree. However, when immigrants to America found the big planetrees of the eastern river valleys, they called them sycamores. This American sycamore is more accurately called a western planetree (*Platanus occidentalis*) to distinguish it from its ancient European/Asian cousin, the oriental planetree (*Platanus orientalis*). The names get muddled, but when called upon to sort them out, you can wisely make these points:

- All but the English sycamores are members of the Sycamore family (Platanaceae) and are correctly called sycamores or planetrees in common parlance.
- But in most of America, "sycamore" usually refers only to the American sycamore (western planetree), the eastern-forest native. In the West, the term might mean California or Arizona sycamores, two other distinguished members of the small planetree family.
- The London planetree, the dominant big-city planetree of America as well as Europe, is a spectacular east-meets-west cross between the venerable oriental planetree and America's own sycamore (western planetree).

a millennium. They can grow up to 175 feet high and 15 feet thick, three-fourths the bulk of champion California redwoods. And they grow commandingly on streets from coast to coast in the United States, as well as on roads and avenues around the globe.

LONDON PLANETREE RULES

A crossbreed of two legendary sycamore species, the London planetree is widely considered to be the world's most reliable city tree. Big, shady, and stylishly mottled, it has not only the charm to grace fashionable boulevards but also the grit to survive their poisons. It is the planetree you are most likely to see in cities, especially the cultivated variety 'Bloodgood'.

From the mighty American sycamore and the ancient oriental planetree came this hybrid, perhaps first in sixteenth-century Spain. Today, it rules thousands of the world's urban avenues and travelers' byways. Without a doubt, it rules London itself, where it has been planted at least since 1663 and now constitutes some 60 percent of the city's trees. Giants more than two centuries old shade the nannies strolling through Kensington Gardens. "Daredevil monoculture," one writer calls this reliance on a single tree type, but the hybrid (in a number of varieties) has proved its mettle by coming through the foulest episodes of London's befouled industrial epochs. Paris, too, has embraced the tree. And consider this: As the most common street tree of Brooklyn, N.Y., the London planetree rules the neighborhoods of that scrappy borough. How many living things can make that claim?

The London planetree got its name from London's love affair with the tree; but this crossbreed, along with crossbred relatives, thrives abundantly in the land of its parent American sycamore. Easily available from nurseries, it is widely planted in Philadelphia and Washington, D.C., including on the Capitol grounds. Manhattan ornaments its Rockefeller Plaza and Bryant Park with it. The treasured Jefferson Street canopy of Corvallis, Oreg., consists of 90-year-old London and oriental planetrees. Soaring London planetrees share streets of California's capital with western planetrees.

The London planetree and its parts are a feast for observers. The tan-gray outer bark, which cannot stretch to keep up with the tree's growth, peels away (*exfoliates*) in tubular curls and reveals patches of the smooth inner bark. The colors of this bark vary according to exposure to sunlight and species variety, but the London planetree will usually show a pretty olive green and sometimes a pale yellow among its mottle, even on the trunk. (American sycamores retain more of the flaky outer bark on the trunk; branches are smoother and show grays, tans, and whites.) All planetrees have enough bright white or colored patches on their upper branches to stand out strikingly from other

The sycamore's smooth inner bark can include shades of tan, white, green, gray, and yellow.

trees, even in summer. In winter, the wide-spreading and twisting, angular branches form a dramatic tracery.

LEAVES AND FRUIT

The warm season brings special sights. The leaves emerge creamy white before they darken to a muted green. Soon they spread like bat wings. Unique to the sycamores is the swollen, hollow base of the leafstalk and the way it fits like a candle snuffer over a pointy-headed little bud.

The leaf itself varies somewhat by tree variety, but it is big—four to nine inches square. With three to five tips (lobes) and large teeth on the edges, it resembles a sugar maple leaf. London planetree leaves have deeper indentations (sinuses) between the tips than leaves of the American sycamore, which look something like broad, webbed duck feet. Planetree leaves flutter prettily in summer, showing their lighter, fuzzy underside. The woolly fuzz, called "pubescence" in the blushless lingo of science, clearly differentiates the planetree leaf from maple leaf.

Most planetree leaves turn dull brown in fall. But something else has been going on to delight the eye. From the unspectacular spring flowers comes a fruit that marks the Sycamore family as clearly as its mottled bark and prompts the nickname "buttonball." Bucky Fuller could have designed this soft, textured sphere about the size of a Swedish meatball. Green at first and brown in fall, it is a cluster of hundreds of seed nutlets (*achenes*), each with a feathery fluff tucked inside the ball and a cap on the external end. Pluck out a nutlet and it looks

London planetree leaf, left, has deeper indentations than American sycamore, right. Two buttonballs (vs. one) mark London planetree.

like a fly for trout fishing. It is beautifully engineered for seed dispersal by wind when the ball breaks up.

The fruits are easy to spot because they dangle from long stringlike stems and usually cling through the winter. Moreover, the number of fruits per group provides the best clue for identifying the planetree types: *One ball:* Almost always American sycamore (western planetree). *Two:* Probably London planetree. *Three or more:* Usually oriental planetree (with deeper leaf sinuses).

ORIENTAL AND AMERICAN PLANETREES: LIVING LEGENDS

Crossbred with the American sycamore to yield the London planetree, the oriental planetree is the venerated species of southern Europe and Asia. On the Greek island of Kos stands a sacred specimen propped up by crutches. Under this tree, according to legend, Hippocrates received the lame and the blind more than 1,500 years ago. While such superannuation may be questionable, the oriental planetree appears often in the literature and mythology of the ancient world. Plato taught his students under one. Today, many a town square is anchored by an old planetree. A community in eastern Spain so reveres the oriental planetree it planted in 1914 that it flaunts it over the Internet.

Across the ocean, the London planetree's other parent earned its own acclaim. The American sycamore grew to enormous girths in the eastern forests. At the time of French exploration, its trunks could be fashioned into dugouts carrying some four tons. George Washington measured an Ohio giant at 13 feet thick. Aged American sycamores tend to rot inside and go hollow, allowing swallows and other animals to move in. Some even housed early settlers while they built a proper dwelling.

Though sycamore wood was much used, pioneers were wary of the tree's fuzzy leaves, which they believed brought allergies and even consumption. The irritant could be borne on the slightest "zephyr," they were told. In this concern, they echoed a second-century Greek physician who warned against the allergenic leaves of the oriental planetree. (The warning holds today for those handling or walking among the fuzzy leafblades.)

Happiest in natural moist bottomlands, where it can grow or rot or split to its heart's content, the American sycamore struggles in cities. Its straight trunk shoots it to heights that get out of hand; its enormous limbs are hazardous in storms. It suffers from anthracnose fungus, which browns leaves and distorts stem growth. Affected trees often grow clusters of leafless sprouts ("witches' brooms") along the limbs. Powdery mildew is another affliction, as are insects. More than a million sap-sucking lace bugs can occupy the leaves of a single tree.

For all that, it is a beloved tree, inspiration for thousands of street namers and these lines of the Indiana state song: "Through the sycamores the candle lights are gleaming / On the Banks of the Wabash, far away." In Gettysburg, Pa., three sycamores still standing at the close of the twentieth century were witness to Lincoln as he made his way to the site of his most famous address. Across from Philadelphia's Independence Hall, the U.S. Agriculture Department grew a living monument from sycamore seeds carried on the lunar orbits of Apollo 14 astronaut Stuart Roosa in 1971.

American sycamore wood has played a colorful role in American urban life. Hard to split, odorless, and colorless, it has absorbed the cleaver's chop in thousands of butcher shops. Other uses have included barber poles, Pullman train paneling, and Saratoga trunks.

CALIFORNIA AND ARIZONA SYCAMORES

Generally smaller and more crooked than its eastern cousin, the native California sycamore gets better marks as a street tree. It makes the select recommended list of the TreePeople (a major urban-tree advocacy group), who laud its "patchy, buff-colored bark on large, often-leaning trunk and gracefully twisted branches." Its leaf sinuses are much deeper than the American sycamore's, and it bears three to seven seed balls per group. A champion specimen in Goleta, Calif., is 90 feet tall.

The California sycamore leaf has three to five long, graceful lobes; the leaf of the desert-tolerant Arizona sycamore is even deeper-cut, with five to seven lobes. The Arizona's seed balls develop in groups of two to four. Sierra City, N.Mex., claims the champion, 114 feet high, with a spread that seems heaven-sent for a desert shade tree: 116 feet. Not for nothing did the sycamore earn its mythological rank as "the tree of protection and favors."

Ailanthus (Tree of Heaven)

Ailanthus altissima

Importance: The most common and tenacious urban tree, considered an exotic ornamental by some, a weed by others. Tree of the novel *A Tree Grows in Brooklyn.*

Family: Simaroubaceae (Quassia). Genus: *Ailanthus.*

Common urban species: ❀ Tree of Heaven (*Ailanthus altissima*) or stinktree, Chinese sumac, ailante, ailanto, tree of the gods, copal, devil's walkingstick, false varnish tree.

Close relatives: ❀ Paradise tree (*Simarouba glauca*).

Typical city location: Backyards, alleys, rail tracks, vacant lots, untended areas. Female tree planted as a street or park ornamental.

KEY FEATURES: A tropical look, with long palmlike leafstalks and curvy branches forming a flat crown. Each stalk bears some 11–30 elongated, pointed leaflets in "alternate" (not directly opposite) pairs.

Leaflets closest to tree have nubby teeth at their bases (see figure, page 71). The stalk's end leaflet may be uniquely shaped; the rest are nubby-toothed or smooth-edged or a mix. Seed fruits look like flattened, twisted french fries with an eye. They cluster in basket-sized bunches, turning reddish in late summer, tan in fall. Leaves have a funky smell when crushed. Female and male flowers often on separate trees. Male flowers produce strong odor.

AVERAGE MATURE SIZE IN CITY: From shrubs of a few feet to trees 60–100' high, 2–3' thick.

RECENT CHAMPION: 64' height, 76' spread, 20' circumf., Head of the Harbor, Long Island, N.Y.

❧ ONE TOUGH CITY TREE

Ailanthus has grown in so many corners of so many cities for so long that just about everyone has a take on it. Kids may imagine it as a palm tree or mistake it for poison sumac. Landscapers see it as a desirable "exotic" for streets and parks or as a squatter to be shooed away. To homeowners, it can be a low-maintenance ornamental or a trash-class weed.

To nearby plants, it's a toxic devil.

Writer Betty Smith saw it as a symbol of hanging tough in the city, featuring it in her coming-of-age novel, *A Tree Grows in Brooklyn* (1943):

> It grew lushly, but only in the tenement districts. . . . It came there first. Afterwards, poor foreigners seeped in and the quiet old brownstone houses were hacked up into flats, feather beds were pushed out on the window sills to air and the Tree of Heaven flourished. That was the kind of tree it was. It liked poor people.

No such baggage accompanied the ailanthus when a Philadelphian imported it from Europe in 1784. A native of Southeast Asia, the

An ailanthus sprouts in the city.

tree derived its name from the Moluccan (Spice Islander) words *ai lanit:* tree + sky. The heaven-reaching height that impressed the Moluccans is reflected in the Latin species name *altissima,* meaning "very tall." The Chinese valued the tree also as a host to silkworms. With so lofty and exotic a nature, the Tree of Heaven was embraced by America's urban landscapers, including the great park designer Frederick Law Olmsted. Chinese immigrants brought the tree to the western states for medicinal uses.

No one took into account the tree's enormous virility. It can reproduce sexually (by pollination) as a toddler, as early as at six weeks old; or it can regenerate itself asexually, sprouting from root and stump. It grows three feet or more a year its first four years. One mature tree can produce some 350,000 seeds annually. The taproot digs in early, exploiting even the meanest soil or rock fragments. When the plant is cut, it resprouts. It sends out toxins to discourage competing plants.

Once established, the ailanthus is harder to kill than the mad monk Rasputin. In fact, The Nature Conservancy lays out this menu of approaches to assassinating the plant: treat with herbicide, feed to a wood chipper, cut with machetes and loppers, dig out roots, girdle the trunk (garrote-style), bulldoze, apply a flamethrower, have cattle graze the young trees. None of these techniques is fail-safe, notes the Conservancy; the surest approach is to pull out all seedlings by hand.

To a tree that resists such assaults, the hardships of city life are child's play. The Tree of Heaven absorbs sulfur and mercury. It has survived cold spells of −33°C and can handle drought. Cement and lime dust? Loves it! Salt is usually tolerated, although New York arborists suspected salt shock in the 1996 death of a number of ailanthuses. No pathogen (disease-producing enemy) seems yet to have the tree's number.

In durability, then, the ailanthus was made in Heaven for city streets. Its shade is dappled, its shape graceful. Landscapers can address the tree's reproductive mania by planting only female trees and keeping males at bay. Unfertilized seeds will fall but not sprout. Segregation also ad-

Nubby teeth at the base identify ailanthus leaflets. Seed wings are twisted, profuse.

dresses the males' social problem—flowers that smell like rancid popcorn in a zoo. Keep those boys by the tracks!

BAD PRESS AND PRETTY POISON

In his *Encyclopedia of Trees,* Hugh Johnson laments the bad press accorded the ailanthus and defends its long plumes as "among the most impressively tropical-looking of any hardy tree's." Most of the trashy associations seem to apply to the young trees, shrubby or spindly, with leafstalks that are easily broken and leaflets that can be reached and therefore crushed and sniffed.

But a mature ailanthus—40 to 60 feet—is a thing of beauty that few connect with the critters sprouting by garbage cans and broken foundations. Look for such mature specimens soaring from a backyard or towering above their weedy juniors in "disturbed" areas—railroad embankments, abandoned lots. The trunks are thick and muscular (a

Monmouth, N.J., champ measured over 13 feet around). The gray bark is textured on young trees by vertical striations, like human stretch marks. The top branches fork widely and horizontally to create a generous crown—sometimes with a flat-topped African-plain acacia look—with leaves clustered at the branch ends. A midsized tree can be thickly foliaged, further thickened and ornamented by yellow spring flowers or summer's yellow-to-orange seed clusters.

The fast-growing tree lives some 50 years, not bad by city-tree standards. It begrudges neighboring plants their longevity, however, by producing a natural herbicide, "ailanthene," in its bark and leaves. Shown to be toxic to some 35 species of plants, this ailanthene brings further defamation of the tree by causing it to be classified as an "invader" plant that displaces native growth. But to scientists seeking a safe herbicide for controlling weeds, ailanthene, which decomposes in four days, is a pretty poison with commercial promise.

Current uses for the tree include erosion control, thanks to the tenacious roots; modeling with its soft wood; and such traditional Chinese medicines as bark tea for diarrhea. (It has also been used as a laxative. Go figure.) While extracts have been given as remedies for a variety of ailments, overdoses are poisonous. But unlike the poison-sumac, with which it is sometimes confused, the ailanthus does not ordinarily cause skin problems from contact with its leaf or flower parts. If leaflets at the base of the stalk have bottom nubs (see figure above) and are not *exactly* opposite one another, the plant is ailanthus, not sumac.

But is it a weed? It's your city. You decide.

Russian-Olive (Oleaster)

Elaeagnus angustifolia, E. umbellata

Importance: A once-favored tree for windbreaks, roadsides, and dry urban spaces, especially in the Midwest and points west of the Mississippi. Nonnative, it is now spreading beyond its welcome. Where not banned or hated, it is still planted for its silvery olive-tree-like foliage, picturesque forms, hardiness, and salt tolerance.

Family: Elaeagnacae (Eleagnus). Genus: *Elaeagnus* (eleagnus).

Common urban species: ❧ Russian-olive (*Elaeagnus angustifolia*) or oleaster, narrow-leafed oleaster, silver tree, wild olive, Bohemian oleaster.

Close relatives: ❧ Autumn olive (*E. umbellata*). ❧ Silverberry (*E. commutata*) or wolf-willow.

Typical city location: Along roads, especially heavily salted ones, highway embankments, waterways. Downtown plantings in high, dry, or poor-soil regions. Parks, parking lots, yards and gardens, industrial parks.

Key features: Small, often crookedly bent and slightly weepy tree with irregular, rounded crown. Often thorny. Trunks single (tree) or multiple (shrubby). Bark tea brown and gray at base, with swirling, peeling strips. Long splits on limb bark.

Leaves are lance-shaped, finger-sized, pearly silver-green on underside, olive green above, toothless edges. The midribs and short stalks of leaves are a soft pearly greenish yellow to white, as are the slender young twigs. Fruit an olive-shaped "drupe," size of a large green pea, velvety silver-yellow becoming shiny. Gray sugary pulp inside around dark pit.

(The *autumn-olive tree* is thornless, with a smaller fruit that turns red. Its leaves tend to be more spoon- than lance-shaped.)

Average mature size in city: 15–40′ high, 20–25′ spread.

Recent champion: 53′ height, 58′ spread, 14′ circumf., near Black Hills Speedway, S.Dak.

❧ The Olive Tree That Isn't

The Russian-olive (or oleaster, Latin for "wild olive") isn't even related to the true olive tree of Biblical and Mediterranean fame. But on a sunscorched roadside where a Russian-olive tosses its pale silver foliage in the dusty wind, you can almost imagine yourself in a dry orchard of the Levant. Get closer and the illusion holds. The tree seems wizened and the bark has ancient character. The leaf mimics the shape and texture and flat gray-green hue of the olive blade. Even the silver-yellow, olive-shaped fruit (August to midwinter) might suggest young olives.

But the Russian-olive belongs to its own family of some 50 small trees and shrubs, and side by side with the true olive (*Oleaceae* family) would show major differences. For one thing, the fruits would hardly match in color or texture—and taste would be a dead giveaway. Russian-olive fruit is a mealy sweet for the birds. As a Washington State botanist told a news writer, "It is not the kind of thing you'd put in a martini."

A FOOTHOLD IN THE WEST

In a vast stretch of America's West, one can hardly drive a road or find a town without Russian-olive trees, which have also stampeded the creeks and rivers of the region. But the tree is relatively scarce in the eastern states. For example, New York's Metropolitan Flora Project lists the Russian-olive in just 4 area communities (including Brooklyn) out of 25.

Much more common in the East is the oleaster's look-alike cousin, the red-fruited autumn-olive, which has become a special nuisance in the Virginia region. Introduced to North America from East Asia in about 1830, the autumn-olive was planted to revegetate disturbed land.

But the Russian-olive, a native of western Asia and central Europe, seems to have come even earlier on the strength of its exotic good looks. And it came to stay. The rugged Russian handles just about any adversity except soggy soil and a wilting fungus that is most damaging in wet eastern climates. The tree spreads easily, resists bugs, and once established is as hard to kill as the street-tough ailanthus. "Mowing seedlings, cutting, burning, girdling, and bulldozing . . . have realized limited success," reports the U.S. Fire Effects Information System.

Before communities planned on killing it, however, they welcomed the Russian-olive as a practical windbreak shrub that also could be raised as an ornamental tree for streets and gardens. As happy in dry soil as in moist, flexing its willowy branchlets in brutal winds, it was a boon to tree-deprived prairie and desert towns, including those with 100-plus-degree temperatures. Mountain towns loved its vigor at high altitudes (to 8,000 feet) and ability to fix its own nitrogen in sterile soil. Equally tolerant of −40°F winters and road salt, it was a natural for the upper-Midwest cities and southwestern Canada.

And so the Russian import took its place by the Great Lakes and points west—and established its own spacious turf. Thanks to wildlife that eats the fruit and disperses the seed in droppings, by the 1920s, the

A pearly veneer covers Russian-olive fruit and undersides of leaves

tree was well beyond its planted range in Utah and Nevada. Colorado was awash in Russian-olives by the mid-1950s.

The fruit-loving birds aren't complaining, nor are the honeybees that visit the small yellow blossoms. A Russian-olive flower, which looks like a tiny inverted jester cap, puts out a supersweet fragrance that some noses find spicy and others cloying. Among city aromas, it may score positive; but with the blossoming comes a problem that is turning many communities against the tree: a pollen from Hell.

Relative to the pollen of, say, orchard trees, the Russian-olive pollen is lightweight and easily wafted from flower parts to the nostrils of allergy sufferers. Writing from "the Russian-olive capital of the Northwest" in Washington State, Don McManman of the *Tri-City Herald* reported that the Russian-olive was worse than the pollen-spewing cottonwood, its river neighbor, for allergenic output. Other writers lament that the irrepressible Russian-olive is starting to displace the preferred tall cottonwoods as they die out along the western streams and rivers (see "Cottonwood" profile). Then, too, the wilting fungus (*verticillium*) and a cankering disease have chipped at the otherwise resistant tree's longevity, making 20 good years on the streets a hard pull.

RUSSIANS GO HOME!

All of which has now villainized the Russian-olive as an invasive weed, "an ineradicable liability." As early as 1975, many communities were deleting the overplanted Russian-olive from their "acceptable-tree" lists. Utah, which boasted a 65-foot champion in Salt Lake City, has declared the tree "a noxious weed." Fort Collins, Colo., chose to physically remove its Russian-olives from town.

Still, arboriculturists exploit the tree's nitrogen-fixing capacity. And there are garden writers who prize the plant as "refreshingly lovely in leaf," a "shimmering" backdrop that "seems to recede into the distance."

Whatever its urban prognosis, Russian-olive remains the closest thing to Babylon along thousands of our dusty roadsides. Urban explorers will encounter it (or its eastern kin, the autumn-olive) for a long time to come. And if they fail to savor its silky, silvery textures and dainty blossoms close up, they will miss a sensation as pleasurable as most martinis, with or without olive.

Cottonwood

Populus deltoides and others

IMPORTANCE: State tree of Kansas, Wyoming, and Nebraska. A celebrated oasis tree for pioneers, widespread in North American cities. Admired for massive size, "restless" whispering leaves. Famous (and infamous) for clouds of cottony seeds.

FAMILY: Salicaceae (Willow). GENUS: *Populus* (poplar).

COMMON URBAN SPECIES: ❀ Eastern cottonwood (*Populus deltoides*) or eastern poplar, necklace poplar, cottontree, whitewood, Carolina poplar. ❀ Plains cottonwood (*P. sargentii*) or Great Plains c., western c., Sargent poplar. ❀ Narrowleaf cottonwood (*P. angustifolia*) or mountain c., bitter c., willow c. ❀ Balsam poplar (*P. balsamifera*) or tacamahac, Canadian poplar, rough-barked poplar, Balm of Gilead (variety). ❀ Fremont cottonwood (*P. fremontii*) or white c. ❀ Rio Grande cottonwood (*P. wislizeni*) or meseta c., valley c. ❀ Swamp cottonwood (*P. heterophylla*) or swamp poplar, downy poplar, river c. ❀ Black cottonwood (*P. trichocarpa*) or bigleaf c. ❀ Carolina poplar (variety) (*P. canadensis*).

TYPICAL CITY LOCATION: Open spaces, especially near water. Railways. Older plantings on streets and (southwestern U.S.) plazas. Edge-of-town roadsides.

KEY FEATURES: *Eastern and plains:* Tall-growing, massive tree, often with long double trunk, roundish overall crown with gnarly limbs showing through. Foliage shimmers and rattles in breezes.

Leaf has triangular shape like a cross section of a Hershey's Kiss, 3–7″ long and across, with rounded edges at base, nubby saw-teeth, and long point. Shiny, bright green, tough-skinned on top, paler below. Yellow in fall. Long leafstalk is flattened like linguine.

Male flowers resemble reddish, 3″ caterpillars. Female fruit a necklace- or bracelet-like chain of small green capsules, later releasing abundant cottony seeds that drift like snow. Old trunk bark develops vertical corky ridges as wide as baseball bats.

Narrowleaf: Willowlike leaves, 2–4″ long by ½–1″ long.

Balsam: Tall trunk, narrow crown, limbs tend upward. Leaf has fine wavy teeth and round stalk.

Fremont: Leaves often wider than long.

AVERAGE MATURE HEIGHT IN CITY: *Eastern:* 60–100′. *Plains:* 50–75′. *Fremont:* 40–80′. *Black:* 60–120′.

RECENT CHAMPION: *Eastern:* 85′ height, 121′ spread, 36′ circumf., Cassia County, Idaho. *Black:* 158′ height, 110′ spread, 27′ circumf., Willamette Mission State Park, Oreg.

❧ CLOUDMAKER, TROUBLEMAKER

Seed fluff clogs a window screen. Little Leaguers watch a fuzz cloud cross the infield. Summer must be approaching, and somewhere in town the big cottonwoods are asserting their right to reproduce—whether the townsfolk like it or not.

Some do, some don't. But here is a tree that welcomed pioneers to

Triangular cottonwood leaves, up to seven inches wide, ride on flattened stalks that catch the wind.

the Great Plains and westward, signaling water and offering shade and firewood along the lonely stretches. A tree that Lewis and Clark hewed into river transportation on their way to the Pacific.

Here is a tree whose green seed-capsule necklaces morph into dreamy summer clouds. And whose pale gold foliage against a deep sky makes Rocky Mountain hearts grow weepy.

The cottonwood flutters its shiny leaves as if to applaud the wind and disperse the sunlight. Native Americans perceived a counseling spirit in the tree and approached it before an undertaking. The Arapaho believed that cottonwoods had cast the stars into the sky.

JUST ADD WATER

All cottonwood species belong to the poplar group (genus) of the Willow family, denizens of river country. Along moist banks, the cottonwoods can spread their shallow, voracious roots, suck up water, and rise to legendary heights of a hundred feet and more. Urban conservationists appreciate the erosion control. Picnickers revere the trees' cathedral heights and shadows, the leaf chittering, the solidity of the old furrowed trunks. In open settings, the explosion of seed parachutes delights young and old.

As urban populations developed, cottonwoods followed people to their habitats as natural migrants or plantings. Communities took to the tree. It was as easy to propagate as shoving a wet pole in the ground— the very technique used with soaked cuttings. In just 15 years, young trees grew big enough to shade the rooftops. The beauty of the cottonwood leaf—usually a glittering broad triangle with rounded teeth and pennantlike tip—brightened the urban landscape. And with their long, linguine-flat stalks, leaves caught the breezes and piped tree music through the streets.

But for these gifts cottonwoods asked a price. They would drink water wherever their aggressive roots could find it—in sewer pipes, septic systems, and waterlines even three or four houses away. (Root mass might be four times the width of the branch spread.) They would rid themselves of dead twigs, littering the ground. They might rearrange a sidewalk to accommodate their hefty surface roots and often-divided trunks. Or clog air conditioners with their thick seed bursts. Or yield massive, brittle limbs to windstorms.

BETTING ON COTTONWOODS

People took a gamble and planted or tolerated cottonwoods in urban regions through most of North America (excluding New England and Florida, where they are uncommon). The 80- to 100-foot eastern cottonwood ruled the eastern half of America. Plains states embraced the western or plains cottonwood, a similar broad-leaved tree that thrived where others would not. Mountain states planted the regional narrowleaf cottonwood, a tree of medium height, slender willowlike leaves, and resiny aromatic buds.

Farther west and in the deep Southwest, the Fremont or white cottonwood gave precious shade with its tall, broad crown. Towns along and beyond the Mexican border planted these and the Rio Grande poplars in schoolyards and plazas and along the streets. *Álamo* is the Spanish name for the cottonwood tree, a stand of which surrounded the famed San Antonio mission-turned-fort in Texas. Double rows of *álamos* graced plazas south of the Mexican border.

AN ULTIMATE SOLUTION

In the East, a male hybrid cottonwood promised a solution to the seed problem. Cultivators in nineteenth-century France had crossed the

KIDS AND COTTONWOODS

Native American children knew the triangular cottonwood leaf as a toy tepee. The leafblade was curled into a miniature dwelling and joined at the seam with a thorn. City kids can make their tepee from a large, wide cottonwood leaf with a flat base. They should snip off the stalk and use clear tape or paste to hold the seam. Like the Native children, they can cut or tear smoke flaps at the top. As they construct a small village of tepees, they might sit still for some cottonwood lore: The idea for tepees was said to have come from the leaf. Hopis carve cottonwood roots into kachina dolls, representing supernatural beings. Plains natives used the roots as rubbing sticks for fire. Beavers chew down whole cottonwoods to dine on the leaves. . . .

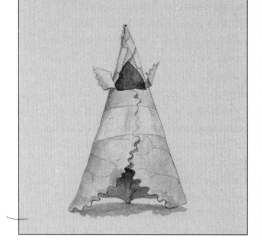

eastern cottonwood with the narrow-crowned European black poplar to create what America would call the Carolina poplar. With root cuttings, cultivators produced a fast-growing, straight-up street tree that would spare residents the seed fuzz. By the 1930s, the tree was rattling its pretty leaves above thousands of urban sites.

But the story was less pretty beneath ground. As thirsty as any cottonwood and more vigorous than many, Carolinas attacked sewer pipes with a vengeance. With other good street trees becoming available, one community after another decided to speed the Carolinas to their rest. The preferred method was girdling, or banding the trunk to choke the downward flow of sugar to the roots—a slow but certain execution of a tree and its shoots.

Cottonwoods met with further troubles in populated areas. Clouds of seeds—3 million to the pound—became ever less romantic to lovers of air-conditioning, and many towns outlawed the planting of the female trees. Structural weakness was another liability. Cottonwoods suffer the debilities of old age relatively soon. A massive century-old tree rotting from the inside can be a picturesque complex of gnarls and hollows, or a disaster—as for a Waco, Texas, boy killed by a cottonwood branch in 1997.

Where nature and commerce collide, cottonwoods often find themselves on the blade of a bulldozer or at the heart of an environmental brawl. In the center of Balmwood, N.Y., a famous but decrepit cottonwood faced doom by town decree until a group of citizens cried whoa. Believed to be the world's oldest eastern cottonwood at 300-years-plus, the landmark tree was 85 feet tall, more than 8 feet

Cottonwood fruit capsules explode with seed fluff to cover the streets.

thick, and still producing new growth, according to an *Arbor Age* account. Passersby from George Washington to Franklin Delano Roosevelt had been part of its history. True, the tree was decayed and straining to support its 80-foot spread, but consulting arborists felt it could be saved with a steel truss and other measures. Up went support cables and 65 feet of steel. The odds were still poor for more than 20 years of survival, but the citizens had asserted their values.

FATE OF THE SPECIES

In 1998, Albuquerque banned in-town cottonwoods as perpetrators of allergies. (Adding to the cottony female output, male flowers—catkins that look like big red caterpillars—produce copious amounts of windborne pollen.) Other American towns may be blacklisting cottonwoods as street species, but the trees still can be found along sidewalks and in unsettled downtown spaces. Considering the number and fecundity of wild cottonwoods, what's going to stop the odd seedling from squatting on hospitable mud? One gardener, seeking advice from an Internet forestry site, asked if there were any way to block the manic seed production. Kill the tree and plant a male, was the arch reply.

But many neighborhoods still treasure their old cottonwoods, including females. The very bark of the eastern and Plains giants, with corky ridges as thick as barge ropes, lends texture to a street. Even gardeners appreciate the cottonwood's ability to green and shade an area in a very short time (given full sun and moisture), while slower, longer-living trees are growing up. The 'Siouxland' is one cultivated variety for planting.

Industry helps keep the tree around. Commercial plantations grow hybrid cottonwoods mainly for wood pulp. Hybrids also occur spontaneously, even in New York's Central Park.

Canada and several border states have their own cottonwood species, the balsam poplar, and in such quantity as to blacken a map that plots their distribution. With its polelike trunk, narrower, lance-shaped leaves, and rounded leaf stalk, the balsam cannot be mistaken for other cottonwoods. The talon-like buds exude a strong, resiny fragrance. A hybrid variety of the tree called Balm of Gilead produces the resin of that name, found in home cough remedies.

Gigantic black cottonwoods have their foothold in the American Northwest, and big-leafed swamp cottonwoods weave through the Southeast and Mississippi Valley. Nor have we named all the species perpetuating the genus. Oddly, the main threat to the flood-loving cottonwoods may be improved flood control, suggests a story in the *Denver Post.* Trailer-park residents in Fort Collins, Colo., survived a 1997 flood by scrambling up mighty, 60-year-old cottonwoods. But these trees are expected to die out. And with flood plains reduced by modern dam construction, fewer seeds will find the water-saturated soil they crave. Already, squat Russian-olive trees are replacing former cottonwood groves along the eastern Plains. When floods come, said one local scientist, don't think of climbing a Russian-olive.

Sugar Maple

Acer saccharum

IMPORTANCE: Native North American tree celebrated for blazing fall foliage, symmetrical beauty, sweet syrup, and hard wood. Present in cities, but happiest as village and suburban shade tree. State tree of New York, Vermont, West Virginia, and Wisconsin. Basis of Canadian flag symbol and Toronto Maple Leafs emblem.

FAMILY: Aceraceae (Maple). GENUS: *Acer* (maple).

COMMON URBAN SPECIES: ❀ Sugar maple (*Acer saccharum*) or rock m., hard m., sweet m., sugartree.

CLOSE RELATIVES: ❀ Black maple (*A. nigrum*). ❀ Florida maple (*A. barbatum*) or southern sugar m. ❀ Canyon maple (*A. grandidentatum*) or bigtooth m., western sugar m.

TYPICAL CITY LOCATION: Streets of small towns and suburbs. City streets where the tree's generous shade and autumn color override risk of pollution damage to tree. Parks, yards, campuses, golf courses.

Key features: A medium-to-large tree with dense foliage. Crown is rounded or egg- or head-shaped, with straight trunk and more-or-less symmetrical spray of upward branches.

Leaves in directly opposite pairs, 4–6″ long, slightly wider; 3 or 5 lobes (points) with coarse teeth, deep, sharp indentations; medium flat green on top, paler underside; fall colors include bright yellow, orange, red, scarlet, and combinations.

Clusters of small flowers make for overall chartreuse hue in spring. Fruit is double-winged samara or *key,* each wing about 1″ long and joined at a wishbone angle. Older bark deeply furrowed, often with long, flat plates.

Average mature size in city: 40–70′ high, 2–4′ thick.

Recent champion: 65′ height, 54′ spread, 23′ circumf., Kitzmiller, Md.

❧ Beauty to Burn

On a searing summer day it burns so that you, shaded by its dense foliage, don't have to. In autumn it blazes with colors that set your soul on fire. The winter hearth glows long after sugar maple wood has turned to embers. And in spring, the tree's juices boil into maple syrup, the ambrosia that warms your pancakes on a lucky morning.

Such burning generosity begs for requital. Happily, it's easy to love a sugar maple, the North American species whose shape and fall foliage are envied by the rest of the world.

Ecstasy is watching its autumn colors explode like fireballs in the woods or towns of the northeastern states, southeastern Canada, or Michigan and Ohio and the Appalachian range. To those describing the spectacle, no image seems excessive:

> . . . patches of yellow-gold merging into saffron, orange into coral, reds beyond reds: crimson, magenta, scarlet, vermilion, ruby—all of it set against the cobalt sky.—Charles E. Little, *The Dying of the Trees*

No medieval European army in all the glory of gorgeous uniforms could compare with the "color parade" the maples put on.—Charlotte Hilton Green, *Trees of the South*

All this passion has landed the tree on the streets of hundreds of towns and villages, since about 1750. Even today, what self-respecting New England village is without its spired white churches and downtown sugar maples? On big city streets, however, the tree is hard put to respond to love's expectations. It finds life all too stressful, suffers burnout.

In woodland settings, the sugar maple is a formidable survivor. As a young tree it can tolerate the shade cast by taller canopy trees. Often it succeeds them, as the taller trees die off or weaken under the shade of the rising sugar maple. Competing with other trees, the maple tends to grow a tall bole (the clear trunk) and push its crown up to a hundred feet and more. It often dominates the forests of its natural regions. There it can fight off pests and live some 300 or 400 years—barring its transformation into bowling pins, dance floors, and other products of the maple-loving wood industry.

On the streets, however, the sugar maple is a less confident tree. Sun exposure and open space give it a shorter bole and rounder, broader crown—vulnerable to the worst heat rays as its dense shade protects strollers. It doesn't like intense city heat and can't bear heavy pollution or salt spray. Its surface roots get restless in tight spaces. Drought destroys it, yet with water it may well exceed its allotted niche.

In modest villages or along spacious tranquil avenues of northern towns like Manchester, Vt., sugar maples bring their pyrotechnic extravaganzas downtown. But in the miasma of crowded cities, the beauties often fade. They suffer leaf scorch and sun scald, or lose their leaves to verticillium wilt, a fungus. Branches die from the tips in. Such pests as cottony maple scale, bladder gall, and Asian longhorn beetles have their way with the stressed-out trees.

Many downtown landscapers now avoid the sugar maple and its similar subspecies, the black maple, or turn to one of the varieties cultivated from hardy individual trees. Among the most popular of these are the thicker-leaved 'Green Mountain' and 'Legacy' sugar maple varieties. Although more urban-tolerant, they are still such fall beauties as should be spared the insults of heavy traffic.

TELLING THE MAPLES APART

Sugar maple leaf, with U-shaped indentations. Wings of keys, about an inch long, form wishbone angle.

Of the world's 120 or so maple species, those most likely to turn up on northeastern city streets are North America's red, silver, and ash-leaved maples and the imported Norway maple (see those profiles). But sugar maples still appear around town, some of them notable. A grove lines the way to the St. Louis Gateway Arch. A tree planted at the White House by Ronald Reagan is among the multitude of sugar maples in downtown Washington, D.C.

For urban observers, distinguishing a sugar maple can be tricky until its fall color gives it away. One can start with the bark, craggier and more deeply furrowed than Norway maple bark, much darker than that of the silver and red maples. The leafblade is about four to six inches wide, not quite as long, and designed by whoever drafted monarch butterflies (see figure). Notice the U-shaped indentations (sinuses) between the lobes. Summer leaf color is bright-to-medium green above, pale green below.

A similar but somewhat darker leaf that droops at the edges probably belongs to a black maple, considered a subspecies of the sugar maple. Look for soft hairs on its leafstalk and leaf underside. Otherwise, the leaf closest to the sugar maple's is that of the Norway maple. A slightly deeper green, it tends to have shallower lobes—up to seven

of them. The two-inch wings of the
Norway maple's fruit or key are much
larger and spread much farther apart
than the sugar maple's, which form a
wishbone angle with a pair of one-inch
wings. A quick way to identify the
Norway maple is to break off a leafstalk or tear the leaf. If milky juice appears, it's the Norway.

North America's approximately
13 native maples include a few other
relatives of the northern sugar maple,
some of which dot the urban landscape. The Florida or southern sugar
maple appears in Texas and the South-

Sugar maple flowers.

east, a medium-sized tree that mimics its northern cousin in form, but
whose leaves are half the size, hairy beneath, and rounded at the tips of
the three to five lobes. Fall color is red and yellow, about the intensity
of prewashed southern football jerseys.

Smaller overall than the Florida sugar maple, the canyon maple of
the central western states has a similar-sized leaf with blunt lobes and
teeth. Of interest to landscapers as a native plant, it can produce striking autumn foliage and a decent maple syrup.

MAPLE TAPPING FOR FUN AND PROFIT

Speaking of that most precious sugar maple syrup, tree sage William M.
Harlow declared that "to taste the cold sweet sap as it drips from the
tree is part of every American's birthright!" But tapping a street maple
is probably not a good idea. Urban dwellers can savor their birthright
on outings sponsored by parks and nature groups around March in
cool regions. Maple tapping works when warming days and freezing
nights act like a pump, expanding and contracting the tree to push the
sap through a taphole in the trunk.

Indigenous North Americans were converting maple sap to syrup

Color Secrets

In autumn, only the leaves of red maple compete with northern sugar maple foliage, and only in a narrow spectrum. What makes the sugar maple leaf so versatile? During the summer, yellow, orange, and other pigments are masked by an abundance of the green pigment known as chlorophyll. Cued by cool weather and shorter days, chlorophyll winds up its annual work of producing tree food (sugar) from light, water, and carbon dioxide. As green pigments quickly degrade, the sugar maple's underlying fiery pigments show themselves. Their chemistry seems stimulated by sugar, soil acidity, and the dryness and sharpness of the cool weather.

Leaf chemistry also severs the leafstalk from its twig before the bright pigments deteriorate, assuring that the streets of sugar maple country are paved with fire and gold.

and sugar long before colonists noted a maple juice that "doth congeal into a sweet and saccharine substance." The skills learned from the natives evolved into today's industrial process, with miles of tubes carrying sappy water from trees to stainless steel evaporators.

The hitch in the romantic act of hand tapping is that the sap water drips slowly, and that some 16 quarts of it have to be boiled painstakingly to make 1 pint of syrup. But, then, if pure maple syrup flowed from the trees, it wouldn't cost its weight in silver.

HARD MAPLE

To the lumber industry, sugar maple is one of the hard maples, a strong, beautiful, lustrous wood that spreads itself throughout the city in flooring, furniture, and countless artifacts. Craftspeople prize two of the tree's quirky grains: bird's-eye, with dots that suggest avian eyes, and curly, a decorative wavy grain.

Humans have long treasured the woods of the hard maples. *Ac*, an ancient word for sharp, might have been associated with the maple pike—the proverbial sharp stick in the eye. From *ac*, perhaps, came the Latin word for maple, *acer*. The Romans feasted off their hard-maple tables. Knotty maple roots made medieval alms dishes. New York State maples supplied a bowling alley craze in Japan. And chunk charcoal from Canadian sugar maple fuels the grills of upscale barbecuers.

Are the put-upon sugar maples becoming endangered? The trees are abundant, but acid rain threatens the maple forests. And global warming seems to be pushing the cool-loving species northward. Watching the trend, one Vermont maple syrup farmer believes that by the time his grandchildren take over, there will be no competition from the lower states.

Norway Maple

Acer platanoides

IMPORTANCE: Probably the most common urban maple. An ample, hardy provider of summer shade. Source species of many cultivated varieties beautifying thousands of North American streets. Bright spring and fall color.

FAMILY: Aceraceae (Maple). GENUS: *Acer* (maple).

COMMON URBAN SPECIES: ❀ Norway maple (*Acer platanoides*). Popular cultivated varieties include (each preceded by *A. platanoides*): 'Crimson King', 'Emerald Queen', Schwedleri, 'Cleveland', 'Columnare', 'Globosom', 'Summershade', 'Parkway'.

CLOSE RELATIVES: ❧ Bigleaf maple (*A. macrophyllum*) or broadleaf m.

TYPICAL CITY LOCATION: Streets, parks, yards, institutional and corporate grounds.

KEY FEATURES: Broken leaf and leafstalk exude white sap, as do reddish buds. Double-winged fruit (samara) is about 2" across; wings form wide angle, sometimes almost in straight line, with flattish seed nutlets at juncture. Small, erect flower clusters (umbrels) create bright yellow-green overall glow in spring.

Tree is broadly rounded or oval, with short trunk, fairly symmetrical shape, and dense overlapping foliage. Dark gray bark develops shallow vertical fissures and network of narrow ridges (vs. scaly, platy bark of mature sugar maple).

Leaf 4–7" long and wide, usually 5 lobes (sometimes 7) spread like hand with hair-sharp tips at ends of major veins; top surface deep green with recessed veins, duller green beneath, both sides smooth; usually yellow in fall; some varieties reddish purple or bronze in spring or summer.

Fruit samaras hang in big clusters.

AVERAGE MATURE SIZE IN CITY: 40–70' high, 25–50' wide, 1–2½' thick.

RECENT CHAMPION: 137' height, 116' spread, 20' circumf., New Paltz, N.Y.

❧ MILKY MAPLE OF MANY FACES

When sunlight filters through this tree in October, the result is magical.
—Henry Mitchell

Unless you live in one of the higher or drier towns of America, those deep-toned maples casting inky shade on your streets are probably Norway maples. How can you be sure? The double-winged seed fruits (samaras), which stay on the tree into fall, measure up to four inches across and look like the legs of a harem dancer doing a split. The ma-

Wings of Norway maple keys spread up to four inches wide. Leaf and stalk exude milky sap when crushed.

ture bark is neatly lined and interlaced, not shaggy and roughly plated like the sugar maple's.

But there's a surer test. Tear a fresh leaf or leafstalk and see if milky white sap oozes out. If so, and if the leaf is about the size of a spread hand, it's a Norway. (Compare the leaf pattern to the maple illustrations here.)

Only one other maple in North America, a native western species, bleeds white; but its leaf, dangling from a 10- to 12-inch stalk, looks like a long-fingered baseball mitt. They don't call it the "bigleaf maple" for nothing. It flaps its autumn orange-yellow most impressively in towns of the Pacific Northwest.

The Norway maple gets its name from the top of its natural range—southern Norway. It grows in forests from the Caucasus and Turkey through Europe, snubbing Great Britain. Europe harvests it for timber, and practically every town and village there plants the tree for shade.

The ambitious Philadelphia plant collectors had specimens in hand by the mid-eighteenth century. Over the years, finding radical new forms and traits among the offspring, cultivators bred these varia-tions into more than 80 named "cultivars" to suit creative gardeners and demanding urban landscapers. What you see on the streets today are likely to be cultivars that have met local tastes and conditions (see sidebar on page 96).

For an imported or "introduced" species, the Norway maple has proved remarkably suited to America's urban environment. (More than suited, say those who see it slowly escaping from the towns into the forests, where it shades out some of the lower woody growth.) Though not invulnerable to maple ailments, the fast-growing tree tolerates wind, frost, air pollution, and a range of soil acidity. It has stood up to heat, drought, shade, salt spray, and poor drainage. All that, and it lights up with tiny bouquets of lemon-yellow flowers in spring, adds a bold dark stroke to summer landscapes, and, if conditions are right, gives a long-lasting show of autumn yellow or gold.

Like a stoic immigrant, the tree has integrated so quietly into the mainstream that it has failed to pick up the usual string of nicknames. It is simply a fixture in urban landscapes throughout America's eastern half and Northwest and along much of southern Canada. It rules the streets of many metro areas, including New York's Bronx, Queens, and Staten Island. Municipal codes of such towns as Ashland, Oreg., and Fort Wayne, Ind., specify Norway maples as recommended or "per-mitted" trees for street plantings, while banning certain native maples.

BREEDING CONTEMPT

Commonality breeds contempt, of course, and the Norway maple has its share of detractors who, at the least, consider the robust tree to be overrated and overplanted. And perhaps there is something monoto-nous about its stocky regular form, like a tree drawn by children. Even the more exciting cultivars—some with narrow forms or purple-tinted leaves—don't satisfy those who favor native trees or extreme diversity among street species.

The very shade that endears the tree to some planters is bad news to others. Norway maple earns a big "dense" in foliage ratings. The

THE SPORTING *PLATANOIDES*

Platanoides means "resembling the plane tree," which isn't much of a species name for the Norway maple—and not even accurate. The tree has its own distinctive traits, including a tendency to spawn mutant offspring or "sports," which can be selected and cultivated into useful variations of the species. Among the most popular of these "cultivars" for urban use are the following half dozen:

'Crimson King'—Purple-red leaves keep color all summer. Leaves of young trees are red.

'Schwedleri'—Leaves emerge maroon, become bronze-green, then orange, crimson, purple in fall.

'Emerald Queen'—Fast growth, good branching, fine fall gold. Larger tree. Leaves emerge pinkish, later dark green and leathery.

'Cleveland' and **'Cleveland Two'**—Compact oval tree form; young leaves marbled with red, later bright green, large.

'Columnare'—Columnar form for narrow spaces.

'Globosom'—Small, rounded, flat-topped form. Young leaves olive or bronze-green.

abundant, sizable leaves overlap, and in some cultivars extend themselves horizontally like awnings. The resulting shade can seem as refreshing as a forest glen or as somber as a Norwegian winter—even menacing, depending on temperament or the neighborhood situation. Combined with the tree's tendency toward shallow surface roots, the shade makes for sparse vegetation anywhere near the trunk. The roots also like to tip sidewalks that get too close.

With one recent exception, the Norway maple has seemed better able to cope with natural pests than other street maples. It has been battered but rarely brought low by aphids, bladder gall mites, leafstalk borers, and cottony maple scale. Even verticillium wilt, the dreaded fungus that kills so many urban maples from the top down, has seemed less lethal to Norways. Certain cultivars show resistance to particular enemies, such as the 'Summershade' variety to leafhoppers or the 'Parkway' to wilt.

But now enter the Asian longhorned beetle (*Anoplophora glabripennis*), a one-inch, beady-eyed bug with long antennae marked like black-and-white crossing gates. Asia had long been troubled by the insect, whose larvae burrow from bark cavities into heartwood and come out again as adults, leaving clean ⅛-inch exit holes and trees with fatally damaged vascular systems.

The insect had never been seen in North America until 1996. It was then discovered munching on Norway maples and horse chestnuts in Brooklyn, N.Y., where 27 percent of the 110,000 street trees were Norways. Except for an invasion on nearby Long Island, authorities seemed to be containing the

Asian longhorned beetles are infesting Norway maples in urban America.

stay-at-home bug by grinding up infested trees. But two years and more than a thousand destroyed trees later, the beetle resurfaced in a leafy Chicago neighborhood—precisely where this writer happens to live. Hundreds of treasured Norway maples bore telltale exit holes, like wounds from a Mafia hit, some of them bleeding thick sap. On block after block, Norway maples were no longer the city's proud street survivors, but fodder for the jaws of giant chippers as forestry officials closed in to stem a national (and personal) tragedy.

RED MAPLE
Acer rubrum

IMPORTANCE: Street and yard tree (in moist regions) beloved for its year-round red features, including fall foliage. Greatest natural north-south distribution of any North American tree. State tree of Rhode Island.

FAMILY: Aceraceae (Maple). GENUS: *Acer* (maple).

COMMON URBAN SPECIES: ❧ Red maple (*Acer rubrum*) or scarlet m., swamp m., soft m.

CLOSE RELATIVES: ❧ Carolina red maple (*A. rubrum* var. *triblobum*) or trident red m. ❧ Drummond red maple (*A. rubrum* var. *drummondii*) or southern red m. ❧ 'Autumn Blaze' maple (hybrid, *A.* x *freemanii* 'Autumn Blaze'). ❧ Silver maple (*A. saccharinum*).

TYPICAL CITY LOCATION: Lightly trafficked streets, yards, parks, campuses.

KEY FEATURES: Medium-to-large tree, roundish or diamond-shaped crown, usually short-trunked in the city. Bark is smooth luminous gray with patterned lines, furrowed when old. New twigs shiny, reddish, with white flecks.

Leaves opposite each other on twigs, 3–5″ wide and long, with three major lobes (points) and sometimes a pair of minor lobes at leaf base; about 15–20 irregular teeth on each main lobe; shallow V-shaped indentations (sinuses) between lobes. Leafblade medium green on top, much paler beneath; brilliant fall red or orange-red, sometimes yellow, or combination. Leafstalk up to 4″, often red.

Bright scarlet buds appear in early March (earlier in southern range), quickly followed by small flowers with tiny red (or yellow-green) petals and drooping red stamens (male flowers), giving overall red hue to crown.

Fruit is a double-winged samara, each wing ¾–1″, joined at angle usually larger than 45 degrees with bulbous seeds at juncture. Reddish at first, brown when ripe in summer.

AVERAGE MATURE SIZE IN CITY: 40–70′ high, 1–3′ thick.

RECENT CHAMPION: 141′ height, 88′ spread, 23′ circumf., Great Smoky Mountains National Park, Tenn.

❧ MORE THAN RED

The scarlet of the maples can strike me like a cry
Of bugles going by.
    —William Bliss Carman

The red, red maple. Native to the wet soils of America's eastern half, it has become one of the nation's favorite—if not hardiest—street trees. Since the seventeenth century, cultivators have been fine-tuning the species into selections that thrive outside the forest and thrill observers with a repertoire of reds.

The red maple leaf has three major lobes with V-shaped indentations. Winged samaras are red when young.

In its moist woodlands, the red maple needs no tinkering. It is reported to be among the least troubled trees in the pest- and pollution-threatened New England forests. It survives in woods contaminated by heavy metals near Sudbury, Ont. No tree claims a greater natural north-south range in North America—from lower Canada to Florida, spilling well over the Mississippi. Its blood-red buds put the first flush of spring upon the continent.

But to assure planters of happy trees outside the forests, cultivators have developed varieties from the hardiest and most reliable individuals. These high-performance breeds have more of what it takes to make it in the cities—to live up to such nursery names as 'Autumn Radiance', and 'October Brilliance'; to bring their rouge charms to the mean streets.

Each season, the tree provides at least one red—or potentially red—feature. In the dead of winter, the shiny reddish twigs of the red maple reward the close observer. By January in the South and March up North, the flower buds explode in a deep red, said to be the inspiration for the tree's common name.

Come spring, small, mostly red flower clusters emerge. The infant leaves that follow tend to be red. The paired seed wings (samaras) come out early, generally red-tinted. Through summer, the slender leafstalks glow a rhubarb red, though the leaf itself is medium green on top and whitish green below. And in autumn the tree switches on its luminous red, scarlet, and crimson leaf colors, which shine well into the darkening days. Next to the irksome urban reds—blinking neons, brake lights, stop signs—the tree's natural hues lift our spirits and rekindle our sense of awe. New York's Parks Department decreed the red maple its "brightest" tree.

BEHIND THE RED CURTAIN

Its redness launched the tree into stardom, but the red maple is no one-dimension celebrity. It can't sing, but it can dance in winds that snap branches on other trees, including the closely related silver maple. The red maple—especially when cultivated—takes a relatively snug, wind-tolerant form, a ball or diamond shape beginning low on the trunk. One writer calls the tree an "intimate" one—"you can reach the branches." And when you do reach them, you'll find leaves with an evocative design. Viewed with leafstalk at bottom, they can suggest a three-toed paw, a cat in a ski cap, a flying Nepalese temple. The teeth along the leaf edges are small and several compared to the few fangs of the sugar maple. The angle between the three main lobes forms a V, versus the sugar maple's U.

Notice that the leafstalks are directly opposite one another on the twigs. Opposite (vs. alternate) foliage is characteristic of maples—as it is of ashes, buckeyes, and just a few other species whose leaves fall (deciduous species).

Young red maples sheath themselves in silvery-gray bark. (Older trees wear a dark, furrowed cloak.) The tight gray bark doesn't quite compete with the second skin of a beech tree, but its pale hue sets off the ruby buds and flowers. The bark is thin and vul-

WHAT'S WRONG WITH THAT TREE?

In summer, the robust green of a red maple leaf often gives way to a sickly yellowing with dark green shadows around the veins. "Aha—a case of manganese-deficiency chlorosis," you can tell your amazed friends. Common in alkaline soil, the deficiency affects the tree's nitrogen intake and chlorophyll production as well as its growth. A professional needs to fortify the soil.

But you can treat another deficiency common in cities: During droughts, give your neighborhood red maples some water. And if you've taken a particular tree under your wing, remember that red maples need protection against mowers and other abusers of the thin bark. Damaged areas will rot.

nerable to damage, however, and can be very quickly defiled in the city. Its surface may show some natural patterns, which to nature writer Charlotte Hilton Green seemed like "broad winding rivers, temples, and white-capped Fujiyama-like peaks."

Mature red maples can be tapped for syrup when the more productive sugar maple is unavailable. Industry considers both the syrup and "soft" wood of the red maple to be second-rate, but it makes good use of the abundant species. For example, those wooden hangers among the plastic ones in your closets—there's a fair chance they were once connected to red leaves.

RED MENACE

A fecund breeder, the red maple can spread itself over forests where other species are dying, or it can launch unplanned families in town. The trees configure their sexual gender in various ways: male or female flowers on separate trees, male and female on one tree, or male and bisexual (complete) flowers on a tree. When the going gets tough, a tree might alter its sexual mix. Red maples as young as four can produce thousands of seeds annually; elders can yield up to a million. Wind carries the falling "whirlybird" samaras for long yardage, and the seeds germinate easily.

A bumper crop of seeds won't menace city streets, where most samaras and leaves join the flow of trash. But red maple is oddly and powerfully toxic to horses and needs to be controlled where the steeds forage. The alluring scarlet leaves cause massive destruction of the horse's red-blood cells. Three pounds of leaves equal one dead animal.

The toxin seems not to affect humans, though leaf extracts are rare even in folk medicine. One brew was used as a medicinal for spleen or liver pain. The best advice may be to drink in only the beauty of the tree, as many notables including Thoreau and Edison have done with gusto. For the delectation of the First Families and their guests, Jimmy Carter planted a red maple on the White House grounds.

MADE TO ORDER

Over generations, red maples adapt to local conditions. Northern trees have structured themselves to bear cold weather, southern trees to tolerate heat. Sometimes the adaptations alter the species enough to create distinct varieties. The largely southern Carolina and Drummond red maples have thicker leaves with woolly undersides. The small Carolina leaf turns gold in fall; the Drummond bears large, broad leaves and samaras twice the size of the northern red maple's.

Cultivators breed trees that emphasize the best of various natural traits, such as brilliant and enduring foliage, handsome shape, or weather tolerance. 'Red Sunset' is a hit among southern and downtown landscapers. 'October Glory' holds its color into November. And the hybrid 'Autumn Blaze' maple grows fast and tolerates drought as well as one of its parents, the silver maple. But come autumn, it does what few silver maples can do:

It blazes.

SILVER MAPLE

Acer saccharinum

IMPORTANCE: A venerable big tree on American streets. Widely planted by earlier generations for its quick growth, shady spread, handsome two-toned foliage, and shaggy bark. Controversial for its tendency to break under stress.

FAMILY: Aceraceae (Maple). GENUS: *Acer* (maple).

COMMON URBAN SPECIES: ❀ Silver maple (*Acer saccharinum*) or soft m., silverleaf m., river m., creek m., swamp m., water m., white m., papascowood.

CLOSE RELATIVES: ❀ Red maple (*Acer rubrum*).

TYPICAL CITY LOCATION: Along residential streets, moist lowlands in parks, waterways, spacious yards, campuses.

Key features: A soaring tree with short trunk, often divided into multiple trunks. Massive limbs form Y-shaped crown with flattish top. On older trees, shaggy, silver-gray bark curls away from tree in vertical strips.

Leafblade has 5 long points (lobes), deeply cut indentations (sinuses) between the points, dramatically jagged edges; medium green on top and contrasting pale silver-green on bottom. To 7" long and wide.

Late-winter twigs sprout reddish bud clusters, clumpy and conspicuous. Leaves then appear in thick clusters.

Fruit is a double-winged samara, or single wing with aborted second wing. Up to 3" long and quite broad, wing is largest of maple "whirlybird" wings.

Average mature size in city: 40–70' high, 35–50' wide, 1½–2½" thick.

Recent champion: 61' height, 82' spread, 32' circumf., Polk City, La.

❧ Big, Beautiful, and Brittle

... it is a favorite, for it ... adds a century to the appearance of a village street.
—Donald Culross Peattie

Urban foresters develop what they call "hit lists" of trees to eliminate from street plantings. High on such lists is the silver maple, a species so beloved by earlier generations that today it towers over thousands of American streets, its abundant, wind-tossed foliage undulating between bright green and silver-green. In Washington, D.C., alone, 11,000 silver maples were planted along the streets in 1883.

Red, radish-sized clusters of silver maple buds in early spring.

Deeply indented silver maple leaf is pale green on its underside.

Too much wind, however, or a crushing ice or snow load, and something snaps in this beautifully composed and friendly giant. Pray that you are not beneath a silver maple when this happens.

Yet, here is a tree that gives lavishly to those who embrace it. A native of moist eastern soils, it grows like magic in cities as in woodlands. Within 20 years, it reaches 50 feet and provides the shade of a majestic tree. In late winter, clusters of small red buds appear on the twigs and swell to the size of radishes, so abundant that the loaded branchlets look like kabobs. Among the first to blossom on city trees, these clumsy buds are as welcome as the sound of baseball. The clusters turn yellowish as their minute flower parts emerge.

Next come the leaves, white folds at first, then green blades as sharply cut as crystal ware (see figure). The leafblade looks more like a five-pointed (five-"lobed") star or splayed hand than the typical maple leaf with broad lobes. Its indentations (sinuses) are deep enough to qualify as "cut-leaf," a deluxe feature in the tree trade but free with your silver maple. The leaf's underside, pale as pistachio ice cream, also sets it apart.

The leafblades hang in clusters from long, droopy stalks. Fall colors, if any, tend toward unspectacular yellow or orange. Sometimes the leaf tips alone turn cherry red.

Silver maple samara with its veiny wings.

A mature silver maple can be identified also by its shaggy bark. Long, vertical, silver-gray strips curl away from the tree at each end, as though slapped on with cheap paste. Vandals can yank these ends free, though the center of the strip may be well attached.

The silver maple fruit develops before the leaves are fully unfolded. As with other maples, it takes the form of a double wing, but often develops one jumbo (up to three inches long) and one stunted wing, the large wing falling separately. As delicately veined as insect wings, they are designed to whirl as they descend. To view the plump seed kernels, break the pair of wings apart and pry open the swollen ends. Don't feel guilty—the tree's huge seed production is one of the knocks against it in cities.

Roots of shaggy-barked silver maple like to heave sidewalks.

MY SWEET EMBREAKABLE YOU

Saccharinum is the scientific name for the silver maple species. As you might guess, it means "sugary," and a superior, fine-grade maple syrup has been another of the tree's gifts. Syrup tapping is not a big part of urban life, however, and does not get this generous tree off the hit lists.

Why are urban foresters gunning for it? The problem is that silver maples break. The wood is hard but brittle. As if the tree cannot accept this tragic flaw, it wants to grow to heights of 100 feet or more. It wants to launch massive upsweeping limbs. It wants to divide a few feet up its trunk into two or more subtrunks bearing enormous numbers of heavily loaded branchlets.

What happens? A stress trauma, and parts of the tree break like candy cane. Branchlets litter the street after a mean wind. A dump of wet snow or freezing rain can take down limbs the size of girders. (This writer once woke to see his subcompact KO'd by a medium branch.) Double or triple subtrunks growing from a short trunk may simply crack apart, like a wishbone. Some say the danger is exaggerated, but these things do happen. Not all at once, but one can see the accumulated damage in winter, when the tall silver maples reveal their amputations and other war wounds.

The tree has minor flaws, too. Its many annoying diseases and pests include wilt, scale, and, lately, Asian longhorned beetle. The wood develops cavities. Lumpy burls and sprouts appear on the trunks. Aggressive surface roots can play havoc with sidewalks and sewers. Young twigs smell a bit like the grave when broken. The tree—so vigorous in its growth that biomass-energy researchers are looking into it—rates only so-so in longevity.

But life is made of trade-offs, and sometimes the romance of big, graceful trees can excuse a multitude of sins. Tree lovers admire not only the upsweeping branches and full crown of the silver maple, but also its distinctive motion, the heavy waves of green and silver that ride the breezes. Songbirds and squirrels flock to it. It is a highly adaptable tree that has grown vigorously even on the streets of western cities. Like certain actors, it sometimes seems more appreciated in urban Europe, where the imported strain turns a sophisticated yellow in October.

Cultivators have developed seedless and less damage-prone hybrids. 'Silver Queen' is a popular variety, with structurally better trunk and branch formation. But the hybrids generally come up short on growth rate and grandeur.

Some experts feel that with timely pruning—of early secondary trunks, for example—the tree would be safe enough in open city spaces. But urban landscapers face a particular menace of our times: liability and lawsuits. Thus, the balance tips against new silver maples on the streets. Planting them there is not only discouraged; in many communities it has been outlawed.

Boxelder or Ash-Leaved Maple

Acer negundo

IMPORTANCE: The outcast of the maple family and one of the most common and adaptable urban trees of U.S. and Canada. Much maligned by landscapers for its weediness, boxelder is a spunky underdog with plenty to interest the observer.

FAMILY: Aceraceae (Maple). GENUS: *Acer* (maple).

COMMON URBAN SPECIES: ❀ Boxelder (*Acer negundo*) or ash-leaved maple, Manitoba m. (in Canada), m. ash, three-leaved m., sugar ash, Plains m., stinking m., poison ivy tree. ❀ (Variety) Variegated boxelder (*A. negundo variegatum*) or ghost tree.

TYPICAL CITY LOCATION: Street and wind-shelter tree in relatively tree-poor Plains and western regions, U.S. and Canada. Elsewhere a very common (if rarely planted) tree along streams and waterways, in wetlands, wooded lots, derelict areas. Cultivated varieties with variegated leaf (white- or yellow-edged) planted in yards, gardens, and parks.

KEY FEATURES: North America's only native maple with more than a single leafblade per leafstalk. The leafstalk branches into one or more pairs of opposite substalks, each bearing a leaflet—a total of 3, 5, or 7 blades, including a leaflet at the tip of the stalk (see figure below). Each light green leaflet is usually V- or U-shaped at the base, with 3 or more pointy lobes higher up. The side lobes are short, the tops long. Size and shape vary.

The tree forms a broad, disheveled crown, often supported by multiple trunks. Single trunks tend to be squat. Light brown bark develops rugged, chunky furrows.

Flowers are petal-less, but the drooping female tassels (on separate trees) are very noticeable. Most maplelike are the winged fruits or samaras that hang in long, profuse clusters. The 2 wings of each samara attach at a tight angle, so that their veiny blades almost touch. The seed cases at the juncture are dimpled, as if pinched when formed. The samaras stay on the tree through winter.

AVERAGE MATURE SIZE IN CITY: 25–50' high, 25–45' wide, 1½–3½' thick.

RECENT CHAMPION: 110' height, 127' spread, 18' circumf., Washtenaw County, Mich.

ৡ ROGUE MAPLE

Among city maples, there are the well-behaved sugar, red, and Norway species that grow neatly along neighborhood streets and put on fall color shows that the whole world applauds.

And then there's the boxelder, rogue of the family. A maple without a conventional maple leaf, but with three or more ashlike blades on its leafstalk. A tree ignobly named for the cheap boxes made of its wood and its supposed resemblance to the bushy elder. A tree that grows helter-skelter and breaks like peanut brittle. A tree with a home-invading bug (see sidebar on page 113).

North America's native boxelder was well enough appreciated when new towns needed a fast-growing, drought- and cold-tolerant shade tree in a hurry. It could be found throughout most of the country. Once planted along the streets, it sprouted to 30 to 40 feet in a few years, spread its foliage wide, and laid a swatch of green on the urban drab of Dallas, Chicago, Denver, and a host of other U.S. and Canadian towns. It could be tapped for syrup. Its winged V-shaped seed fruits—maple samaras—dangled like baubles in great pendant clusters and stayed all winter to please the eye. For all its problems, it had no lack of treeness and found a place even in tree-rich cities such as Washington, D.C., and Seattle.

Flamelike boxelder leaflets of the Maple family's only compound leaf.

But as other hardy species came along and the boxelder revealed more flaws, the tree fell into disrepute. To get any respect from urban landscapers, it either had to be the only maple tolerant of local conditions, or a dolled-up variety of its natural self. Otherwise, it was scorned with a vengeance: "Where they are neglected or continue to be planted, the character of the town must be cheap and ugly" (Julia Ellen Rogers). "[Has a] tendency to attack by several sucking, defoliating, and boring insects" (G. H. Collingwood). "There is no excuse for planting this tree" (Kansas Board of Agriculture).

ITS OWN CHARMS

Today, there may be no excuse for planting the tree where other more shapely and less problematic species will flourish. Even to outlaw its planting, as has been done, makes sense in neighborhoods vulnerable to falling branches. But the tree at least deserves its place in the woodsy and scruffy areas of town, where urban naturalists can observe its charmingly eccentric features.

Dangling curtain of boxelder samaras. Wings form tight angles.

For example, its leaves. Why did a North American maple come up with multiple, flame-shaped leaflets instead of the classic hand-shaped blade celebrated on the Canadian flag and the Toronto Maple Leafs' jerseys? The "pinnately compound" boxelder leaf, with its one to three pairs of opposite leaflets and an end (*terminal*) leaflet along the stalk, does mimic the ash leaf and justify "ash-leaved" and other ashy names for the tree. But take a three-leaflet boxelder leaf and hold it with the end leaflet at top; how many ash leaves look like a hand puppet? A pointy-eared elf? (Some people think it looks like poison ivy, too; but if the leaflets are exactly opposite each other, it is not.)

There is whimsy in the varied leaflets themselves. Sometimes, just one lonely point (lobe) pops out of a side. Or whole rows of lobes, more like teeth, appear along the edges. The top lobe often divides into several points, like a flame.

To fully appreciate the leaf structure, cut a few sprigs off a summer tree about 12 to 18 inches from the end leaflet and place them in a vase of water. The leaflets, which can seem relaxed on the tree, will soon snap to attention. With light coming through the prominent veins on the leaflets' bottom surfaces, the geometry of the whole arrangement is enchanting.

The tree's winged samaras put on their own show. They have developed from the drooping female flowers, which look something like long-haired moppets or forkloads of spaghettini. The many flower strands produce a small curtain of samaras, dozens of double-winged seed carriers per cluster. The wings almost touch, unlike the wider-spreading samaras of most other maples. They will turn from an airy light green to delicate brown for their winter sojourn on the tree. Squirrels will lick their chops at the sight, but landscapers will wince at the thought of all those seeds making new invasive boxelders, which they can surely do.

BETTER-LOVED BOXELDERS

When fall hits the eastern half of North America, the dull brown boxelder leaf is an embarrassment to the royal-hued maple family. But boxelders of the West, including interior California, often take on superior variations, including tints of red and yellow autumn color. Drought tolerance has made boxelder a hero of dry-country Xeriscaping, or landscaping that preserves water resources. Naturalist Donald Culross Peattie found this "small bastard maple" to be "a true friend of man and beast in the West."

THE BOXELDER BUG

Among the many pests that raid the boxelder is *Leptocoris trivittatus,* a half-inch, red-striped bug that calls the species home—except when it's in *your* home during the winter. Leaving their nymph-stage offspring on the (female) trees, the adults migrate to nearby houses and hide in attics, basements, window casings, and other crevices. On warm winter and early-spring days, they may emerge in large numbers to crawl and fly around your rooms or gather on sunny exterior surfaces. Other than to give you goose-flesh, spot your draperies, and prejudice you against the boxelder forever, they do no harm. A vacuum solves your problem, if you prefer not to await their return to the tree.

Cultivated since 1688, the tree claims its share of old giants and even a heritage tree or two. During the War of 1812, a boxelder in Michaels, Md., held lanterns used to decoy British gunners.

The Count of Galissonnière thought enough of the tree to introduce it to France in 1760. French cultivators and others found that they could breed an extravagantly variegated (multicolored leaf) variety from the boxelder species. With leaflets of rich green framed by bold patterns of white, yellow, gold, or pink, these varieties have been snapped up by urban gardeners—many of whom are disappointed when the tree ages and the leaflets lose their variegation while the species develops its usual flaws. Proving that you can always take a tree out of nature, but you can't always take nature out of a tree.

White Oak: English, American White, Bur, California Valley

Quercus robur, Q. alba, Q. macrocarpa, Q. lobata

Bur oak.

IMPORTANCE: Trees of legendary strength, longevity, and utility. Brawny and picturesque. Objects of art, myth, and worship. Frequent symbol of all trees and of forestry. State tree of Maryland, Connecticut, and Iowa (American white). Illinois state tree (bur). Prized asset in urban communities.

FAMILY: Fagaceae (Beech). GENUS: *Quercus* (oak). SECTION: *Quercus,* formerly subgenus *lepidobalanus* (white oak).

COMMON URBAN SPECIES: ❧ English oak (*Quercus robur*) or common oak, Norman oak. ❧ American white oak (*Q. alba*) or eastern white oak, ridge white oak, stave oak. ❧ Bur oak (*Q. macro-carpa*) or mossycup oak. ❧ California valley oak (*Q. lobata*) or California white oak, weeping oak.

TYPICAL CITY LOCATION: Specimen trees of parks, campuses, golf courses, cemeteries, private residences and grounds.

KEY FEATURES: In white oak group, leaf lobes almost always rounded; no bristles at lobe tips, as with red oaks.

    English oak: Pair of earlike lobes at base of leafblade, instead of usual V-base. Tallish acorn (shallow cup) on long stem.

    American white oak: Mature bark forms light gray, vertical 1–1½" strips. Acorn about ¾" in shallow, warty cup.

    Bur oak: Acorn cup has burry fringe. Leaf's large middle notches (sinuses) give blade a "pinched waist." Corky ridges often line twigs.

    California valley oak: Small leaf, 2–4", with 7–11 lobes and hairy underside. Long rocket-shaped acorn, to 2½".

AVERAGE MATURE SIZE IN CITY: 30–70' high, 20–80' wide, 2–5' thick.

RECENT CHAMPION: *White:* 96' height, 119' spread, 32' circumf., Wye Mills State Park, Md. *Bur:* 96' height, 103' spread, 27' circumf., Paris, Ky. *California valley:* 63' height, 99' spread, 29' circumf., near Covelo, Calif.

❧ THE SHOW OAKS

Most of the oaks you'll find on urban streets are red oaks (see profile), the oak group that transplants easily and shoots up smartly even in heavy traffic. The white oak group is different. Now and then, one of its species gets street duty, provided its deep taproot and sprawling surface roots can be accommodated. But more often the urban white oak sits on a chunk of hallowed ground—a churchyard, courtyard lawn, spacious park site—there for you to cherish and admire as a tree that has seen it all.

    Age brings awesome dimensions. Brawny, barrel-chested trunks. Horizontal boughs that challenge gravity, seeking a force "worthy enough to be worth resisting," as oak lover Oliver Wendell Holmes phrased it. Such heroic girth and serpentine limbs have long been associated with the supernatural. As trees that appeared to attract lightning (possibly owing to negatively charged, damp and rotted interiors), the oaks were convincingly divine to the ancients. Aryans, Greeks, and Romans held the trees sacred. The Celtic Druids wove them into their religion, setting their holy ceremonies in the macabre shadows of the oak groves.

Classification in the white oak group, however, depends on botanical rather than divine traits. All oaks produce acorns as their fruit, but the white oaks produce them within three seasons, spring to fall (red oaks take at least five seasons). Thus, white oak twigs are bare of acorns over the winter. The interior of the white oak acorn cup is smooth (red oak cups are silky-haired inside). The lobes of white oak leaves are usually rounded, never ending in a bristle like the sharp lobes of red oaks.

There are other botanical distinctions, none contributing to immortality. Yet, because white oaks tend to grow slower and older even than the long-lived red oaks, they become conspicuous witnesses to history. Within their group are the legendary old oaks of central Europe and England and their big, superannuated North American cousins.

THE THOROUGHLY ENGLISH OAK

In America, landscapers disseminate the English oak mainly by way of slim cultivated varieties such as 'Attention!' or 'Fastigia', which can fill a tight urban space. But the wide-spreading, ancient oaks of England are the true stuff of Anglo-American heritage. English oak and its sister species, the Durmast oak, covered a third of England just 500 years ago. These were the mistletoe-clad trees sacred to the Celts (the Latin genus name *Quercus* is thought to derive from the Celtic *quer* and *cuez,* "beautiful tree"). These were the oaks that sheltered William the Conqueror and saw the battles of Henry IV; the trees that at age 100 could yield near-indestructible timber—the wood (allegedly) of King Arthur's table, of great cathedrals, and of three-decker English warships, some of which were said to require 3,500 trees.

Though the oak woods were tragically diminished, many of England's 500-year-plus heritage oaks were alive and as broad as banquet halls at the close of the twentieth century. One that did not quite make it was the 1,000-year-old Robin Hood's Larder, in whose trunk the hero supposedly stored his hunting catch. In the late eighteenth century, a group of schoolgirls on a field trip started a fire from a boiling kettle and severely burned the tree, which blew over in 1966.

English oak leaves have earlike lobes at their base. The inch-tall acorn sits on a shallow cup.

Imagine the burning ears of the mortified schoolgirls and you won't forget how to identify the English oak leaf. The base of the leafblade, instead of being V-shaped as on most other oak leaves, is formed of two small pendant lobes, so earlike you could hang little earrings on them. Otherwise, the two- to five-inch leaf is as unexceptional as the craggy old trees are wondrous, its color a blotter green that in fall becomes, in the words of a British naturalist, "the grey ghost of a brown that has been." Acorns are large, well over an inch long, with shallow cups.

Native to most of Europe and to lands east, English oaks are adaptable trees that may yet boom in urban North America. Aside from the columnar varieties and numerous isolated specimens—as in Olympia, Wash., and North Bend, Ohio—much of the English oak action in the United States is experimental. Don't tell the State Department, but in tests at Michigan State University, young English oaks outgrew and outperformed American white oak species in both forest and urban settings.

REVENGE OF THE AMERICAN WHITE OAK

Seeking timber to replace its depleted stocks of English oak, the British navy turned up its nose at poorly seasoned American white oak shipped

The five to nine lobes of the American white oak leaf are rounded. The acorn cup is shallow and warty.

by the colonists. But the superb white wood of that tree (and its close kin) underpinned the structures of an emerging nation. By 1812, Massachusetts white oak was considered good enough to support the guns of the frigate *Constitution,* whose victories over the British earned it the name "Old Ironsides."

American white oak, widespread through the eastern half of the United States and southeastern Canada, wins many a vote as the continent's king (or queen) of deciduous trees. Though not first in size, beauty of foliage, or durability of wood, its total points in these categories would be hard to top. Few species can challenge its longevity or the spectacle of 30- to 50-foot horizontal limbs and 10-foot-thick trunks. Older trees form a distinctive bark whose relatively light gray color prompted the name "white oak." The bark divides into long, narrow vertical plates, like strips of shaggy bandage.

The list of famous old American white oaks reads like a DAR honor roll. Several Revolutionary-era trees were only middle-aged by the rebellious 1960s. A representative few heritage trees:

- Charter Oak, Hartford, Conn.—In 1687 housed the Connecticut charter being hidden from the British to resist amalgamation of the states. (Died in 1856 to tolling bells.)
- Kilmer Oak, New Brunswick, N.J.—Reputedly inspired Joyce Kilmer's immortal poem "Trees."
- Christopher Columbus White Oak, New Hope, Pa.—500 years-plus, a sapling when Columbus arrived.
- Raleigh, N.C.—Oak born ca. 1340. Beneath it, President James K. Polk wrote a public letter opposing annexation of Texas.
- Gettysburg Oak, Gettysburg, Pa.—300-years-plus, withstood the Civil War battles of 1863.

■ Tree That Owns Itself, Athens, Ga.—An oak was willed its own land by property owner. It died in 1942 and its offspring inherited the land.

On most oaks in the white group, the lobes and indentations of the leafblades remind one of jigsaw puzzle pieces, though probably no two patterns will ever mesh. The five to nine lobes of American white oak leaves vary from deep-cut to mere bumps. Leaves on higher branches tend to be more deeply lobed. The mature blades are four to nine inches long, up to four inches wide.

Summer color is bright green on the upper surface, gray-green on the lower. In autumn, the foliage often colors a sensational wine red before the blades turn bronze and brown. In typical oak fashion, many leaves refuse to fall until spring. (According to one legend, an angry Satan chewed notches into oak leaves when he lost a bet that all the leaves would drop.)

If the tree is old enough to produce fruit (20 to 50 years), its ripe acorn will be up to 1¼ inches long with a warty cup covering just its bottom quarter. The acorns fall to the ground in autumn. Hold an acorn with cup at top; it looks like a green grape wearing a tan astrakhan cap.

American white oaks send down a long water-seeking taproot, one of the big obstacles to street transplants. But the species still spreads itself around town in the form of wood—tough, resilient, water-resistant, and gorgeously grained. Highly varnished American white oak floors were de rigueur around 1900, the Golden Oak Era. Today the wood is still prized—CONDOS WITH OAK FLOORING!—but now polyurethaned.

A close relative of white oak is more commonly planted in cities. Swamp white oak (*Quercus bicolor*) transplants willingly and puts out fine yellow and red autumn foliage. Look for a very pale, felty undersurface on the lustrous dark green leaf, and flaky bark with untidy twiggy tufts. Some of the 5 to 10 shallow leaf lobes may be pointed, rare among the white oaks.

BUR OAK, LORD OF THE PRAIRIES

Shaggy acorn cups and big leaves with pinched waists distinguish the bur oak.

Reaching the prairies, the North American pioneers came upon an oak species that, standing alone or in regiments, seemed the un-challenged ruler of these vast spaces. This was the bur or mossycup oak, so named for the unique burry fringe around the top of its acorn cup. Thanks partly to cork layers insulating the trunk and branches, these slow-growing, long-living oaks could resist the fires that swept through mid-western prairies and forests. With roots that mirrored the tree's aboveground dimensions, the bur oak could withstand windstorms as well as droughts. Travelers were enchanted to find parklike "oak openings" with only low growth beneath the tenacious bur oak stands.

Soon the Great Plains settlers were hacking at the huge trees for their excellent white wood, or planting them where it was worth waiting 20 to 30 years for a shade tree that resisted drought, cold, and fire. Today, some of these very trees stand in mid-American cities, resisting pollution as well. Patient urban landscapers are raising new bur oaks. Minneapolis, Denver, Washington, D.C., and Boulder are among the cities graced by bur oak plantings. Seattle fares less well; the trees struggle, and the city's largest bur oak was "hideously decapitated in 1984," reports Arthur Lee Jacobson.

The tree's distinctively shaggy acorn—also one of the largest acorns at up to 2½ inches—is absent on trees under 35 years old or so. But other features, including corky ridges on the twigs, identify a youthful tree. At its largest, the leaf is about a foot long and six inches wide, biggest of all the oak leaves. The typical blade is thick, firm, and fiddle-shaped, narrower toward the stalk and with a pinched midsection formed by a pair of large, deep notches (sinuses). The pinched waist often divides the leaf into two different lobe patterns. Sometimes the upper lobes are more subtle. Leaf color goes from dark green to dull, blotchy yellow-brown in fall.

Older bur oak trunks show a characteristic deep furrowing, creating rough vertical plates up to four inches wide. Mature branches drop some of their bark, leaving a patchy surface. On ancient trees, lower limbs may extend so massively that they touch the ground and form secret summer hideaways.

A number of early-American bur oak celebrities made it well into the twentieth century; some are greeting the third millennium. The Council Oak in Sioux City, Iowa, was some 150 years old when Lewis and Clark held council with Native Americans by it. Beneath an oak in San Marcos, Tex.—now known as the Sam Houston Kissing Bur Oak—Houston kissed the young women who brought him a flag.

WESTERN MONARCH: CALIFORNIA VALLEY OAK

Native to just one state, slow-growing, wide as a freight car, and weepy when mature, the California valley oak is not your all-American street tree. But where it does appear in interior valley communities up and down the Golden State, it demands recognition as a national treasure.

By some measures, the valley or California white oak is the largest North American oak

Stout California or valley white oaks can live half a millennium.

From Little Acorns . . .

. . . come big oaks and a flood of lore. Seventh-century laws regulated swine feeding in England's acorn woods. . . . Hunger-driven humans fed on acorns by drying them and boiling tannin from the bitter kernels. . . . Herbalists made a diuretic from acorn powder in wine. . . . Virginians used "oke ackorne's" to loosen up. By "boyling it long it giveth an oyle which they keepe to supple their joynts," noted one observer.

An acorn is the fertilized, ripened ovary of the tiny oak flower. What were leafy scales around the flower become the cup. "The cup . . . is not the least attractive feature," says a British nature writer, and its scales or warty bumps—distinct for each species—do make for fascinating close-up study. Oaks produce some of their best acorn crops well after age 100—middle age—but the fruits cannot travel far without the aid of animals. Some estimates credit squirrels with planting two-thirds of the dropped acorns.

Other parts of the tree besides acorns and wood have their own stories: bark as a source of tanning chemicals and astringent medicines; and galls, the insect-triggered goiters seen on leaves, for their part in ink production, dyes, tanning, and medicines.

tree. It can live a good 400 to 500 years. Trunks 14 feet thick and crowns 180 feet high have been reported on old trees. Monstrous lower limbs snake out 50 feet, often with pendulous "weeping" shoots. To secure groundwater in its dry terrain, the tree fulfills the poet Virgil's notion of an oak:

> High as his topmost
> boughs to heaven
> ascend,
> So low his roots to
> hell's dominion
> tend.

Roots as deep as 80 feet have been measured. No tree has longer acorns on average; the valley oak's is a sleek 1½- to 2½-inch rocket on a bumpy ½-inch launching cup. Native California Indians roasted and ground the sweet acorn kernels as a food staple. Farmers drove hungry pigs to the trees for seasonal acorn pig-outs.

Even the bark is massive, five to six inches thick on old trees, deeply furrowed and often broken into rectangular plates. The only thing small about the tree is its leaf, at 2 to 4 inches relatively puny among oaks but not without character: It has 7 to 11 deep, curvy lobes and a hairy lower surface. Owing to its modest leaf, the big spreading valley oak has been called the "American elm of California."

A two-inch rocket, the valley oak acorn is, on average, the largest acorn.

Like the elm, this noble tree is seriously endangered; not so much by disease—bad enough, in the form of leaf mildew and twig dieback—as by decades of cattle grazing and real estate development in the fertile valleys. A town's old specimens may be revered, and Bicentennial valley oaks such as one in the City of Live Oak, Sutter County, are protected. But development marches on, stomping roots, lowering water tables, leaving even "rescued" trees to die prolonged deaths in compacted, depleted soil.

Luckily, valley oak wood is poor and often rotten, or barely a tree would be left standing. Even so, practically no new valley oaks are reaching sexual maturity except in concerted conservation projects. California Oak Foundation programs and other projects give hope. The state highway agency launched a million-tree planting project in 1994. Meanwhile, by 1998, winegrowers in Santa Barbara County had plowed under some 2,000 valley and other oaks to make way for new vineyards. In response to protests, the vintners offered to plant 20,000 replacement trees. If all goes well, what was lost will be replaced—in about year 2198.

Red Oak: Pin, Northern Red, Willow, and More

Quercus palustris, Q. rubra, Q. phellos, and others

Pin oak, with downward-tending lower branches.

Importance: A group of majestic, fast-growing native oaks ranking high among North America's street trees. Several are favorites in Europe. Group includes official trees of New Jersey (northern red oak), District of Columbia (scarlet oak), and Prince Edward Island Province, Canada (northern red oak).

Family: Fagaceae (Beech). Genus: *Quercus* (oak). Section: *Lobatae,* formerly subgenus *erythrobalanus* (red oak).

Common urban species: ❧ Pin oak (*Quercus palustris*). ❧ Northern red oak (*Q. rubra*) or red oak, common red oak. ❧ Southern red oak (*Q. falcata*) or Spanish oak. ❧ Scarlet oak (*Q. coccinea*).

❀ Shumard oak (*Q. shumardii*) or swamp red oak. ❀ Willow oak (*Q. phellos*). ❀ Laurel oak (*Q. laurifolia*). ❀ Shingle oak (*Q. imbricaria*) or northern laurel oak. ❀ Water oak (*Q. nigra*).

TYPICAL CITY LOCATION: Streets, parks, campuses, open grounds.

KEY FEATURES:

Pin oak: Single straight trunk (on street trees), drooping lower branches; C-shaped spaces (sinuses) between 5–9 leaf lobes.

Northern red oak: Shallow V-shaped leaf sinuses, 7–11 lobes taper toward tips and point away from leaf base; "ski tracks" on upper bark; 1" acorn.

Southern red oak: End leaf lobe like long "witch's finger."

Scarlet oak: Multitoothed, flared lobe tips, O-shaped sinuses; acorn cup shaped like a top.

Shumard oak: Tufts of hair on bottom leaf surface.

Willow oak: Narrow finger-sized leaf with no lobes.

Leaves of the following are dark green and leathery. *Laurel oak:* Leaf shaped like dulled spearhead or spatula, no lobes, or crown of 3 lobes. *Shingle oak:* Leaf shaped like spearhead, no lobes. *Water oak:* Varied leaf, spreads wide from narrow base, sometimes with 3–7 short, bristled lobes.

AVERAGE MATURE SIZE IN CITY: 35–70' high, 35–70' wide, 1–4' thick.

RECENT CHAMPION: *Pin:* 110' height, 112' spread, 20' circumf., Henderson County, Tenn. *Red:* 134' height, 81' spread, 21' circumf., Great Smoky Mountains National Park, N.C. *Willow:* 123' height, 100' spread, 23' circumf., Memphis, Tenn.

ᘍ THE STREET OAKS

Among the 600 or so oak species worldwide are many trees of dazzling brawn. An elite few of these, in the right place at the right time, have inspired the kind of awe and legend attached to gods and heroes. Such trees are mainly of the white oak group (see profile), ancient monarchs with historic names and sites.

The trees of a second major group are lords in their own right. These are the red oaks, formerly called black oaks for their occasionally somber bark. Growing from seed to full-chested towering giants, strong of limb, crisp and colorful of foliage, they, too, have dazzled forest and countryside observers. Many forest red oaks stretch to more than 120 feet as they reach for the sun. A southern red oak in Upson County, Ga., has a crown the width of a football field, one of the widest-spreading trees in America.

No one can question the majesty of red oaks in their natural habitats. In the last few centuries, however, several species have been tested as urban trees—and many have taken to the streets like kids out of school.

FINDING YOUR OAK

How do you tell a red oak? Look at the edges of a full-grown leaf. In the red group, leaf veins usually end in a sharp tip with a little hairlike bristle ("arista") that extends slightly beyond the edge. On white oak leaves the edges are rounded where the veins meet them, with no bristles in sight. This little whisker is a big key to the world of oaks.

To make sure your tree is an oak in the first place, look for signs of an acorn. All oaks—and virtually only oaks*—make acorns. No other fruit can be confused with that smooth and pointy-headed nut nested in a textured cup. Acorns are a reliable identifier of oaks, but not always easy to find. Urban plantings tend to be youthful trees, and some oaks must reach senior-citizen age before producing their first fruit. (Fruiting results from fertilization of the spiky female flower by wind-borne pollen from the catkin male flower on—ideally—another tree.)

Acorns of the red oak group take at least from spring to the following year's spring to mature. White oak acorns take only from spring to fall—a critical difference between the two groups. Even if acorns have developed, urban wildlife and street action can make them scarce. If no acorns appear on the branches, check the ground below for their remains. Fragments of the acorn cup confirm the tree's oakness and give further clues: Downy cup interiors mean red oaks; shiny-bald inte-

*The western tan oak, which belongs to another genus, is the only other North American tree producing an acorn.

riors, white. Full, nested acorns help distinguish species partly by the size and position of the cup relative to the nut. The half-inch pin oak acorn, for example, sits in a very shallow cup, more like a saucer.

If acorn-scrounging leads nowhere, do your best with leaf comparisons. Oaks often hold some leaves well into winter, especially on the lower branches of younger trees. Look for the tree's most typical leaf shape and study a sample (see figures). Brace for bouts of confusion. With their bristles, red oak leaves are distinct from those of whites; but among the reds, the distinctions between species can be subtle. Also, leaf shape tends to vary wildly on individual trees and within a species. And to confound even the experts, oak trees commonly crossbreed to form hybrids.

But do not despair. Street oaks are usually bred in nurseries, and some will be true to textbook form. These make good starting points in an oak apprenticeship. Though many godlike red oaks occupy urban territory—New Jersey's Palisades Parkway, for example—the average street oak is less an object of awe than one of pleasing form and foliage. It is more likely to be a tidy 30- to 40-foot specimen than an explosive 80- to 100-foot giant. Its limbs, though sturdy and often horizontal, are not the sideways trees that seem to grow from the classic oaks.

PIN OAK

Among street landscapers, the graceful pin oak wins popularity contests hands down—or branches down, which is one of its ornamental features. Urban pin oaks develop a pyramidal or oval shape, with the lower branches swooping downward, the middle branches outward, and the top branches upward. Left alone, the downward branches would reach almost to the ground, forming a pettiskirt around the trunk. Park trees get to keep that skirt, but along the streets pin oaks have their hems raised to accommodate traffic.

Skirt or none, the pin oak reigns as the most popular street oak in America, dominating many eastern and midwestern avenues. It is Seattle's number-one oak. New York's Central Park is a pin oak haven. Not only does the tree resist pollution and disease, but it also scores high in transplantability. If a tree won't transplant readily from nursery to street, say no more about it to a city landscaper. Within the red group, pin oaks and northern red oaks have especially fibrous shallow roots for grabbing what nutrients are available in a city's so-called soil. Most red oaks transplant better than whites, which is why reds draw street assignments while the whites stick to cushier settings.

A native of wet places (*palustris* is Latin for "of marshes"), the pin oak does fine in Cementland if it gets sun and acidic soil. Most oaks favor an acid tilt in their setting and suffer malnutrition in alkaline soils. A malnourished pin oak quickly goes chlorotic, and an alarming number of midwestern pin oaks are showing the symptoms—yellowed leaves with green around the veins. But a healthy tree is a stately one. Its distinctive leader trunk rises straight as a mast to the top of the crown, supporting an abundance of branches. Leafless twigs or spurs grow like pins from the trunk, probably giving the tree its common name. The lustrous dark green leaf extends its five to nine narrow lobes like arms, each ending in three or four sharp bristled fingers. Deep C-shaped spaces between the lobes allow fragmented sunlight to filter through. Shades of rust and red appear in fall.

Pin oak travels well to Europe, where it was popular even before Americans urbanized it in the early twentieth century. Since then, notable urban pin oaks have included a White House specimen planted by President Eisenhower and 225 trees along Memorial Drive in Cleveland, Miss., honoring World War I veterans.

Posting their observations of a pin oak on the Internet, Oregon elementary school students noted that in winter "it is rather baron." Perfectly understandable for one of the aristocratic oaks.

NORTHERN RED, SOUTHERN RED, SHUMARD, AND SCARLET OAKS

Another aristocrat of the forest, where it is the tallest oak, the northern red oak thrives in urban settings as long as soil drainage is adequate. As the cold-hardiest red oak, it stars in the frigid cities of North America. In Europe, it tops all introduced American oaks in popularity.

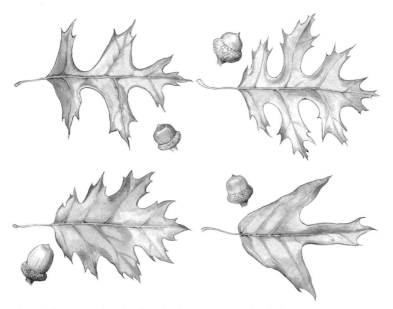

Sharp lobes tipped with a bristle characterize red oak leaves. Clockwise, from upper left: pin oak, with big, C-shaped notches; scarlet oak, with long toothy lobes; "fingered" southern red oak; and northern red oak with shallow notches and lobes angled toward tip.

In an ample urban setting, the tree grows fast and develops a rotund crown starting fairly low on the trunk. Branches veer off horizontally. Higher up, the trunk usually divides into secondary trunks. Often the upper trunks and branches are lined with distinctive "ski tracks," the vertical plates and furrows of the mature bark.

Northern red oak foliage is dense. Leaf shape varies on a given tree, but falls within a general form of 7 to 11 lobes that angle toward the end of the leafblade. Each lobe tapers to its multibristled tip. Narrow V-shaped spaces between the lobes go no more than halfway to the midrib, making for a more generous leaf surface than the pin oak's. About four to eight inches long, the leaf feels more papery than leathery. Leafstalks are often red, while the blade colors brown-to-orange in fall, even crimson or gold. From a distance, the foliage often has a burnished metallic or dry-roasted look.

Northern red oaks usually wait 25 to 50 years to produce their first acorns. At about an inch long, the nut is twice the size of the pin oak's, with a more bulbous cup covering just the base. Once a tree gets going, it can yield up to 1,600 nuts in a good year—which excites few besides the wildlife dining on the seed. Acorns of the red oak group are too bitter for most other palates. Those of the white oaks are relatively sweet, beloved by pigs, and sometimes consumed by humans as a nut or flour.

Northern red oaks stand out in hundreds of urban sites, such as Boston's VFW parkway and the White House and Capitol grounds. New Jersey and Prince Edward Island Province honor it as their official tree. As a grass-parkway tree, it has handled pedestrian traffic, air pollution, and road salt; but compacted, poorly drained soil gets it down. Lately, the dreaded oak wilt fungus (*Ceratocystis fagacearum*) has been a nasty adversary, especially in the tree's northwest range and southern extremes.

A related species, southern red oak or Spanish oak, can take over nicely where the heat is too much for the northern red. The two species overlap in the mid-Atlantic states, but the southern red oak shades many an urban space in the coastal South. The leaf immediately distinguishes it from its northern cousins: the end lobe—opposite the leafstalk—is like a long finger flared sharply at the tip, a witch's finger. (Another distinctive form, like a pear with a three-point crown on the fat end, sometimes appears.) The acorn of this full-bodied oak is just half an inch long and wide, with a shallow cup.

The Shumard oak is another southern answer to the northern red oak (and scarlet oak—see below), which it resembles. A valuable lumber oak, it has been embraced as a hardy city species. Look for tufts of pale hair on the underside of the leaf.

Scarlet oaks, aptly named because they flame scarlet in autumn, would probably sweep their urban relatives off the streets if they transplanted as well as pin oaks. But they do not, and so reign mainly in the woods of America's southern mountains and northeastern coast. If grown from seed or pampered, however, they can thrive in gardens and parks; thus, they are showing up in cities from the American Northwest to eastern Canada and south to Georgia, including Washington, D.C. In fact, scarlet oak is the official tree of the District, where the twenty-third president, Benjamin Harrison, planted one at the White House.

If fall color doesn't reveal the scarlet oak, look for extra bristled teeth flaring out from the lobes—noticeably more than the pin and red oak's—and deep O-shaped notches between the lobes. Acorn cups shaped like tops enclose about half of the ¾-inch nut. A penknife would reveal scarlet-colored inner bark, but tree scraping should be left to the wildlife.

NO-LOBERS: WILLOW, SHINGLE, LAUREL, AND WATER OAKS

They are oaks, they are red oaks, but they have their own way of going about a leaf. The willow oak is probably the most common of a group of southernish trees with no (or minimal) lobes on their firm leaves, and no guarantee of a conspicuous bristle. But the trees grow their strong branches like oaks, and the acorns gestate for more than a year, as with other red oaks.

Oaks though they are, willow oaks imitate willow trees in leaf shape, long twigs, fondness for riversides, and easy hybridization. But unlike true willow, willow oaks make fine, upright, long-lived street trees, only occasionally growing too large for their sites or succumbing to disease. The willow oak leaf is about finger-size, shiny green, smooth-edged and pointy-tipped, with a slight bristle. Baby leaves and autumn leaves are yellow. The tree's profusion of spiky foliage gives it a fuzzy pastel texture, light and beautiful. The shallow-cupped acorn measures about half an inch.

Native to humid southern areas and much planted in the urban South, the willow oak adapts slowly but happily to the parks of New York, Philadelphia, and cities of the lower Midwest. It can be found in Boston and Cape Cod. First Lady Hillary Clinton added one to the White House oak collection.

Shingle oak leaves, some twice the size of the willow oak's, are shaped like the head of a spear (lanceolate). They unfurl from a narrow cylinder in spring, become dark green, shiny, and firm, and add exotic

Firm leaves and small acorns of southernish red oaks. Clockwise, from left: willow oak, two forms of laurel oak, and shingle oak.

luster to the upstanding qualities of an oak. The species is of medium height and growth rate, but individuals can soar. One in Cincinnati surpassed 104 feet. French colonists were among those who axed the midcontinental trees to make shingles, and the name stuck. Now the shingle oak is happy to green the streets and let vinyl do the siding.

Like the spearhead-shaped leaf of the mountain laurel, the laurel oak leaf is usually smooth-edged and leathery dark green. But instead of pointed, it tends to be rounded at the tip, like a tongue. The tree is described as "nearly evergreen," meaning it may cling to its green foliage almost until the new season's leaves appear. Its abundant ¾-inch acorns have shallow cups. A popular shade tree in the southeast, it grows biggest in Florida and can be found as far away as Houston and southern Illinois.

Some people call the laurel oak a water oak, but a similar and even more popular southern shade tree claims that name—along with the nicknames possum, punk, and duck oak. "Duck" may refer to the leaf shape, narrow at the stalk and spreading wide at the tip, sometimes with pointed "toes" along the sides and tip. Water oak bark is distinctively tight, appearing almost smooth. A memorial water oak in Selma, Ala., by the Brown Chapel AME church, marks the site where Martin Luther King, Jr., changed American history.

Two forms of water or duck oak leaf, suggestive of a duck's foot.

Transplantable, fast-growing, and lustrous green, the water oak becomes a hulking beauty, often hung with parasitic mistletoe. People who pause beneath the mistletoe for a kiss, however, should be advised: Water oak limbs can be brittle or decayed, and their wood—like that of most oaks—is brutally hard and heavy.

Live Oak: Live (Southern), Coast, Canyon

Quercus virginiana, Q. agrifolia, Q. chrysolepis

Live or southern live oak, typically hung with Spanish moss.

IMPORTANCE: Long-lived evergreen oaks that grow dramatically thick and broad. Beloved (if sometimes threatened) as urban specimens. Live oak draped with Spanish moss a symbol of the American South; state tree of Georgia. Coast live oak a California icon, source of Oakland city name.

FAMILY: Fagaceae (Beech). GENUS: *Quercus* (oak).

COMMON URBAN SPECIES: ❀   Live oak (*Quercus virginiana*) or southern live oak, Louisiana live oak.   ❀   Coast live oak (*Q. agrifolia*) or California live oak, encina.

CLOSE RELATIVES: ❀   Canyon live oak (*Q. chrysolepis*) or goldcup oak, iron oak, maul oak.

TYPICAL CITY LOCATION: *Live:* Broad avenues, highways, yards, parks, squares, private yards. *Coast:* Parks, highways, old plazas, upscale housing tracts.

KEY FEATURES: In urban settings, moderate number of limbs that start low on trunk and grow massive with age. Leaves are firm, leathery, shiny, dark green on top surface, and stay on tree through the winter; old leaves often shed in spring as new leaves replace them.

 Southern live oak leaf is mussel- or football-shaped, 2–5" long, with smooth or sparsely toothed (spiny) edges. Acorn becomes dark brown, slender, to 1", on long stalk, matures within calendar year. Limbs often draped with Spanish moss.

 The 1–4" *coast live oak* leaf is convex, like an umbrella (or upside-down dinghy), often with spiny teeth. One-inch acorn is conical, light chestnut brown, matures in one growing season; cup is thin, fuzzy at bottom and inside. Bark is deeply furrowed, dark brown.

 Canyon live oak identifiable by golden fuzz on doughnutlike acorn cup. Egg-shaped acorn matures over 2 years. Leaf is relatively flat. Bark is smoke gray and relatively unfurrowed.

AVERAGE MATURE SIZE IN CITY: 40–60' high, 60–100' wide, 3–6' thick.

RECENT CHAMPION: *Live:* 55' height, 132' spread, 37' circumf., near Lewisburg, La. *Coast live:* 70' height, 150' spread, 24' circumf., Encino, Calif.

❧THE DEFIANT ONES

They defy classification. They defy time, gravity, and the elements. They defy autumn's tug on foliage.

 These are the big live oaks, an elite few within the small group of North American evergreen oaks. Although these evergreens gradually replace their old leaves with new ones, in winter the trees are plump with foliage. Compared to the leaf-dropping (deciduous) oaks with their skeletal frames, they look alive—and thus the name.

 The live or southern live oak, whose Gargantuan proportions are so often lightened by Spanish moss, is to the American South what the

English oak is to England: the soul of a land embodied in a tree. In the shadow of a live oak's colossal spread, it is always midnight in the garden of good and evil—a place of glory and dark secrets.

A related species, the coast live oak, works its magic on tree lovers in California. There it grows from the Bay Area south, along the coastal regions. Another thick-limbed, wide-spreading evergreen, it symbolizes strength and majesty, natural beauty—and high and low moments in the history of oaks and people.

A third species, canyon oak, reflects the gold of the Golden State. Not only do its yellow leaf colors intensify in fall, but also fuzzy golden scales cover its acorn cup. The most widely distributed of California oaks, it covers some 1.2 million acres in that state alone and grows from Oregon south to Mexico and west to Texas. It is "mined" as lumber and fuel and coveted as a jewel in the urban landscape.

Each of these majestic trees has scrubby versions, and each hybridizes with certain other oaks—often frustrating identification. Their classification within the oak genus is a work in progress: The latest consensus seems to be that southern live oak belongs in the white oak group, coast live oak with the red oaks, and canyon oak in an intermediate class—golden oak (section *protobalanus*). But the trees go on acting in their own ways, sometimes defying the group rules. In its northernmost ranges, the southern live oak may even de-evergreen itself, shedding its leaves in fall.

Scattered around the West and Southwest are about a dozen other evergreen oaks. Some, like the Engelmann oak, can grow large and show up in cities; others can barely claim to be trees. Our three trees deliver wonder enough for a live oak apprenticeship.

LIVE OAK: ALIVE AND WELL IN DIXIE

In and around New Orleans, the live oaks line up as if for Mardi Gras. Audubon Park and City Park are like staging points for these giant floats—trees 75 feet high, wide as a boulevard, with limbs that look like transcontinental oil pipes. Driving west out of town, Charlotte Hilton Green (*Trees of the South*) took stock of some 5,230 live oaks within 170

miles, not counting the bayou by-ways and inland plantations. A little more west and one reaches Houston, with its breathtaking Main Street esplanade of live oaks in four rows.

The eastbound traveler moves through Gulfport, Biloxi, Mobile, Clearwater (Fla.), town after town that has thought of itself as a city—if not *the* city—of live oaks. Along the southeastern coast, one can hardly escape live oaks until the northern end of Virginia. And not

Sturdy two- to five-inch leaves of the live oak with dark acorn.

just ordinary 100-year-old, 80-foot-wide live oaks, but dozens of such celebrated heritage trees as the Treaty Live Oak along Prudential Drive in Jacksonville, site of councils between settlers and native tribes.

Why so many of these noble trees? For one thing, the live oak is simply doing what comes naturally—thriving in its native sandy lowland soils; taking in stride hurricanes, floods, droughts, and salt air, thanks to its deep roots, strong wood, and waxy, leathery foliage. For another, the live oak is a fecund plant, putting out an annual and often abundant crop of acorns or sending up sprouts from its roots, or both.

But history, too, played a role in the tree's profusion. Starting around 1800, the young American republic set aside great tracts of coastal live oaks as a resource for naval war vessels. The ships needed unbreakable angle braces for their joints, and nothing seemed stronger than the "knees" of live oak—the crotches between the huge extended branches and short, thick trunks. These wood braces served for generations, but when iron and steel displaced them, the live oak tracts—not a good source of straight lumber—were ceded to the Interior Department. So immense growths of live oak persisted, while thousands more trees were planted for their aesthetic value in town and country, including as grand entranceways to the plantations.

Typically 40 to 60 feet high and up to twice as wide, the tree is striking enough in itself: Low branches may swoop along the ground before angling up; its "joyous leaves of dark green" (Walt Whitman) are shaped like mussel half shells two to five inches long; the slender dark brown acorns resemble little gourmet olives. But in a stroke of design genius, nature teamed the tree with Spanish moss (*Tillandsia usneoides*), a shaggy, unlikely member of the pineapple family. Festooning the live oak branches, Spanish moss has the jewelry-like effect of glamorizing its host. At the sight of such moss-draped canopies along the boulevards of, say, Savannah, Ga., one can only cry, "Lawdy!" and "Glory be!"

Happily, the moss asks for no more than a platform from which to absorb atmospheric moisture. Only when rampant moss interferes with the tree's photosynthesis does it need some discipline, which can be achieved with spraying. Urban live oaks are relatively high-maintenance trees anyway, requiring regular pruning and thinning. Ancient trees sometimes need cabling to keep the hypertrophied parts intact.

Live oaks host other mosses and mistletoe, as well as defoliating, galling, and boring pests. But the trees are more likely to be laid low by a sapwood fungus known as live oak decline. A deep freeze can also bring them down, with 0°F considered the point of no return. Yet, planted live oaks have survived as far north as Little Rock, Ark., and even in some Pennsylvania gardens.

In any climate, what the trees abhor is soil compaction or thirsty plantings near the roots. The "duff" or displaced foliage that live oaks drop in spring is ground cover enough, says one landscaper; otherwise, let the unplanted area beneath simply frame the beautiful picture.

COAST LIVE OAK: A MOVIE STAR

As the most conspicuous tree in the low woodlands of southern California, the coast live oak has landed many a part in Hollywood film productions. In girth and breadth it is a full-blown Orson Welles of a tree, but one that maintains its vigor at ages beyond 200. Its usual film role is to represent the Great Western Outdoors, but with its crooked, twisted, picturesque forms, it can also do exotic forests and haunted groves.

Coast live oaks grow fast as saplings. With decent sunlight, ample space, and protection, they can thrive in urban settings within their natural range. An ongoing Internet debate concerns the amount of watering they should get. Established trees get their water via several deep main taproots; they like their natural dry season and can develop a nasty fungus if watered. But according to one gardener, planted trees appreciate a drink now and then.

Californians have associated the robust tree with country living; they like to see it in their neighborhoods. Where developers can promote coast live oaks—as in the San Fernando Valley—buyers have come flocking, leading to more development and too often a thinning of the trees.

California's shipping commerce had already taken its toll on coast live oak from San Francisco to the Mexican border. These were the landmark groves and oceanfront trees of the earliest Spanish missions. But coast live oak was unmatched as a clean- and steady-burning fuel, and seagoing vessels soon demanded forests of it. In towns, the wood fetched prices that few landowners could resist. Communities like Santa Barbara eventually lost their rich groves. Today, the coast live oak is considered stable in its northern ranges but declining in the south. The state of California and the Nature Conservancy count it as one of the state's rare and imperiled natural communities.

"Brawny, angular, and low-limbed" describes several western oaks. To distinguish the coast live oak, remember its connection with shipping. The leaves are like little upside-down boats. With the shiny dark green side in water, a plucked leaf would bob along like a dinghy one to four inches long. Its curled-in edges often have small spiny teeth—good rowlocks for Lilliputian oars.

Coast live oak acorns are shaped like dunce caps or the domes of the celebrated Conehead family. They are light chestnut brown and ¼ to 1 inch long. The cup scales feel papery, a little fuzzy at the bottom. A fuzz also lines the inside of the acorn shell. Though often classed as a red oak, the species defies the group rule for acorn development: It produces its mature fruit within one growing season, not two. From August to October, it aborts its damaged acorns, then drops most of the

ANCIENT OAKS

So many are the celebrated (southern) live oaks that a National Live Oak Society keeps tabs on them, with a register of trees authenticated as 100-years-plus. Among the most famous trees:

- Middleton Oak, Middleton Oak Gardens, near Charleston, S.C. A giant with 10-foot-thick trunk. Available as a setting for events, seating up to 100 guests beneath its spreading boughs.
- Angel Live Oak, St. John's Island, S.C. A tentacled tree monster that looks like the oldest living thing east of the Mississippi (legend has it at 1,400 years), even if in fact it is not.
- Jim Bowie Oak, Opelousas, La. A 300-years-plus specimen, near the museum that's the former home of Bowie, who died at the Alamo. One of several heritage oaks whose offspring are available for planting from American Forests (see "Resources").

good ones beginning with winter rainstorms. However, it waits until May to drop its last acorns, giving itself a second season to sow offspring.

CANYON LIVE OAK: HARD BEAUTY

Like the coast live oak, the wide-ranging canyon live oak was seized upon for shipbuilding and fuel, but also for such rugged implements as wheels, axles, and plow beams. Its wood was hard enough to split other wood. So many mauls (heavy hammers) were made from it, the tree became known as maul oak.

Considered one of the most beautiful of the western oaks, the tree grows tall in its natural canyons, with long trunk and compact crown. It can handle altitudes up to 9,000 feet. Given space in town—where it is prized as an ornamental—it eventually develops the oak's classic spread, some 70 to 80 feet wide, on a short trunk. Its smoke-gray bark remains thinner and less furrowed than that of the coast live oak.

On their top surface, the leaves are bright yellow-green and highly glossy. Golden or dull-silver hairs tint the bottom surface. Compared to the curled-in leaves of the coast live oak, the blades are flatter, more spearlike, and have about twice as many veins. Spiny teeth often line the edges.

Canyon live oaks first flower at about 15 to 20 years, after which they can be identified by their acorns, which drop in late summer or autumn after two growing seasons. The shallow acorn cups are doughnut- or turban-shaped and covered with distinctive tawny-golden hairs. The egg-shaped nut varies from about one inch long to a freakish three inches.

These were among the acorns that Native Americans baked after removing the bitter tannins and grinding the nuts into mush or flour. Modern tests have confirmed the good flavor and nutrients of baked goods incorporating this flour. Still, a maul oak cookie doesn't sound like one you would bite into lightly.

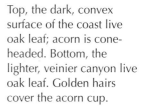

Top, the dark, convex surface of the coast live oak leaf; acorn is cone-headed. Bottom, the lighter, veinier canyon live oak leaf. Golden hairs cover the acorn cup.

Weeping Willow (and Dry-Eyed Cousins)

Salix babylonica and others

IMPORTANCE: A group of trees whose long, drooping twigs and leaning craggy trunks have made them into romantic symbols, evocative of mourning, beauty, and grace even in urban settings. Willow bark yielded the original aspirin ingredient.

FAMILY: Salicaceae (Willow). GENUS: *Salix* (willow).

COMMON URBAN SPECIES: ❀ Weeping willow (*Salix babylonica*) or Chinese w., Babylon weeping w., Napoleon w. ❀ Golden weeping willow (*Salix* x *sepulcralis* 'Chrysocoma'). ❀ Wisconsin weeping willow (*Salix* x *pendulina* 'Blanda') or Niobe weeping w. ❧ Sepulchral weeping willow (*Salix* x *sepulcralis* Simonk). ❧ Thurlow weeping willow (*Salix* x *pendulina* 'Elegantissima').

Close relatives: ❧ Black willow (*Salix nigra*) or scythe-leaved w. ❧ White willow (*Salix alba*) or European white w. ❧ Crack willow (*Salix fragilis*). ❧ Scouler pussy willow (*Salix scouleriana*) or western pussy w. ❧ Pussy willow (*Salix discolor*). ❧ Peachleaf or almondleaf willow (*Salix amygdaloides*).

Typical city location: Single trees or rows along watery landscapes. Cemeteries, golf courses, yards, campuses.

Key features: Of the hundreds of willow species, many are shrub-sized. The relatively few big weeping species are wide-spreading trees with twigs that hang straight down like stringy hanks of hair. Their often-multiple, often-leaning trunks become thick and lined with deep, swirling furrows.

Leaves of most species are about finger-length or longer and finger-wide, with a ¼–½″ leafstalk, minute fine teeth, and a long pennantlike tip. Many are curved or crescent-shaped. Commonly, they are darker green on top than bottom, and may have soft hairs on the bottom or both sides. They turn yellow in fall. Often two tiny holes or *glands* are found on the leafstalk, and some stalks have *stipules,* or a pair of minileaves at the base.

The strandlike twigs are usually bendable and brightly colored, especially in spring, when different species may put out yellow, red, or purple shoots, among other colors. Distinctive buds have just one scale, like a miniature fingernail close against the twig. Male and female flowers (on separate trees) appear with the first leaves. Velvety male "pussies" are distinctive. Fertilized female flowers develop spikes of small capsules that emit hairy seeds. (See text and sidebar for features of specific breeds.)

Average mature size in city: 25–50′ high, 30–60′ wide, 2–4′ thick. (Pussy willows 12–20′ high.)

Recent champion: *Weeping willow* (*S. babylonica*): 117′ height, 116′ spread, 26′ circumf., Detroit.

❧ ACTORS PLAYING SAD

The willows dip
Their pendant boughs,
Stooping as if to drink.
　　—William Cowper

It's like coming upon actors rehearsing a tragedy. One weeping willow mourns at water's edge, grief mirrored on the glassy surface. Another heaves its golden tresses in despair. Suddenly, as if a director shouted "Break!," the willows seem to drop the pose and relax, sunning their bright-colored twigs. Their leaves flutter like small pennants, candy green on one side, ice-cream pale on the other.

These trees are hanging loose and happy. It may be that big willows can evaporate some 400 gallons of water a day from their leaves. But cry tears? Don't believe it.

LAUGHING WILLOWS

The linking of willows with grief is a recent twist in their long involvement with humans. To early civilizations, a willow meant a happy hearth, protected by wattled willow roof and walls. It meant happy feet in the form of willow-twig footwear. The name "willow" has nothing to do with grief or loss, but derives from an Anglo-Saxon term meaning pliancy, as in willow twigs. Although the renowned Babylon weeping willow got its common name from the sorrowful trees of Psalm 137—

> *By the rivers of Babylon, there we sat down, yea,*
> *we wept, when we remembered Zion.*
> *Upon the willows in the midst thereof we hanged up our harps.*

—the trees were not willows, say the botanists, but probably Euphrates poplars.

Today's weeping willows can rejoice in their status as "specimen" trees, meaning trees that are planted mainly to look terrific in an appropriate setting. As such, they get their favorite spots, with full sun, plenty of water, and room to stretch their wide-spreading, fibrous roots. In such comfort they grow fast—doubling from 10 feet to 20 in three years—and display some of the brightest spring colors in the bark of their new twigs.

The male and female flowers, on separate trees, are of soft "pussy" texture, the males becoming bright yellow with pollen. Leaves appear early and stay well into fall, when they turn a pretty yellow. The weeping branchlets almost touch the ground and form a vaulted bower for urban sweethearts and picnickers—or a chapel for mourners. The tree lends not just mass, shade, and color to the selected

Finger-sized or larger, weeping willow leaves are like graceful pennants. Tiny glands may appear on stalks (detail).

spot, but the dreamy romanticism that has long inspired artists and myth makers.

ROMANCE OF
THE BABYLON WEEPING WILLOW

In China, where the *babylonica* species—mother of weeping willows—grew wild, Han Dynasty poets sang of such trees, as did many bards over the next two millennia. The species came to England in the eighteenth century, supposedly when poet and gardener Alexander Pope spotted a twine of live willow twigs on a package from the Mediterranean. He planted the sprig, and, since almost any live willow cutting will root in moist soil, it became the celebrated Babylon weeping willow of his Twickenham Garden. (It was later chopped up for tourist trinkets.)

SORTING THE WEEPERS

Willows are famously many and mixed, but here are some clues toward identifying the common large weeping types:

Babylon: Extremely long weeping branches and olive-to-brown twigs, hairy stalks, leaves ⅓–¾" wide, medium green above, paler below, with long tip.

Golden: Long weeping branches, twigs yellow-gold, leaves shiny above, soft white with hairs below.

Wisconsin or Niobe: Not as weepy as Babylon. Green twigs, leaves dark glossy green, leafstalks hairless.

Sepulchral: Less weepy than Babylon. Leaves stay green far into fall.

Thurlow: Long weeping branches, yellow-brown twigs, leaves dull green, to ⅞" wide.

Many a weeping willow, including those of Washington, D.C.'s East Potomac Park, are said to have descended from a Babylon willow on St. Helena, Napoleon's place of exile. Napoleon brooded and later lay buried beneath the tree. One writer argues that the original willow broke in 1821, was replanted on Napoleon's grave from cuttings, and did not survive souvenir hunters. However, the American Forests Famous & Historic Trees Program (see "Resources") does offer seedlings descended from a Napoleon willow cutting brought to the States in the 1870s.

The Babylon weeping willow remains one of the world's most revered and beloved trees—at least by those who don't have to deal with its blight and canker diseases, insect infestations, messy twigs, aggressive roots, brittle boughs, and short life span—the liabilities of all willows. Most of the big weeping willows seen in cultivation are hybrids with the *S. babylonica* (see sidebar), which itself lacks some of the hardiness of crossbreeds and prefers the southern states.

One of these hybrids, the golden weeping willow, might surpass the Babylon in popularity, as it has done in England and some northern states. A cross between *babylonica* and a yellow-twigged variety of the white willow, this weeping hybrid boasts golden twigs and branches, whereas those of the Babylon species are olive brown. It is a tougher tree, more resistant to cold. And it is potentially bigger, often growing

50 to 75 feet high to the Babylon's 30 to 50 feet, with a hefty spread. Arthur Lee Jacobson reports "a very wide specimen behind the [Weightwatchers!] building" in his *Trees of Seattle.*

FRISKY GENUS

Trees of the willow genus, *Salix,* can reproduce either asexually (by a cutting of a twig or branch rooted in the soil) or sexually (by seed of fertilized flower). And they do both with gusto. Willows habitually drop pieces of twig, so that trees along moving water manufacture flotillas of shoots to take root in muddy banks, a great adaptation by nature. Riverside communities are usually grateful for the erosion control. Ducks, too, say thank you. They like to nest between the big surface roots.

Planters can stick twigs and branches in the ground for laughably easy propagation, and cultivators can graft stock from differing trees into new varieties and hybrids. In sexual reproduction, the female flowers receive male pollen via wind or insects and are less than choosy about their willow mates. When their seeds ride out on fluffy parachutes, one never knows the exact breed that will sprout. But to sprout at all, the delicate seeds must land quickly on moist, sunny land.

Some 200 species of willow are known, about 100 in North America. It is a genus still becoming, with enough hybrids to torment even the experts who try to classify them. But only about 40 to 50 types tend to reach tree size. Knowing two or three common types in your urban area is a good start.

WHY THEY WEEP

Not every common willow weeps or even sniffles. What makes the Babylon willow so distinctive is its natural weeping habit. Most willow twigs sprout rather perkily off their branches. But every so often a nonweeping species will produce a weeping mutation, a tree whose branch buds angle away from the "leader" trunk or main boughs. Or whose shoot tips react to gravity by drooping, rather than heading upward on the strength of "reaction" wood—wood that strengthens itself to counteract gravity. These mutations may then be cultivated to produce a weeping variety or hybrid, which gains the appended name "pendula." For example, the weeping golden corkscrew or dragon's claw willow (*Salix matsudana* 'Tortuosa Aurea Pendula') not only dangles its twigs, but (as the term "Tortuosa" denotes) twists them. Look for this popular, contorted variety as a garden, campus, or cemetery specimen.

WILLOWS AROUND TOWN

Modest neighborhood yards often sport a sizable weeping willow, whose runaway roots and messy twigs can spark some lively feuds. In a number of towns west of the Rockies, small globular willows appear on so many front lawns they look like rows of vanity bulbs. But the larger weeping varieties are the troublemakers. On an Internet garden forum, a woman announced she was thinking about planting a weeping willow in her sunny backyard. She was practically flamed by respondents. "Willows are water thugs!" shouted one adviser.

The weeping thugs often escape to muddy urban areas, or are planted in park, institutional, or corporate settings where their roots can run wild. Ponds and lagoons are the obvious settings. A weeping willow reflected in water may be a landscaping cliché, but it is still a diamond in the city's rough.

THE DRY-EYED WILLOWS

By nature, the big nonweeping willows haunt waterways, creeks, and swamps and the moist lowlands of parks. The most common, America's native black willow, tends to be an unruly 50-foot brute with dark, massive, furrowed trunk. It plops down any which way it likes, leaning close to the ground or even lying on it. But from its seemingly lazy trunks and boughs—some of them half dead and hollow—come sprays of lively shoots with their cheerful scythe-shaped leaves and minileaves (stipules) at the base of the leafstalks.

Black willows tend to lean low, but their shoots often grow upward.

Peach or almond willow is another good-sized native found from Ohio west. The light green and wide (up to two-inch) leaves seem more peach- than willowlike, and the twigs are dark orange or red-brown.

Crack willow, introduced to America some time ago and used for charcoal and gunpowder, can be a burly tree—but the twigs snap with the twist of your fingers or a good wind. The three- to six-inch leaves are dark green on top, silvery below. Look for dot-sized glands on the leafstalks.

The western Scouler willow doesn't scowl; it was named for naturalist John Scouler, and in spring it graces the landscape with a litter of soft "pussy" catkins, earning the alternative nickname of "western pussy willow." Its leaves are often spatula-like, widest toward the tip. From shrub-size to some 80 feet tall, the tree is largest of the various species known as pussy willows.

Salix discolor is the shrub or small tree that Northeast and Midwest

America calls pussy willow. It earns that honor with the biggest "pussies," or silky male catkins, of any willow, about an inch long. It decorates many a small urban front yard, at risk of being plucked for someone's vase.

White willow is the great willow of Europe, long naturalized here and a component of many hybrids, weeping and not. The biggest willow around a number of cities, it can reach 100 feet in height and measure almost 10 feet thick, as did a trunk in Michigan (and one in Prague). Soft white hairs put a silvery sheen on the young leaves, which are later blue-gray. To Shakespeare, it was the willow "that shows its hoar leaves in the glassy stream."

English cricket bats come from a variety of white willow, but the tree's most famous product may be a compound called salicin. White willow bark and leaves, which contain it, were a cure-all prescription in ancient and folk medicine. In 1899 salicin extract was developed into aspirin, the most successful of all pharmaceuticals. Aspirin is now made synthetically.

Amateurs trying to identify hybrid willows might need that aspirin, or at least a mellow recording of "Willow Weep for Me," to calm themselves down. It is a frustrating endeavor—for we have not even touched on such shimmering-leaf willows as "shining" and "bay," or the prolific Carolina, ward, bebb, and scores more that might turn up within the city limits. Advice: Do the best you can, then sit by a willow and enjoy a good book.

LOMBARDY POPLAR

Populus nigra cv. 'Italica'

IMPORTANCE: A dramatically narrow tree whose branches gush upward to form a dense spire of shimmering foliage. Fast-growing, nonseeding, a widely popular tree for borders and vertical effects. Usually stands about 15–50 years before succumbing to canker disease.

FAMILY: Salicaceae (Willow). GENUS: *Populus* (poplar).

COMMON URBAN SPECIES: ☘ Lombardy poplar (*Populus nigra* cv. 'Italica') or Mormon tree.

CLOSE RELATIVES: ☘ Black poplar (*Populus nigra*).

TYPICAL CITY LOCATION: On borders between properties. As a screen to hide fences and absorb noise. Against buildings and walls. In confined yards and landscaping strips. Lining roadways and private drives. Background or vertical accent in designed parks.

KEY FEATURES: Narrow geyserlike form. Thickets of slender branches starting close to tree base and hugging the straight trunk as they rise skyward. Top branches frequently bare of foliage in mature trees.

Fluttering triangular leaves about 1½–3″ long and slightly broader at base, lustrous green on top, pale green beneath, not hairy, fine blunt teeth. Vivid yellow in fall. Leafstalks slender, flattened on sides, 2–3¼″ long.

Bark smooth and greenish gray (sometimes whitish) on upper branches; rough and brown-black on older trunk. All planted trees are male, with reddish 2″ caterpillar-like flowers.

AVERAGE MATURE SIZE IN CITY: 30–60′ high, 10–15′ wide, 1–3′ thick.

RECENT CHAMPION: None on American Forests *Register.* Heights of up to 150′ and trunk widths to 6′ have been cited. Michigan's champion is 81′ high with 20′ spread.

❧ NOBLE SENTRY, BRIEF FLAME

Measured by the growing pace of most trees, the Lombardy poplar shoots up like a geyser. In the 15 years it takes some oaks to grow 10 feet, the Lombardy becomes a 40- to 50-foot pillar of green flame, burning yellow in fall. Wasting little energy on outward growth, it holds its thickets of branches close to the trunk and pushes them skyward to create a narrow upright form known as "fastigiate." Among deciduous trees, none are more erect.

The Lombardy has long stood sentry along borders and fields. Its dense branches begin at the base of the trunk, often accompanied by new sprouts (suckers) from the assertive roots. Lined up, Lombardy poplars form a wall that nature can raise to 80 feet and more in one generation. Unfortunately, while the next generation watches, the wall is likely to be breached by a fungus that brings dripping, suffocating death to the trees.

Thus, the flame that rises so nobly is a brief one, often burning no more than 15 years before the cytospora canker disease—or a borer beetle—begins to bring it low. Landscape and garden authorities continually advise against planting the tree, recommending more resistant, longer-lived fastigiate species such as the Bolleana white poplar (see "White Poplar" profile). But to tens of thousands of planters, the Lombardy means "instant tree" and remains the upright sentry of choice.

MADE FOR THE CITY

Lombardy poplars fit narrow urban spaces as if invented for them. Parks commissioner Charles Stover worked 250 of the trees into New York's Hell's Kitchen during his 1910–1914 reign. In the slits between today's skyscrapers, slimness counts, as do style and grace. With its lithe form and dancing leaves, the Lombardy suits *la dolce vita* of downtown.

One would expect no less of a tree whose ancestor grew near fashionable Milan, Italy—though probably in a rustic setting along the Po River on the Plains of Lombardy. Sometime before 1750, cultivators from northern Europe encountered an unusual male tree. They believed it had sprung from one of the local black poplars; but unlike those vigorous, wide-spreading poplars, this offshoot grew narrowly upright. Thought to be a mutant (sport) of the black poplar species, the tree came to be classified as an Italian (*italica*) variety of *Populus nigra* (black poplar) and known commonly in English as Lombardy poplar.

Most botanists agree that the Lombardy had grown in Asia some time before being brought to Italy. But whatever the trees' ancient origins, the northern Europeans craved what they saw along the Po and took cuttings home with them. Soon scions of this Lombardy male were being propagated throughout Europe. The resultant trees delighted planters with their form, shimmering foliage, and strength as borders and windbreaks.

The tree spread quickly to America, propagated from the same male stock. Philadelphia

Lombardy poplar—"an exclamation point in landscape architecture."

gardener William Hamilton acquired one in 1784. Thomas Jefferson chose the tree to line Pennsylvania Avenue during his presidency. By the twentieth century, it was embraced throughout the continent, wherever it could grow from a cutting and stand tall. Mormons planted so many in their western settlements that "Mormon tree" became one of the few American nicknames for the variety. The tree seems to have responded to the honor by reaching extraordinary ages and sizes in Mormon country (Utah), where trunks five or six feet thick support vigorous gushers of foliage.

MAKING A POINT

The triangular lombardy poplar leaf, about the size of a matchbook.

Some believe the Lombardy to be the most widely planted ornamental tree in America, though it is fast being replaced. Still, along many urban fringes one sees Lombardys breaking the flat lines of factories, warehouses, industrial parks, golf courses, ball fields, schools, housing tracts, malls, airports, waterways, rail lines, and roads. And if these plantings are to last just 25 years or so, no one seems worried about it. There will be other trees, reconfigured landscapes, other people to worry.

In the suburbs, Lombardys (or close hybrids) are sometimes as common as cedar fences, serving to screen one property from another without such unneighborly annoyances as overhanging branches and grass-killing shade. But they do get ratty with age. One Internet correspondent bemoaned the condition of her exhausted 70-foot Lombardy, coveting the "leafy green" vigor of the neighbor's 50-footer. (She was advised to take down her 40-year-old giant before it killed someone.)

In downtown areas, the trees are especially striking when planted against a flat surface, say, a windowless concrete or brick façade. A row of Lombardy poplars underscores a building's upward aspiration, as architects might say. Against bland surfaces, the trees undulate, whisper, turn bronze in spring, then green and pale green, then gold. Elsewhere in town, even standing alone, the Lombardy serves as an exclamation point in landscape grammar.

The Lombardy leafblades are "deltoid," roughly like the triangular Greek letter delta. But they are smaller than most poplar leaves, about the size of a matchbook, and in the wind, they gyrate wildly on long and slightly flattened leafstalks. Clattering against one another, flashing their pale undersides in waves, they seem determined to live life to the fullest in their brief allotted time. You gotta like that in a city tree.

DYING UGLY

After life in the fast lane, the Lombardy most often faces a grim ending. With that in mind, a group of urban foresters in Oregon named the tree one they would most like to see *less* of. In doing so, they outlined the progress of the tree's canker disease: Rain splashes oozes of spores from old cankers onto leaves and bark wounds; infection spreads and forms new cankers on branches. The cankers grow until they girdle the branches and cut them off from nutrients. The tree dies from the top down, sometimes pushing out new sprouts from the trunk in desperation. No cure is known.

Of course, no tree death is pretty, but there are other problems with the Lombardy. Especially in Canada and the northern United States, poplar borer beetles bring woe to the tree, burrowing into the heart of the trunk and exposed roots. Ugly discharges of sap mark the burrow entrances. The wood structure is weakened and the tree dies or breaks.

Lombardys also share the poplars' trait of aggressive, wide-spreading, water-thirsty roots. A virtue in erosion control, the root system can wreak havoc near buildings. According to a tale from a British law firm, a Lombardy sucked moisture from the base of a house during a 1989–1990 drought and caused the structure to subside. Insurance proceedings began, and the tree was cut down. (Happily—except for the tree—a period of rainfall refreshed the soil and the house miraculously "floated" back into position.)

Poplars also transpire (evaporate moisture from their leaves) at a feverish rate, which calls for all the more water from the soil. Glands at the tips or sides of leaves may even exude drops of water, so that the trees are said to cry. In Roman mythology, "weeping" black poplars bemoan the death of young Phaëthon, whose pride led him to drive and lose control of the sun chariot. To save the world from burning, Jupiter slew Phaëthon and cast him into a river. Phaëthon's sisters, sobbing along the riverbank, were turned into poplars.

Could the mutant Lombardy poplar be Phaëthon's avenging spirit? See how it stabs at the heavens, how Jupiter strikes it down when it rises too high. A tempting fancy, and one in harmony with the tree's affinity for full sunshine: For Phaëthon, father was the sun itself.

Myths grow like leaves from the great trees. The Lombardy poplar is one tree you can find in town, listen to, and study as your own imagination soars.

Trembling (or Quaking) Aspen

Populus tremuloides

IMPORTANCE: A dramatic tree with chalky-white bark and the most wind-sensitive leaf of any broadleaf species. Brilliant yellow in fall. Widest natural distribution of any tree in North America.

FAMILY: Salicaceae (Willow). GENUS: *Populus* (poplar).

COMMON URBAN SPECIES: ❧ Trembling aspen (*Populus tremuloides*) or quaking a., quiver-leaf a., small-toothed a., American a., Canadian a., quakie, popple.

CLOSE RELATIVES: ❧ European aspen (*P. tremula*) or common a. ❧ Bigtooth aspen (*P. grandidentata*). ❧ White poplar (*P. alba*). ❧ Gray poplar (*P. canescens*).

Typical city location: Malls and plazas (especially in western or mountain towns), hillsides, edges of park thickets, sunny open spots including vacant areas, golf courses, cemeteries, and parkways where suckering (tree sprouts from roots) is not a problem or can be managed.

Key features: Waferlike leaves that dance in any breath of air; almost round, 1½–3″ across, with small point at tip; fine regular teeth around edges; shiny light green on upper surface, paler matte green below; radiant gold in winter. Leafstalks are long, slender, ribbony, pinched flat, catching breezes and fluttering the leafblades.

Foliage begins high on trunk and forms a modest rounded crown. Trunk rises polelike with slight taper.

Bark greenish white to bright white with narrow black horizontal lines and black scarring from lost branches or other trauma; does not peel like paper birch bark. Base of older trunk becomes black, furrowed, and warty.

Average mature size in city: 20–60′ high, ¾–1½′ thick.

Recent champion: 109′ height, 59′ spread, 10′ circumf., Ontonagon County, Mich.

❧ Mover and Shaker

One expects to find shaking and quaking in New York City, but not necessarily a forest tree that trembles in all five boroughs day and night for three seasons a year.

Yet there it is, the trembling or quaking aspen, growing in New York City and almost every county within 50 miles (according to the New York Metropolitan Flora Project), not to mention a total of 38 states, including Alaska, and every province of Canada.

The trembling aspen is the most widely distributed tree species in North America, the only transcontinental broadleaf tree, growing naturally from Newfoundland to California and Mexico. In the United States, it misses only the Southeast and south-central states.

You can almost hear it: Those millions of trembling aspens, each with thousands of nervous leafblades quivering on ribbony stalks in the least air current, the thin but firm leaf surfaces brushing together in a transcontinental *hshhhh*. In fall, the round leaves rustle like mini-tambourines, golden against the skies.

NO QUIVERING AT CROSSWALK

In cities, most of this leaf action takes place in sunny spaces away from downtown sidewalks, because the trembling aspen—pretty as it is with its lollipop foliage and straight white trunk—rarely works as a street tree. It doesn't like compacted soil or partial shade, hosts a ton of diseases when stressed, and would be lucky to live 15 years without intensive care. Its favorite survival stunt is suckering, or sending up new tree sprouts from its roots—and nobody wants an aspen thicket at curbside. The smooth bark, which scars easily, invites neighborhood calligraphers. Male trees would litter the sidewalks with their spent catkins (caterpillar-like flowers). Females would pump cottony seeds into the air from their dangling bracelets of seed capsules. And the lovely rain-like whisper of the trembling leaves would be lost in the roar of traffic.

As a rule, when aspens come to town they wind up along highways and in parks, cemeteries, and other roomy sites where their natural traits can shine: A golf course needs thirsty trees in high-moisture areas. Eroding gravelly hillsides need roots. Corporate or institutional landscapers like the naturalistic feel of light-toned aspens against dark conifers. Some cities are lucky enough to have forested parks edged with aspens.

In addition to suckering, aspens can reproduce through wind-borne seed, but the tiny perishable seed must find a quick bed of moist soil in the sun. In 1870, one seed swathed itself in the wet dust of a Greensburg, Ind., courthouse roof. A bushy, freakishly old aspen was still hanging in there in the 1990s.

Seeds tend to incubate in a city's so-called "disturbed" spaces or wastelands, where sun and mud are plentiful. Aspens will take refuge here and even more willingly in burned-out areas, "perpetually re-stocking the land that man has ruined," as one writer puts it. In nature, aspens are among the first trees ("pioneers") to spring up after a forest fire. They rise quickly in the full sun and provide cover for such shade-loving trees as maples and conifers, which will eventually grow to shade and replace the aging aspens.

In aspen territory, any scorched earth can draw the trees. As Napoléon invaded Moscow, Russian patriots burned the city down rather than leave it to the French. It is said that the ruins were taken over by the European or common aspen, a close cousin to the trembling aspen.

The wide-ranging European aspen figures in at least two successful urban trees: the upright European aspen, a columnlike variety from the Swedish forests, and gray poplar, a cross between European aspen and white poplar, common along French roads.

As for the trembling aspen, it can be made to work in towns where few other trees grow readily. In parts of the Rockies, Great Basin, and Southwest, elevation or climate limits the choice of urban trees. Landscapers often nurture the local native aspens. Though it prefers well-drained moist settings, the tree does well in high, dry areas, and the golden foliage—especially of a western variety (*aurea*)—brings mountain splendor to the streets.

In Flagstaff, Ariz., a white-barked young specimen gleams against a dark background—not of conifers, but of a sprawling blue Wal-Mart superstore. Another aspen takes center stage at a café plaza in Flagstaff's charming old-town area. Where gunslingers once quaked in their boots, boot-wearing urbanites now sip espresso—and leave the quaking to the tree.

ANCIENT TREMBLER

No one knows how long the aspen has been trembling. The poplar genus, of which the aspen is a member, has been around some 100 million years. Quaking aspen pollen at least 16,000 years old has been recovered in the U.S. Midwest. Individual aboveground aspen trees live only some 50 to 60 years, but the root system from which they and their clones spring is an organism that grows and endures to eerie extents. One such root system in Minnesota is estimated to be 8,000 years old.

Another in Utah has some 47,000 stems.

The aspen's age, distribution, and distinctive traits have assured its place in folklore. Why does the tree tremble? In sadness and shame, says one legend, because Jesus Christ was crucified upon a cross made of aspen. Another tale has Jesus cursing the tree for its arrogance. Folkloric comparisons between the wagging leaves and women's tongues were often made—and perpetuated by tongue-wagging men.

Folk healers with a homeopathic bent prescribed quaking aspen for quaking palsy victims. The patient pinned a lock of hair to the tree and chanted, in effect, "You shake so I don't have to." Folk remedies from the tree in-

Trembling aspen's waferlike leaves on ribbony stalks. Unlike birch bark, the bright white bark does not peel.

cluded a bark tea for menstrual cramps and bowel and urinary disorders. (The inner bark, a favorite of beavers, is quinine-bitter.) In Canada, early settlers chewed the bark to make a poultice for bleeding wounds; hunters masked their (no doubt formidable) human scent with an aspen extract; and parents lined baby cradles with soft rotted aspen wood. Mohawk, Cree, Delaware, Fox, and Chippewa tribes used aspen medicine for, respectively, worms, coughs, weakness, and nose colds, and to prevent premature childbirth.

Although aspen wood is soft and weak, settlers built cabins with the logs and Mormon pioneers made aspen furniture. Its resistance to splintering and ability to shred makes it useful for boxes, matches, and padding. One contemporary firm shreds the wood into Sani-Chip rodent bedding.

Today's major aspen product is pulp for magazine paper. Along with trembling aspen, the industry harvests a slightly larger relative, bigtooth aspen, so named because its leaves are edged with wavy motor-gear-like teeth. The bigtooth grows mainly in the Northeast and Great Lakes areas of the United States. It rarely makes its way into town.

THE PERFECT TREMOR

Many types of leaves tremble, especially those of the poplar group. Each species has its own style. Big glossy cottonwood leaves clatter, sounding like applause. The white poplar leaf blinks green and white as it flips over. But the aspen leaf, a wafery wind catcher that pivots at right angles to a wind-catching stalk, stands alone as a metaphor for protracted shaking: ". . . hand did quake and tremble like a leafe of Aspin greene" (Edmund Spenser).

Onandagas called the North American aspen "nut-ki-e," meaning noisy leaf, but its scientific name and most of its common names refer to its motion. It trembles, quakes, or quivers depending on air movement and the maturity of the leaf. *Tremuloides* is Latin for "like *tremula*," which refers to the European *tremula* ("trembling") aspen. Nature writers describe the motion as "like sparkling water," "like ripples on the surface of a stream," and "like thousands of butterfly wings." But the words mean little until you hunt down this tree and see for yourself what trembling is all about.

White Poplar

Populus alba

IMPORTANCE: A strapping poplar tree whose leaves flip from dark green to white as the breezes turn them. Upper bark usually a burnished white with black diamond pattern. Distinctive and urban-tough, the tree has appealed to planters since colonial times.

FAMILY: Salicaceae (Willow). GENUS: *Populus* (poplar).

COMMON URBAN SPECIES: ❀ White poplar (*Populus alba*) or abele, silver p., woolly p., maple-leaved p. ❀ (Cultivated variety) Bolleana poplar (*P. alba* 'Pyamidalis'). ❀ (Cultivated variety) Silver poplar (*P. alba* 'Nivea').

CLOSE RELATIVES: ❀ Gray poplar (*P. canescens*). ❀ Quaking aspen (*P. tremuloides*).

TYPICAL CITY LOCATION: Roadsides, highway embankments, parks, cemeteries, seaside acreage, waterways, property borders, old and abandoned dwellings.

KEY FEATURES: Upper side of mature leaf is dark green and leathery; bottom side and stalks are coated with feltlike white hairs. (Young leaves are woolly on both sides.) Leafblades 2–5″ long. Shape varies considerably, from arrowhead to maplelike, with dulled points (lobes) or large wavy teeth. 'Nivea' variety shows mostly the maplelike (palm-shaped) leaf. Leafstalk is long, thin, flexible, partly flattened.

Bark of higher trunk and branches tends to be smooth white (sometimes greenish gray) with many horizontal rows of diamond-shaped black marks. Does not peel like birch bark. Lower trunk becomes black and furrowed. Suckers often sprout from trunk base or roots.

A many-branched tree; may have multiple trunks. Crown spreads wide, with open spaces.

Male flowers resemble 4″ purplish caterpillars. Female flowers (on separate trees) produce hanging bracelets of small seed capsules, which release tiny black seeds attached to tufts of hairs.

AVERAGE MATURE SIZE IN CITY: 40–80′ high, 2–3′ thick.

RECENT CHAMPION: 93′ height, 86′ spread, 22′ circumf., St. Charles, Ill.

❧ TWO-TONE IMPORT

A native of Eurasia, the spirited white poplar has made its way to North America to join the local *Populus* clan, which includes the cottonwood and aspen poplars. A big drinker with rambunctious roots, the tree has charmed Americans since colonial times with its flashy two-tone foliage and stylish white bark. No tree has quite the look of a white poplar when even a breath of wind makes a flip card of every leaf—dark glossy green, then soft and silvery white.

Unlike today's homeowners, settlers would have welcomed the tree's habit of splaying its roots in search of water. Acreage was abundant, sewer lines unknown. The roots merely reinforced the soil. The white poplar's habitual "suckering"—throwing off new offspring from its roots— would have created a pleasing thicket, helped drain swampy land, and formed a windbreak. But as towns rose, the trees' plumbing came into conflict with residential pipes, and the root system became "invasive." White poplars were exiled to the borders of housing plots if planted at all. Many escaped by seed to the woods or abandoned areas. Those planted in town today are mainly for erosion control, binding highway embankments and other slippery slopes.

LOOKING FOR ABELE

A common English name for the white poplar is the somewhat mysterious "abele." It is thought to be of Dutch origin or perhaps related to the Flemish botanist Matthias de l'Obel, for whom the tree inspired a title-page device and a motto, *Candore et spe*— Candor and hope. To M. l'Obel, the leaf's white underside symbolized candor, and the green

THE SWEATBAND TREE

How did the white poplar leaf get its two tones? An evolutionary trail may be lacking, but mythology fills in. It seems that Hercules, fresh from a victory, seized a poplar branch and wreathed it around his head. He wore this crown on a descent into Hades, and in the infernal heat his perspiration blanched the undersides of the leaves while the hellish smoke blackened their upper surfaces. Somehow the pattern stuck.

In another tale, Pluto, the king of the Underworld, changed his beloved nymph Leuce into a white poplar upon her death. (*Leuce* is the Greek name for the tree, from *leukos* or "white.") Listen carefully for her sighs as you visit this species.

The narrow Bolleana variety of white poplar is more durable than the look-alike lombardy poplar.

side hope. Consider that as you gaze at the full winking foliage of a big abele: *candor-hope, candor-hope, candor-hope,* flashing like a digital billboard.

Although the tree has established itself in most of temperate North America, today's urban explorer might have to treasure hunt in parks and open areas to find a wide-spreading beauty. In nature, abeles prefer to be off by themselves.

A few cultivated varieties are much easier to spot in town. The Bolleana poplar, for example, is a narrow, upward-gushing tree frequently replacing the shorter-lived Lombardy poplar (see that profile) as a border planting. This and the silver poplar variety 'Nivea' are handsome ornamentals: glorious when sunlight flickers on the two-toned foliage and textured white bark; wistful as they bow to November winds and spend their (sometimes) reddish or pale yellow autumn leaves.

In spring, male abeles announce themselves with carmine red flowers (catkins), caterpillar-shaped and up to four inches long. Wind-borne catkin pollen drifts to the yellow-green female flowers on separate trees. From the fertilized flowers come hanging charm bracelets of minute green capsules, the fruit typical of poplars. The capsules will later release cotton-tufted seeds. The male catkins fall to the ground.

After the flowers come the leaves—foliage that delights sight and touch. Many other tree species produce two-tone leaves, dark on top and light on bottom. But the abele provides one of the most striking contrasts, on a leaf that rivals the trembling aspen for its restless tossing and twisting. Young growth is the whitest, with twig, buds, stalk, and leaf bottoms seemingly sprayed with talc. The whiteness comes from an abundance of tiny smooth hairs, which feel as velvety to the touch as an equine muzzle. Such woolliness is known as *tomentose* among botanists, and the coating itself the *tomentum.*

At maturity, the leaf surfaces are lustrous forest green (upper) and silky, silvery green (underside). Before the usual summer afflictions curl and spot them, the leafblades seem like new Naugahyde cutouts, and rather inventive ones. Many of the shapes mimic the maple leaf but never achieve the depth and sharpness of true maple lobes. Some look like a small maple leaf worn dull by salt winds, others like a rectangle thinking about becoming a maple leaf. All have hairy undersides.

DOWNSIDE

The downside of a downy side, of course, is that it catches dirt. Various writers have noted that the white poplar leaf gets unsightly as it collects soot and grime on its woolly bottom. But few city observers will be put off by a little grunge on a tree that still sparkles overall. Nor will they worry about the suckering that so discourages cottage gardeners. The more one cuts back these new sprouts or threatens the parent, the more vigorously the offspring seem to grow—"until," says one intrepid gardener of old, "the grubbing hoe and axe have been resorted to." And even then one may not see the last of this persistent tree.

The white poplar tolerates drought, semishade, smoke, salt air, and some deicing salt. It is relatively disease-resistant, cankering less than the Lombardy poplar. It can bind sandy or marshy soil. As for vandalism, what self-respecting initial carver would compete with the black

Dark green on top and silvery white on bottom, white poplar leaves put on a show when they flutter.

diamonds engraved across the tight white surface of the bark? The upper white bark is difficult to reach anyway on older trees, whose bottom fifteen feet look diped in runny cement.

As a street tree, the species may need some work. But for city landscapers seeking biodiversity, the white poplar and its cultivated varieties (including a weeping 'Pendula') offer tough, yet romantic trees for selective use.

Birch

Betula papyrifera, B. pendula, B. nigra, and others

European white birch, with drooping shoots.

IMPORTANCE: The great tree of cold northern climes, famous for its often white, waterproof, peeling bark and its many historic uses. Serves as a brilliant ornamental in urban landscapes, though short-lived and subject to infestation. State tree of New Hampshire, provincial tree of Saskatchewan and Quebec.

FAMILY: Betulaceae (Birch). GENUS: *Betula* (birch).

COMMON URBAN SPECIES: ❧ Paper birch (*Betula papyrifera*) or paperbark b., canoe b., white b. ❧ European white birch (*B. pendula*) or silver b., common b. ❧ River birch (*B. nigra*) or red b. ❧ Gray birch (*B. populifolia*). ❧ 'Whitespire' (*B. platyphylla* 'Whitespire', a cultivated variety of Japanese white birch).

TYPICAL CITY LOCATION: Parks, yards, plazas, waterfronts. *Gray birch:* Waste sites, roadsides, sandy areas.

KEY FEATURES: Birches are usually medium- to large-sized trees, light in density, with distinctive whitish or red-brown peeling bark; spade-shaped (as in playing-card suit) leaves, firm-textured, with two or more sizes of sawteeth; and, from late summer through spring, tassel-like (male) catkins at the tips of twigs. Short woody spurs project from the small branches. Often grown as multiple-trunked trees.

Paper birch: Bark on large branches and young trunk is smooth ivory or creamy white, marked with thin raised horizontal lines (lenticels). Peels in curls and large ragged sheets as trunk expands. Orange inner bark. Leafblade 2–5", rounded at base.

European white birch: Very thin drooping shoots (new growth) off the branchlets. Warty twigs. Red-brown bark becomes satiny white with black diamonds and vertical fissures, little or no peeling. Leafblade 1–3" long, cultivated varieties with long curved tip, often sharply and deeply indented along sides, rich yellow in fall.

River birch: Symmetrical branching. Young bark reddish brown or darker; mature bark (especially of cultivated varieties) peels in extremely shaggy flakes of pink, peach, orange, brown. Leafblade glossy, 2–4", wedge-shaped at base.

AVERAGE MATURE SIZE IN CITY: 25–60' high, ½–2' thick.

RECENT CHAMPION: *Paper:* 107' height, 76' spread, 19' circumf., Point Aux Barques, Mich. *River:* 111' height, 96' spread, 13' circumf., Lamar County, Ala.

❧ BARK *AND* BITE

In more sexist times, male poets portrayed the white-barked birch tree as meek and demurely feminine. For Coleridge, it was "the Lady of the Woods." James Russell Lowell called it the "most shy and ladylike of trees." They saw femininity in the silkiness of the tree's bark, the grace and delicacy of its branch structure, the fluttery lightness of its foliage. The bark was often virgin white. And when exposed to oppressive heat, most species soon fainted away.

Yet these same poets might have known the tree's toughness in their youth, when disciplinarians applied a birch switch to the lads' tender parts. Birch has no greater virtue, said a 1551 herbal, than "for the betynge of stubborn boys, that either lye or will not learn." But its rugged virtues are many. It endures the brutal northern climates better than any other deciduous tree. It has long served for weapons, shelter, snow crossing, water travel, and fuel.

Feminine associations still crop up, as with the "Mother's Tree" birches planted on Mother's Day in various U.S. locales. Arlington National Cemetery is the site of the National Mother's Tree, a birch. But, in fact, each birch tree packs both female and male sexuality: erect female catkins beneath dangling male tassels. Fertilization produces legions of tiny biwinged seeds. The seedlings become the staunch pioneer trees of burned-out forestland and moist wasteland.

Robert Frost ("Birches," 1916) knew the truth of birches, how they bend without breaking, how the snow-white trunk could take a world-weary climber toward Heaven, until the tree dipped to set him down again, renewed.

BEAUTY'S MIXED BLESSING

Ladies or not, some half dozen (of about 60) species of birch are blessed with features that have made them irresistible to urban landscapers. The three most common species in America are the paper birch and European white birch, both white-barked trees for colder zones, and the heat-tolerant river birch, a shaggy brown-barked species whose pink-barked 'Heritage' variety is planted in cities as far south as Florida and Texas.

Each of these species boasts an airy branching pattern and a graceful leaf—dark green, double-sawtoothed, and more or less spade-shaped. But what has most attracted human attention is the distinctive bark. For the amazingly waterproof and durable bark of the paper birch, Native Americans stripped the trunks of the great forest trees to fashion canoes, wigwams, containers, torches. Eurasians exploited their native white birch for the silvery, parchmentlike bark and its

Birch leaves. From left, cutleaf European white b.; European white b.; river b. (glossy, with V-base); paper b. (rounded base).

herbal and tanning oils. And for white or curly bark to ornament lawn and garden, modern landscapers have brought water-loving birch species into urban settings, where dry and compacted soils often lead to tree stress and fatal infestations.

The bark qualities that stir wonder also inspire bark abuse among the naïve or mean-spirited. The chalky white surface of a paper birch tempts carvers. The curly ends of peeling (*exfoliating*) bark invite stripping—often injuring the tree, which at best heals the wound with a grungy dark patch. Children love to peel off a pretty white strip, sometimes to make miniature canoes. Birch bark for casual use or kicks should come from fallen trees or limbs, whose resinous bark is preserved long after the wood rots. Intact bark has been found even on fossilized birch wood in Siberia.

THE NATIVE PAPER BIRCH

The North American paper birch vies for the title of champion of the white barks, along with aspen, white poplar, and the European white birch. You can gather some of that whiteness without peeling the bark; just rub your hand on the trunk and see the residue. Lacking the tannin of the inner bark, the outer bark layers are made up of clear cells and air spaces that reflect light in all directions, which makes for the perception of white. The whiteness prompts landscapers to set the tree against dark background conifers, a stirring sight often encountered in nature.

The outer bark's cellular structure—alternate layers of smaller and larger cells—might also account for the characteristic peeling, as the larger cells are more easily ruptured by environmental changes. The inner bark, layered with cork cells, insulates the tree from cold. It waterproofs anything made from the bark—including the celebrated birch canoe. (Because the stripped bark curls in on itself, the canoes were built white-side-in.)

Paper birch is one of several birches with thin raised horizontal lines, like long dashes, circling the bark. These stretched-out breathing pores known as lenticels add to the high design of the tree. As the tree ages, it

Peeling, waterproof, white bark of North America's paper birch.

gets dark and rough on the lower trunk, but by then the tree may be well along on its brief life in the city, some 30 years. The most dazzling ornamental specimens—often grown with two or three trunks—are probably young adults. Juvenile trees are still shiny reddish brown.

Paper birch comes in several natural variations, named according to region: the western, mountain, Kenai, Alaska, and northwestern paper birches. From its smaller birch, Alaska draws a commercial syrup—medicinal-tasting in this writer's opinion, but divine in a butter-toffee confection known as Birch Logs.

EMBRACING THE EUROPEAN WHITE BIRCH

In the northern cities and to some extent in the American Southwest, the European white birch is treated like a native daughter—or son—and embraced as an ornamental. The tree doesn't always survive the embrace, being one of the birches most vulnerable to stress and infestation. But it remains the most commonly planted birch in the United States, owing to its fine white bark and a romantic drooping posture. (The *pendula* in its scientific name, *Betula pendula,* means hanging down.)

Also known as silver birch, the tree grows abundantly in the northern regions of Europe and Asia and has long been part of daily life and lore there. Branches, sacred to the Nordic god Thor, were hung in homes to ward off evil. Lapps and Finns perfected the art of "birch switching" or branch whippings as a finale to the sauna sweat. The light but strong wood served for such everyday artifacts as broom handles and cradles. The bark became cloaks and leggings as well as a writing surface. (The name "birch" relates to the Sanskrit *bhurja,* "a tree whose bark is used for writing upon.")

From the tree's abundant sap came various alcoholic brews, some still made today. The Russian people mastered the distillation of oil from the outer bark, creating a major product known as birch tar for preservation of leather. The thick brown liquid, with a balsamic odor, gives Russian leather its distinctive smell.

White birch tea contains oils of the leaves and shoots, which were thought to dissolve kidney stones and treat other ailments. In her 1996 *Leaves in Myth, Magic and Medicine,* Alice Thoms Vitale recommends a skin wash made from a palmful of birch leaves steeped in a cup of boiling water for two or three minutes (five to eight minutes for acne).

The European white birch arrived in Virginia before 1752 and was thoroughly Americanized in the 1920s, when Calvin Coolidge planted one on the White House grounds. (Washington is too hot for the paper birch.) Now it can be found in most U.S. regions—excluding the Southeast—and even as an escapee to the woods. One can distinguish it from paper birch by the fine shoots that droop straight down, the warty young twigs, and the bark, which barely peels and is marked by diamond-shaped cracks. Observers be warned, however, that birch trees crossbreed readily, and many specimens will be a blend of species and their characteristics.

Still, two cultivated varieties stand out clearly in American landscapes: the 'Crispa' or cutleaf weeping birch, whose deeply indented leaf edges and extreme drooping make it a favorite ornamental; and the 'Purpurea' group, as flashy a show of purple-bronze foliage as can be seen against silver-white bark.

Such beauty pays a price in vigor. Of European white birches in general, horticultural writer Michael Dirr notes that "the tree should not be stressed—you might as well send a formal dinner invitation to the bronze birch borer." For the species, stress means conditions unlike the tree's natural cool, moist, and well-drained settings. The cultivated varieties especially need pampering: dedicated watering, fertilizing, spraying, pruning. Otherwise, as Dirr notes, the borer reduces them "to rubble." (It attacks paper birch, too.)

It is sad to see an infested birch and all too easy to play diagnostician. Deteriorated brown foliage usually means birch-leaf miner, a bug that tunnels through the leaves. It is rarely fatal. But a balding crown and tunnels puffing up the bark inevitably signal bronze birch borer (*Agrilus anxius*)—and the end. The wormy larvae cut off the sap flow as they tunnel from the top down. When they emerge as adults, they chew a D-shaped hole in the bark—D for Death to the host.

THE FEISTY RIVER BIRCH

Only the shaggy brown river birch seems truly adapted to cities, holding its own with urban heat blasts and the deadly borer. Native to the streams and rivers of eastern America, the river or red birch is one fine tree for the neighborhood. Not only is it hardy in all U.S. climate zones, but it is fast-growing, nicely forked, wind- and ice-storm-resistant, and ornamental. The shimmering, glossy green leaf has a silvery or bluish underside. Often the fall color is golden yellow.

River birch bark practically explodes into flakes of brown, salmon, orange, and peach.

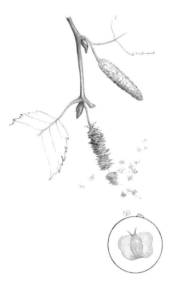

Fertilized female birch flowers, or strobiles, break up to release buglike winged seeds.

River birch bark is naturally platy or flaky; in cultivated varieties, it peels in colorful flakes of brown, salmon, peach, orange, and lavender—as if some child had gone wild with crepe paper. The superb 'Heritage' variety provides a pinkish-white bark, a bonus for regions deprived of the paper and European white birches.

River birch will give a good two decades as a street tree if its low branches are trimmed and the soil is acidic and watered. Twenty years isn't bad on the street. It may live more than 50 years in more watery settings, such as golf courses and river parks.

Alone of all birches, the river birch drops its seeds in spring, a strategy developed so that river floods can carry the offspring to new territories. In cities, the seeding conelike fruits make for a keen spring observation.

BARKING UP OTHER BIRCHES

Among other birches seen around town is the 'Whitespire' or Japanese white birch, recognizable by its narrow, pyramidal form, leathery dark green leaves, and elegant chalk-white bark that does *not* peel. Descended from a single tree in Japan's Yatsugatake Mountains and tweaked by cultivators in Wisconsin, it gets mixed reviews of its supposed heat-tolerance and resistance to bronze birch borer.

Gray birch is a persistent tree of northeastern North America. It grows like a weed in urban spaces, rarely cultivated. Smallish and short-lived, it can nevertheless grace a landscape with its multiple trunks of white or lustrous gray bark with profuse black scarring. The leaf is a glossy triangle with a long "pennant" tip.

The bark of many wonderful birches comes up a shade short for urban stardom. Two northeastern species worth hunting, however, are the yellow (*B. alleghaniensis*) and sweet (*B. lenta*) birches. Both reward the finder with a delightful wintergreen oil in the broken or chewed twigs. Yellow birch bark is gray-yellow and peeling. That of the sweet birch is dark gray-brown.

Whichever birches you pursue, be grateful for their presence and concerned for their future. Global warming could be pushing them northward, away from cities where once they could handle the heat.

AMERICAN BEECH
(AND ITS EUROPEAN KIN)

Fagus grandifolia (and *Fagus sylvatica*)

IMPORTANCE: One of the magnificent, long-lived members of the royal family Beech, which includes beeches, oaks, and chestnuts. Beloved for its skin-smooth (often initialed) bark, commanding and harmonious form, vivid leaf colors, and creaturelike surface roots. Not urban-tough. Usually an isolated specimen tree in town.

FAMILY: Fagaceae (Beech). GENUS: *Fagus* (beech).

COMMON URBAN SPECIES: ⚜ American beech (*Fagus grandifolia*) or red b., white b., beechnut, "initial tree."

CLOSE RELATIVES: ❧ European beech (*Fagus sylvatica*) or common b., and its varieties: purple or "copper beech" (*F. sylvatica* f. *purpurea*), weeping (*F. sylvatica pendula*), and fernleaf (*F. sylvatica* 'Asplenifolia').

TYPICAL CITY LOCATION: Parks, campuses, cemeteries, private grounds.

KEY FEATURES: Round or bell-shaped form. Low branches heavy and horizontal; higher branches bowed slightly downward. Leaves cluster in horizontal planes. Bark is tight, skinlike at any age, light blue-gray, with some dark mottling. Muscular surface roots suggest fantastic anatomical limbs.

Leafblade 3–5", spear-tip shaped, lustrous sea green above, lighter below, with 9 or more sets (often 13–16) of straight veins ending in spiny teeth. (*European beech* leafblade has 5–9 sets of veins, slightly curved and ending in wavy leaf edge.) Leafstalk ½" long or less. Slender, ¾", thorn-sharp buds.

Fruits are ½–¾" triangular oily nuts, usually two inside a green-brown prickled husk (cupule) that opens at first frost and drops nuts.

AVERAGE MATURE SIZE IN CITY: *American:* 50–70' high, 45–60' wide, 2–4' thick. *European:* 50–70' high, 35–45' wide.

RECENT CHAMPION: *American:* 115' height, 138' spread, 24' circumf., Harwood, Md.

❧ A. L. ♥ A. B.
(ALL LOVERS LOVE A BEECH)

No tree has so fair a bole as . . . the beech . . . with its neat, close, tight-looking bark, like the dress which athletes wear.
   —Henry David Thoreau, *Journals*

To children in the darkening woods, the fleshlike trunk and muscular roots can be petrifying. But to lovers, the bosomy smoothness and overall splendor of the American beech is simply heart-melting. Many a

Winter reveals the bell-shaped branching structure of the beech.

couple commemorate their meltdown by carving hearts and initials into the canvas of pewter-gray bark. Such markings, which may last for centuries on the long-lived tree, have become as much associated with the species as its edible beechnuts.

Beech love is far from new. Some 2,000 years ago, according to Pliny the Elder, a Roman aristocrat romanced a European beech tree in a sacred grove of Diana on the Alban Hills. Confusing the tree with the goddess, he embraced it, kissed it, lay in its shadow, and poured wine on its trunk. Today's tree lovers may be less physical, but no less passionate. In 1998, for example, protesters campaigned for months to rescue a century-old beech from the bulldozer at a University of Connecticut campus. (They failed, but salvaged 40 new-growth twigs for repotting.)

America's appreciation of its beech—the only *Fagus* species native to North America—took an odd turn when colonists encountered the eastern beech forests where the trees soared over 100 feet and shaded out most other undergrowth. The settlers came to realize that beech groves, with dense layers of fertilizing leaves on the ground, marked some of the richest agricultural soil. And so they lopped down the trees to make farms. As lumber, the wood lacked tensile strength, but made for excellent fuel and small artifacts.

Beech groves still exist, mostly in well-drained forest regions of America's eastern third. Like maple, the beech comes to dominate its turf by tolerating shade when young, piercing the canopy as a taller neighbor expires, and finally shading its own sun-dependent neighbors into extinction. With male and female flowers on the same tree, it produces an abundance of seeds; but few of these beechnuts escape the more than 30 wildlife species that relish them. Instead, the tree reproduces by growing suckers from its roots, vigorous suckers that become mighty colonies of interconnected beech trees.

The American beech looks like a rugged tree that could handle urban life, but in fact it is very particular where it puts its burly feet. Wiggling its toes in roomy forest loam, the tree is huge and hardy, resists pests, and can live 300 or 400 years. But in the compacted or disturbed soils of the streets, the tree is miserable and shows it.

Even if healthy, the beech is the wrong tree for traffic routes. In good soil and open sunlight, it spreads wide and protects its trunk with low branches that bring massive foliage almost to the ground. Other than in such groomed communities as Newport, R.I., the American beech appears in towns mainly as a "specimen" tree. Carefully placed and tended, it usually stands alone in parklike landscapes to be admired—and, when no one is looking, initialed.

LOVELY OF LEAF

The mature American beech offers much more to admire than its famous bark. Its branches radiate evenly into a near-perfect bell jar outline. Many a nature writer has waxed lyrical over its foliage. "An unearthly pale pure green clothes the tree in a misty nimbus of light," croons Donald Culross Peattie of the first spring foliage. The bright young leaves soon lose their ethereal fuzz, darken to a sea green, and expand to about five inches of exquisite geometry. Some 9 to 16 sets of veins run straight as rail ties to the leaf edges, where they end in sharp points. The lustrous, papery leaves cluster in distinctive horizontal planes, like layers of awnings catching the light.

When autumn turns the foliage to a mountain of gold, poets scramble for words. And the beauty goes on. Through winter, the lower branches retain many of their leaves, now coppery or whitish. Early settlers treasured even the fallen leaves, stuffing their mattresses with them. "The smell is grateful and wholesome," wrote one pioneer, "they do not harbor vermin, are very elastic, and may be replenished annually without cost."

Also worth noting are the beech's slender buds, like ¼-inch pointy cigars; the male flowers, miniature pom-poms on a string; and the woody prickled fruit case, whose four valves open like a pair of beaks to release the triangular, oil-rich nuts. Called "beech mast," the nutritious peanut-sized nuts of American and European beeches have long fattened hogs and fowl. Stone Age people ate beechnuts. Other societies have favored them as a treat. *Fagus,* the Latin (and scientific) name for the beech genus, came from a Greek word for eating. The tree you eat is how some ancients saw it.

A DOWNTOWN BEECH FROM EUROPE

The American beech has one major variant known as Carolina beech (var. *caroliniana*), a southern tree with smaller, thicker, darker leaves. But otherwise it is happy to be who it is, where it is: It spawns no varieties for cultivation, and in foreign plantings proves a poor traveler. The closely related European or common beech is just the opposite. Offspring often vary in interesting ways, and dozens of the best ones have been cultivated into superb varieties that thrive far from their Eurasian homelands.

Brought to North America before 1752, the tree and its cultivars are generally better adapted to city conditions than the American beech. This tolerance, along with the charm of such cultivars as weeping, fernleaf, and copper (purple-leaved) beech, has assured the pres-

Beech leaves and nut. From left, American b., with spiny teeth; pointy nut in bur; European b., with wavy edges; fernleaf European b.

ence of fine beech specimens in coast-to-coast urban America and Canada. Two European fernleaf beeches, planted by the First Ladies Johnson and Nixon, grace the White House grounds.

Like the American beech, the European beech is a large, slow-growing tree, similar in form, flower, and fruit. But its foliage quickly distinguishes it from the North American species: The leaf edges are wavy, not pointy-toothed, where the veins meet them; and vein sets usually number in single figures (five to nine) rather than double. The bark is eye-catching, but no match for that of the American beech. It is darker and rougher, often likened to elephant hide.

Beeches that form a giant weeping heap or sport exotically colored or filigreed leaves are always European varieties. Some observers consider the copper beech, with its deep reddish-purple foliage, to be one of nature's stateliest beauties. Tree expert Hugh Johnson dismisses it as "the biggest red thing there is to grow." Johnson also finds the weeping beech "a monstrosity," but urban communities tend to treasure their old specimens. One giant weeper in Flushing (Queens), N.Y., was honored on its 150th birthday in 1998—and died a year later.

A runty, contorted European beech variety (*F. sylvatica* 'Tortuosa') is actually called "monster" or "parasol" beech. Striking when snow-covered, its branches twist like "snakes in a frenzy," wrote a staff member about the Arnold Arboretum's specimen in Massachusetts.

CARVED IN HISTORY

For all their sacrosanct beauty, beeches have suffered trunk abuse from carvers dating back at least to Virgil (70–19 B.C.), the Roman poet who asked,

> *Or shall I rather the sad verse repeat*
> *Which on the beech's bark I lately writ?*

In northern Europe, ancient runic inscriptions on the bark might have prompted the English name "beech" via Germanic words for "book" or "letter." The Polish word for beech is *buk.*

One famously inscribed American beech grew in Tennessee, between Jonesboro and Blountville. The tree bore the carved notice, "D. Boon cilled A BAR On Tree in thE Year 1760." Frontiersman Daniel Boone would have been 26 at the time, young enough to cut a boast into live bark. The 70-foot tree fell in 1916 and was made into souvenirs, though by then the carving had been obscured by scablike "wound cork" typically manufactured by the beech.

Tempting as it is to leave one's mark on a beech trunk, bonding with the tree can be achieved by sight and touch alone. Our suggestion: Savor the beauty, massage the bark, and let the tree inscribe itself on *your* being.

Common Hackberry (and Sister Sugarberry)

Celtis occidentalis (and *C. laevigata*)

Importance: An unassuming elm-family tree that increased its urban presence after Dutch elm disease ravaged the big elms. Like its southern sibling the sugarberry, it gives shade, brings birds, survives in poor soil, and deals stoically with a host of its own afflictions.

Family: Ulmaceae (Elm). Genus: *Celtis* (hackberry).

Common urban species: ❧ Common hackberry (*Celtis occidentalis*) or northern h., American h., beaverwood, nettle-tree, false elm, bastard elm. ❧ Sugarberry (*C. laevigata*) or southern h., lowland h., Mississippi h., Texas sugarberry, palo blanco.

Close relatives: ❧ Netleaf hackberry (*C. reticulata*) or western h.

TYPICAL CITY LOCATION: Newer plantings (especially of varieties) on streets and in parking lots and open yards. Older trees in parks, wetlands, out-of-the-way areas.

KEY FEATURES: Young bark is smoothish and light gray, but soon develops corky warts and abundant warty ridges. Tree is modest- to medium-sized, with dull light green foliage. Spreads wide like elm, but more O- than V-shaped. Tufts of twigs or "witches' brooms" appear on branchlets. Twigs slender, brownish with white flecks.

Fruit a shiny, pea-sized drupe on thin stalk, with cherrylike stone inside; skin becomes dark purple (common hackberry), or yellow-red (sugarberry).

Leafblade 2–5" long, half as wide, with 3 prominent veins arising from ¼" leafstalk, long pointed tip, and rounded base that is clearly lopsided in relation to stalk. Toothed mainly along upper edges, may be smooth or partly toothed at base. (Narrower sugarberry leaf tends toward smooth edges.) Bumps (nipple galls) common on leaf undersurface.

AVERAGE MATURE SIZE IN CITY: 30–60' high, 20–45' wide, 1–2' thick.

RECENT CHAMPION: *Common hackberry:* 94' height, 88' spread, 20' circumf., Mason City, Ill. *Sugarberry:* 81' height, 114' spread, 25' circumf., Society Hill, S.C.

ࡩ A DECENT NOBODY, WITH WARTS

The hackberry is not familiarly known by the inhabitants of the regions where it grows, else it would more commonly be transplanted to adorn private grounds and to shade village streets.
—Julia Ellen Rogers, 1926

Like happiness, the common hackberry is what you find when looking for something else. It is a here-and-there tree, rarely seen in large stands. Urban explorers might be drawn to its broad shade, but few seek it out as a thing of beauty or romance. It thrives in hundreds of U.S. towns and cities, but lives up to its historic name as "the unknown tree."

Some of the world's 75 or so hackberry species have been cultivated since the seventeenth century; yet when North American settlers came upon one of the native hackberries (about seven species have been identified), they would often record it as an "unknown." Sugarberry, the American South's version of the common hackberry, was regarded as *bois inconnu* (unknown wood) by French settlers.

The common hackberry is no showboat. A medium-height member of the Elm family, it has none of the vaulting splendor that marks the American and other grand elms. Its branches rarely explode into the elm's forked patterns; instead, they seem unsure of their direction and, thanks to a

Hackberry leaves suggest elongated elm leaves. Dull yellow-green, they often house jumping lice in whimsical "nipple galls." Fruit is a dark drupe.

mite, tend to culminate in bunched-up twigs called "witches' brooms." (Hackberries of New York's Central Park are good examples.)

The leaves have the graceful lancelike shape of elm foliage, with lopsided base and long curving tip. They brighten the spring landscape, but their summer color dazzles no one. Small male and female flowers emerge on the same tree and do their job without pageantry. Fruits are not the gossamer wafers that fly from elms, but barely conspicuous pea-sized drupes, dangling singly from cherrylike stalks. Fall foliage is a pallid yellow. Only the bark, a tight skin that develops warts and corky ridges, might call attention to itself like some bestial hide.

Lacking the grandeur and lore of the great elms, the common hackberry must be valued for what it is: an open-armed refuge from city heat. A puff of green amidst the gray. A tough customer that can survive droughts as ruthless as the 1934 Kansas killer. A kin of elm that doesn't get Dutch elm disease. A noninvasive, fairly fast grower that will oblige planters in almost any kind of terrain—acid, alkaline, wet or dry, muddy or rocky—though it grows best in rich, moist earth. (Except for an aversion to alkaline soil, the sugarberry is equally adaptable in its own region.)

Young hackberries shoot out long arms of drooping leaves in an overall pyramidal form. Over the next two decades, they evolve into pumpkin- or head-shaped trees, some 40 feet tall and broad. They can and do grow much larger, even 100 feet high, given moisture, sun, nutrients, and room for the deep roots.

Though it doesn't like surprise frosts, the hackberry outdoes many street trees in holding on to its big limbs. It often serves for a gold watch number of years before succumbing to injury-induced rot and other ailments. Whatever its shortcomings, the hackberry is a decent, amiable species doing its best amidst the world's clamor. What more appropriate tree to shade the boyhood home of America's fortieth president than the Ronald Reagan Hackberry in Dixon, Ill.?

HACKBERRY WATCHING—WARTS AND ALL

Like all of urban nature, the modest hackberry yields its share of delights to the caring observer. The gray bark, which starts out as smooth as beech bark, soon grows the curious wartlike bumps. Later, the bark develops choppy vertical rows of corky ridges to create the trademark look of the mature trunk: like Godzilla with the worst case of sunburn peel you've ever seen.

Hackberry leaves often host eraser-size "nipple galls," the dwellings of minute jumping lice. Located on the underside of the leaf, the hard and well-sealed galls take on amusing shapes, like cartoon fireplugs or baby bottle nipples.

In summer the observer might also spot a hackberry emperor butterfly (*Asterocampa celtis*), a species stuck on this tree and colored to match it. The male butterflies like to perch on tall sunlit objects—including an observer's head—to watch for females. Other visitors include robins, cedar waxwings, and birds of some two dozen other species, none of them indifferent to the "unknown tree." They come for the hackberry fruit, which in fall ripens to a morsel about the size of a raisin. In fact, the edible berry tastes slightly like a raisin or date when the scant flesh is nibbled off the stone pit. By winter, when few other fruits still dangle for famished birds, hackberries are as popular as a street fair.

As with the mulberry tree, however, the birds' droppings are among the hackberry's less attractive aspects for humans. Yet, in the beautiful scheme of nature, feasting birds distribute the hackberry species by processing the stone pits in their digestive tracts and drop shipping the seeds along their migration routes. Without such a delivery service into Canada during spring migrations, Ontario and Quebec would probably have one fewer broadleaf species for its woods and towns.

Hackberry bark looks as if it were pinched into warty ridges.

HACKBERRIES AT THEIR BEST

The sugarberry tends to be a taller, slimmer tree than its northern sibling, but a cutback version is often found in small city yards. Many street landscapers are shunning both siblings in favor of cultivated varieties that resist witches' broom and other problems of the species. Most likely to be seen are the varieties 'Chicagoland', with large leaves and an erect "leader" trunk; 'Prairie Pride', featuring dark, leathery, lustrous leaves; 'All Seasons', lemon-yellow in fall; and the hybrid 'Magnifica', with dark green leaves and few berries to attract those nasty birds.

The American Southwest has some of its own hackberry species, smaller trees, notably the netleaf or western hackberry seen in parks and playgrounds. Look for the raised netted veins on the leaf underside and an orange-red fruit. Thickleaf hackberry, a western variety (*crassi-folia*) of common hackberry, shades some arid Texas towns.

NAME THIS TREE

As if to aggravate its identity problem, the hackberry has been too often named something it isn't. Great Britain calls its species the nettleleaf, based on the nettlelike roughness of the leaf, an exaggeration. "Hackberry" itself is thought to derive from "hagberry," a Scottish name for a cherry species. The genus name *Celtis* was Roman naturalist Pliny's term for the lotus tree, but the hackberry is hardly the pollen-spewing lotus of Greek mythology that brought sweet forgetfulness. It is a tree with its own rugged ways, and one worth remembering.

SWEETGUM
Liquidambar styraciflua

IMPORTANCE: A popular street tree coast-to-coast, noted for unique star-shaped leaves, outstanding fall colors, and spiny "gumball" seed fruits. (Also for decorative wood and medicinal resin.)

FAMILY: Hamamelidaceae (Witch-hazel). GENUS: *Liquidambar* (sweet-gum).

COMMON URBAN SPECIES: ❀ Sweetgum (*Liquidambar styraciflua*) or American sweetgum, star-leafed gum, red-gum, gumtree, alligator-wood, blisted, sapgum.

CLOSE RELATIVES: ❀ Formosan sweetgum (*L. formosana*) or Chinese s. ❀ Oriental sweetgum (*L. orientalis*) or Turkish s.

TYPICAL CITY LOCATION: Streets, parks, parking lots, yards. *Larger specimens:* Watery recreation areas, campuses.

KEY FEATURES: Leaf is star-shaped, usually 5 points (lobes) but often 7; about 4–7" across; long slender leafstalk; fragrant when crushed; texture smooth, lustrous, hefty; edges dully sawtoothed; color bright green in summer with outstanding range of rich fall colors. Leaves are alternate (not opposite) on twigs and drop late in autumn or in early winter.

Distinctive woody, spiny fruit, 1–1½" wide. An aggregation of beaky, seed-containing capsules. Droops all winter from a spindly stalk and looks like a large brown burr.

Twigs and small branches may have conspicuous corky flanges or "wings," but not always. Bark medium gray and roughly furrowed (smooth on many West Coast specimens).

Young trees take on reliable, narrowly conical shape, sometimes plump at bottom; in later years, upper crown spreads quickly to form irregular roundish or paddlelike shape. (Lofty forest trees are bare one-half to two-thirds up the trunk.)

AVERAGE MATURE SIZE IN CITY: 35–60' high, 20–40' wide, 1½–3½' thick.

RECENT CHAMPION: 136' height, 66' spread, 23' circumf., Craven County, N.C.

❧ A STELLAR PERFORMER

They say that the American sweetgum is overplanted in some towns, even in the warm coastal areas where landscapers have their pick of dreamy species. But the virtues of this native tree make it very hard— and sometimes pointless—to resist.

Its foliage alone earns it a place in the pantheon of street trees. Not only does the sweetgum leaf form a symbolic star, but a big shining star, a star that keeps its heft and luster for up to three seasons, and a star that explodes with autumn hues even in mild temperatures. How many other trees bring the colors of an eastern October to the California coast? Very few.

Woody, beaky sweetgum fruit and star-shaped leaf with its long stalk.

The sweetgum leaf may be less than geometrically correct as a star—sometimes its small bottom "legs" sprawl sideways and its "arms" are more pudgy than angular—but it strives to be interdenominational. Though its most common form is as a five-pointed (lobed) star or pentagram, the arrangement of these points suggests the six-pointed Star of David. Often, two additional base lobes appear, as if equipping the star for new-millennium duty.

The virtues of the leaf go on. Its edges are ornamented with a serrated pattern. It rarely succumbs to damaging pests and disfiguring diseases, as do so many deciduous (falling) leaves. It emits a camphory fragrance when crushed, a hint of its contribution to the tree's celebrated sap or "copalm balm" (see sidebar). In autumn it comes up with brilliant designer colors. Depending on tree variety and local conditions, leaves turn shades of yellow, ochre, orange, burgundy, scarlet, crimson, purple, blue, and brown. The color pageant may be less spectacular than that of the sugar maple's, since not all leaves turn at once or with the same intensity. But sweetgum coloration can dazzle into early winter, when the maples are bare.

A Balm "Beyond Belief"

"It relieves wind in the stomach and dissipates tumors beyond belief," reported the sixteenth-century herbalist Francisco Hernandez. "Added to tobacco, it strengthens the head, belly, and heart . . ."

What supposedly performed such miracles? It was the resin extracted from Mexico's sweetgum tree, a tree the Aztecs called *xochiocotzo-quahuitl* and which Europe would name *Liquidambar* (liquid amber) *styraciflua* (flowing with storax or aromatic resin).

As a guest of the Aztec emperor Montezuma, Hernando Cortés puffed a smoke of tobacco infused with the resin. Perhaps this gave him the "belly and heart" to subjugate his host.

The sweetgum of Mexico (and North America) does not actually flow with the resin known as storax, a time-honored perfumy balm from Turkey's oriental sweetgum. But it does produce a similar resin known as styrax or copalm balm, which has often substituted in commerce for the oriental balm.

When the sweetgum's bark is cut, it exudes a yellowish gum used in the manufacture of syrups and ointments. Though Hernandez may have overstated its medicinal properties, it long served as a folk treatment for skin irritations and wounds. At one point, Alabama was producing a pound of resin per tree in its styrax industry.

According to country lore, a flavorful chaw of gum could come directly from a bark wound. But lately, when nature writer Janet Lembke coaxed some gum out of a tree, she reported that it smelled like cinnamon, tasted like cardboard, and stuck to her teeth through two brushings.

TOP CREDENTIALS

More than just a pretty face, American sweetgum comes to town with a sterling résumé. Its natural range is impressive: a swath of eastern America, from Connecticut south to Florida and west to Missouri; and another strip from Texas through Mexico into Central America. It is a tough tree, one of only three surviving species (along with Chinese and Turkish sweetgums) from an ancient genus of some 23. It is a vigorous tree, growing up to 165 feet high and 5 feet thick in its forest habitats. In cultivation, it can flourish so abundantly that in 1997, one Florida nursery rushed to give away some 4,000 young sweetgums that were starting to shade its other, slower-growing stock.

Easy to establish as urban plantings, saplings grow from 12 to about 30 feet in as few as six years, given plenty of sun, moisture, and ample root space. Reliably, they take a neat conical form until middle age pushes the upper crown into the broad, irregular spread of a big shade tree. Established trees handle most soils, poor drainage, and the usual urban stresses and deprivations while still warding off natural invaders.

Already prized for its resin and lumber, the sweetgum was cultivated in about 1680 and soon made its way into European parks and gardens as an ornamental. One of its early appearances in U.S. cities was in the form of paving blocks hewn from the tree's heavy wood. It did not distinguish itself as a road surface, but by the twentieth century, its foliage was lighting up American parks and streets.

Frederick Law Olmsted included it in his first plantings for New York's Central Park. Cincinnati, Louisville, and other cities along the Ohio River pioneered in sweetgum plantings, which spread through the Midwest. Back east, Philadelphia planted it in proud rows along Independence Mall. Southeastern towns, where sweetgum already squatted along roadsides and cleared areas, could hardly avoid planting it. In Texas and Arkansas, its fall color was a blessed sight.

Western cities have swelled the sweetgum's urban empire. Five percent of the public trees in tree-rich Sacramento, for example, are sweetgums. Each fall in such cities as Los Angeles and San Francisco, sweetgums blaze on downtown streets among yawnably evergreen melaleucas and Australian willows.

As a species, sweetgum has the further virtue of producing mutant offspring with advantages for urban use. From one rebellious orange-headed tree on Palo Alto's Bryant Street came the 'Palo Alto', a cultivated variety much used in California. Among other cultivars are the 'Burgundy', with fall foliage of that color, 'Variegata' or 'Gold Dust', its green leaves streaked with yellow, and the cold-hardy 'Moraine', a speedy, uniform grower with wine fall foliage.

THE SPINY SIDE

Male sweet-
gum flowers.

If the sweetgum is such a star, why doesn't *every* city in North America give it top billing? For one thing, it's a star that shuns the most frigid circuits. It sets its natural limits at Danbury, Conn., in New England, and southern Illinois in the Midwest. True, some icy towns in Massachusetts, Maine, Ontario, and elsewhere try their luck with the tree. But they work with stock from the northernmost range or the cold-hardiest cultivated varieties. At about −35°F, however, just about any sweetgum will call it quits.

But why should cities such as Sunnyvale, Calif., blacklist sweetgum as a street tree? The answer is in the unusual fruit, which some communities consider a liability. Like the American sycamore's "buttonball," the sweetgum fruit is a ball-shaped cluster of seeds and seed-dispensing apparatus. But unlike the soft sycamore ball, the sweetgum fruit ripens into a woody sphere covered with projecting hooked beaks. The beaks—each pair originally female parts of the flower—are now the tips of seed-containing capsules. In fall, the beaks open and winged seeds fall out. The "gumballs" remain on the tree through much of winter; but when they fall en masse and roll along the ground to disperse more seeds, they can spike a bare foot or twist an ankle as quickly as citizens can holler "Lawsuit!"

Thus many a nervous urban forester dismisses the sweetgum tree as a "litterer"—a snub that irritates those who find wonder, not bother, in a tree's intricately engineered mechanisms. "There is . . . no justification for simply eliminating such species of trees from city planting," says landscape architect Henry F. Arnold. "There are places where their special characteristics far outweigh the inconvenience of removing the organic litter."

Cultivators have developed a fruitless sweetgum, but at the price of a winter delight. The sweetgum's seed balls are fruits with character, bobbing like miniature maces from the tree's bare branches. Children like collecting them; craftspeople gild them as decorations. Clever gar-

deners use them as cat-
resistant mulch.

Often, but not always,
sweetgums come up with
still another visual treat:
corky wings or quirky
growths of bark along the
branchlets and twigs. In
the late 1800s, New York
peddlers offered these
branchlets as "alligator
plants." Neither plant nor
alligator is known to have
sprouted from them.

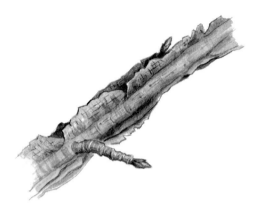

Some sweetgum twigs develop corky wings
and an "alligator" look.

For all its merits, the
American sweetgum seems to have been a lost cause of statesman
Alexander Hamilton, who had a passel of lost causes before losing his
life in a duel. Hamilton, reportedly, was so enamored of the sweetgum
that he wished it to become the nation's emblematic tree. It did not
happen, nor, surprisingly, is the sweetgum the official tree of any state.
However, about 80 miles east of the Alabama state capital (Montgomery), in a bucolic region of rolling hills and dense forests, sits the
proud town of Crawford, population 650. Its official tree, Hamilton
might be pleased to know, is one with aromatic resin, striking fall
color, and a star-shaped leaf.

Ginkgo (Maidenhair-Tree)

Ginkgo biloba

IMPORTANCE: A treasured survivor from the dinosaur era, virtually un-
changed from its 100-million-year-old fossil forms. Easy to identify
by fan-shaped leaf and eccentric branching. Widely popular in
cities, where it resists most hardships and diseases and turns golden
yellow in fall. Fruit of female tree infamous for its stench and slim-
iness. Leaf extract said to aid memory.

FAMILY: Ginkgoaceae (Ginkgo). GENUS: *Ginkgo.*

COMMON URBAN SPECIES: ❀ Ginkgo (*Ginkgo biloba*) or maidenhair-
tree, golden fossil tree, stink-bomb tree.

CLOSE RELATIVES: None.

TYPICAL CITY LOCATION (MALES ONLY): Along commercial and residential streets, in parks, plazas, and cemeteries. Older trees in romantic or sacred sites.

KEY FEATURES: Leaf is fan-shaped, about 3" across, sometimes with a notch dividing it into 2 lobes (thus "biloba"). Numerous veins radiate out from the base to the edges, with no central vein (midrib). Slightly leathery texture, yellow in fall. Slender leafstalk about 3", allows fluttering of leaf in breeze.

 Young trees shoot out straight branches, mostly at upward angle; leaves grow from stubby pegs along most of branch. Sparse branching and varied angles of young tree may give gawky look. Older trees round out, eventually forming full or tapering crown, stout trunk.

 Fruit of female trees—rarely seen in cities—crabapple-sized and apricot-hued, rancid-smelling when opened.

AVERAGE MATURE SIZE IN CITY: 40–80' high, 30–60' wide, 1½–3' thick.

RECENT CHAMPION: None on American Forests *Register.* Moderate growth rate, but old trees frequently exceed 100'. Notable ginkgoes have been reported in Milan (125' high), Hyde Park, N.Y. (12' thick), and Philadelphia and Tokyo (10' thick).

❧ THE MEMORY TREE

Thou queer, outlandish, fan-leaved tree . . .
 —Jacob Bigelow

Three young ginkgo trees shade the patio of a Chicago café and the neighborhood students who gather there. The trees' sparse branches are ruffled with foliage along their length. They jut out like water sprays at crazy angles. The fan-shaped leaves flutter on slender stalks, adding a whisper to the student chatter and radio music.

 The trees and students have this in common: They represent the

The ginkgo's leathery, fan-shaped leaves grow from stubby pegs.

sole surviving species of their biological family. *Homo sapiens* lost its closest related species about 40,000 years ago. *Ginkgo biloba* had a family of other fan-leaved species until the glaciers wiped them out perhaps 1 million years back.

As the student chatter would reveal, humans are still wrestling with matters of heritage and identity. But the ginkgo knows—at least genetically—who it is and was. One of Earth's oldest plant species, it spanned the temperate forests more than 200 million years ago. And judging by fossil remains, it has not changed its essential character for perhaps 150 million years. The species in earshot of the students looked much the same among the wallop of pterodactyl wings.

Genes that remember 150-million-year-old instructions ought to be worth bottling—a notion that inspired a popular product of New Age therapy: ginkgo biloba extract. About 50 pounds of dried leaves yield a pound of the medicinal. Although ginkgo had long been valued in Asia and Europe as a treatment for everything from asthma to bedwetting, only recently did it explode on the U.S. scene as a supposed aid to memory and moderator of Alzheimer's disease.

Studies seemed to show that ginkgo leaf compounds encourage the release of a dilating agent in the brain's blood vessels, thus improving oxygen and nutrient intake. The compounds may also prevent blood platelets from clumping. While Western physicians generally have hedged their bets on ginkgo, manufacturers trumpeted its virtues in such late-1990s products as MegaMind, Memory Mate, and Food for Thought.

FROM FOREST TO CITY LIFE

Some time after the era of the dinosaurs, the ancient ginkgoes retreated from the glacial regions to a final sanctuary, the nonglacial forests of eastern Asia. Interaction with the tree might have come early in human history, but one of the first known mentions of it is in an eighth-century Chinese agricultural work. A 1587 Chinese herbal described the ginkgo accurately as *ya-chio-tzu*—a tree with leaves like a duck's foot. Revered by Buddhists, ginkgoes were cultivated and preserved in temple gardens, where seventeenth-century Western visitors first encountered them. The Chinese named the tree *yin-kuo,* referring to the silvery nut inside the fruit.

A century later, Europe had its first imported ginkgoes, prized enough so that a Parisian gloated over five seedlings he had conned from a tipsy horticulturist in London. In 1784, after a (sober) transaction with an English supplier, Philadelphian William Hamilton planted the first known ginkgo in America in his Woodlands garden (now Woodlands Cemetery). A ginkgo in Manhattan's Inwood Hill Park is thought to be New York City's oldest, dating to about 1850.

The name "maidenhair-tree" came from a perceived resemblance between the ginkgo leaf and those of some maidenhair ferns. The tree does echo some traits of ferns and pines. Like conifers, it is classified as a gymnosperm (naked-seed), but it is very much its own plant. By the 1900s, ginkgoes had shown urban planters their ability to survive pests, drought, storms, ice, city soils, and some pollution. Architect Frank Lloyd Wright's favorite tree, it made its way into city landscapes across North America, as happy in southeastern Canada as in New Orleans.

Like its ancient ancestors and primitive ferns, the ginkgo reproduces by means of flagellated sperm cells. Carried by wind-borne pollen to the female flowers, the sperms swim a short distance to fertilize the ovules. However, it is the interface between ginkgo and *Homo sapiens* that has perpetuated the tree, for the species stopped reproducing in the forests some centuries ago.

No one is sure why the tree is absent from the wild, but neither is anyone worried about its persistence on the globe. It is hard to find a dead ginkgo. One of the trees is said to have survived the atomic blast in Hiroshima. Many cultivated ginkgoes are 5, 6, even 10 centuries old, and the vast dispersion of robust, propagated trees assures their habitation. Symbolically, the U.S. Agricultural Department planted an avenue of some 90 trees on its Washington grounds. The enormous Jacobs Field baseball stadium in Cleveland is fronted by rows of ginkgoes. In Japan alone, the ginkgo has been planted in seemingly every park, palace grounds, and holy place, as well as in rows along major boulevards.

Asians are among those who appreciate the gastronomic qualities of the fruit nut. Shorn of its rank flesh, it is boiled for soup or roasted as a nutty treat to be snacked when liquor flows. A Japanese custardlike dish called *chawanmushi* contains the nuts. In her charming book *Leaves,* Alice Thoms Vitale passes along a recipe for ginkgo porridge, using the nuts, honey, and rice. It is probably good for you.

THE FEMALE "PROBLEM"

For all its virtues among Asians, the fruit of the ginkgo almost cost the tree its place in cities across America. The ginkgo is a dioecious species, meaning that its male tassel-like catkins and its stubby female flowers appear on separate trees. Only female flowers, when fertilized, produce the ginkgo fruit—and soon after they do there is something very rotten wherever the trees stand. The oval, one-inch, tan-orange fruits drop from the twigs, and quickly the ripened slimy pulp is exposed for all to smell and slip on.

How terrible is the smell? Comparisons range from "rancid butter" (which, like ginkgo pulp, contains butyric acid) to "vomit." A University of Delaware Website describes the fruits as "odoriferous land mines." Most sources agree that the stench can never be removed from clothing that has touched the pulp, and that skin rashes can result from contact with the open fruit.

Add to all this the liability of sidewalks greased with the slime of an abundant fruit fall, and it is clear why urban landscapers specify male cuttings, or why some communities ban the females, or why a California neighborhood amputated the many street ginkgoes it had planted years earlier as seedlings. The trees—unidentifiable as to sex when young—turned out to be fruitful femmes.

Male ginkgoes also have received a bit of discipline to bring them in line with urban tastes. In progressive cultivations, unruly sizes and shapes are bred out and reliable forms bred in. Among the resulting varieties are 'Autumn Gold', with a broad pyramidal form at maturity and reliable fall color; 'Princeton Sentry', shaped like a tall column; and 'Fairmount', with a dense conical body.

Ginkgoes mature into lovely forms with abundant folliage, the better to yield leaf extract for supposed memory enhancement.

These are the pleasing types of ginkgoes you are likely to see on city streets. They are fruitless and less imposing than the older breeds, but they retain the ginkgo's endearing qualities: fluttering fan-shaped leaves, "plumose" or plumelike foliage patterns on the branches, and a brief but stirring display of golden fall color. You may be fortunate enough to see some of the great ancients as well, in parks, special gardens, or arboretums. The stout, fissured trunk will be topped by a huge head of foliage, some of it sticking out like unruly spikes of hair. You might even find a female one day, in some open area, where you can tell her you are sorry about her, er, exclusion from polite society.

MULBERRY

Morus alba, M. rubra, M. nigra

The broad white mulberry tree. Older trees tend to lean.

IMPORTANCE: A group of wide-spreading shade trees including the white mulberry, a now-common urban species that influenced world history as host to the silkworm. Sweet juicy berries are magnets for wildlife. Fruitless varieties are beginning to dominate urban planting.

FAMILY: Moraceae (Mulberry). GENUS: *Morus* (mulberry).

COMMON URBAN SPECIES: ❀ White mulberry (*Morus alba*) or silkworm m. ⚘ Red mulberry (*Morus rubra*) or purple m., American m. ⚘ Black mulberry (*Morus nigra*) or common m.

CLOSE RELATIVES: ⚘ Russian mulberry (*Morus alba* var. *tartarica*). ⚘ Paper mulberry (*Broussonetia papyrifera,* not a true mulberry, but comparable) or tapa cloth tree.

TYPICAL CITY LOCATION: *White mulberry:* Residential streets (especially fruitless and weeping varieties); roads, streets, and gardens of old U.S. eastern towns; parks and cemeteries. *Red:* Urban nature areas; sunny sites where tree has escaped from woods or crossbred with white mulberry. *Black* and *Russian:* Gardens and ornamental sites of Pacific Coast and other western areas; also roadsides, abandoned spaces. *Paper:* Urban gardens, especially in U.S. South.

KEY FEATURES: *White* and *red* species tend to be big, wide-spreading trees. *Black* and *paper m.* smaller and bushier.

White m. leaves generally glossy on top, smooth and hairless top and bottom; *red m.* leaves rough on top, hairy on bottom. Leaves of both species vary in shape from heart and oval to mitten-like to many-lobed, often asymmetrical; *white m.* leaves 3–5", *red m.* to 9".

Leaves of *paper m.* very rough on top, fuzzy on bottom, to 11". *Black m.* leaf heart-shaped at base.

Mulberry leafstalks exude milky latexlike sap when broken. Bark of *white* and *red m.* rough, scaly, and ridged; *white m.* bark yellow-tinged. *Paper m.* bark smooth, tight, etched with interlacing yellowish lines.

Mulberry fruit looks like blackberry, to 1" long; white, pink, lavender, or almost black; soft fruit falls to ground when ripe.

AVERAGE MATURE SIZE IN CITY: 20–50' high, 30–60' wide, 1½–3' thick.

RECENT CHAMPION: *White:* 59' height, 73' spread, 24' circumf., Johnson City, Mo. *Red:* 63' height, 78' spread, 22' circumf., Edmond, Okla.

≥ FRUITY SHADE TREE— HOLD THE WORMS

In Asia, a white mulberry tree might be identified by the silkworms feasting on its leaves. Not in America. Brought to the colonies from China in a doomed effort to produce domestic silk, the tree species has migrated to urban spaces to become the most common of the city mulberries. The worms are gone, thriving only in nations able to manage this fickle silk spinner. For urban observers, mulberry identification now takes other paths.

In one, the tree first reveals itself as a shade umbrella, a luxuriant crown of foliage often wider than it is tall. The crown consists of glistening, lime-green, mitten-size leaves, which alternate along the twigs on thin 1½- to 2-inch leafstalks. Some leaves are actually shaped like mittens, others like hearts, and the rest like hearts with U-shaped bites taken out of them. All have medium-sized, loosely matched teeth along the edges, and many are cupped inward like little boats.

The variety of leaf shapes—from symmetrical to fanciful—is a charm of the tree. So is its overall form, the crooked branches wobbling far out from a short, craggy, sometimes leaning trunk, the lower branches drooping when full. Reportedly, author D. H. Lawrence was so charmed by the mulberry he confessed to climbing one au naturel.

In early summer, (female) mulberry trees further identify themselves with explosions of blackberry-like fruit, catching the eye of winged and legged creatures alike. These clusters of white, pink, red, or darker berries shout "Mulberry!" loud and clear, cuing the Mother Goose ditty, "Here we go round the mulberry bush . . . so early in the morning."

There is another way to recognize mulberries: by slipping on the crush of slimy, sidewalk-staining fruit that has ripened and fallen from the tree. Or discovering on your parked car the seeds (and stain) of the berry as nature intended them to be dispersed—via the guano of birds. At the sign of the chalky white and purple splatter, you are in mulberry country.

The raw white mulberry fruit—up to an inch long and so appetizingly plump and succulent—can be eaten by humans, but its sickening sweetness and absence of flavor and tartness is one of the great gastronomical letdowns. Mulberries "do quickly putrefie in the stomach, if they be not taken before meat," reported an early critic, perhaps referring to the purported cathartic qualities of the fruit. But one should perform one's own taste tests. Red mulberries are said to taste better than white, and the black mulberry and certain hybrids are considered good enough for commercial processing into jams, preserves, and even wines.

Glossy leaves of the white mulberry take a variety of notched shapes. Fruits measure about an inch long.

The sensible mulberry for street or yard is a fruitless male, but males can make their own trouble. Their flowers, lacking the nectar to attract pollinators, rely on wind to carry their fertilizing pollen to a female mulberry flower. Thus, like the males of many tree species, they produce a storm of pollen to assure success and torment allergy sufferers.

Mulberries score high on most tests for an urban tree. They grow fast, look good, and give shade. Once established, they tolerate drought, salt, compact soil, high winds, and air pollution. They handle insects and disease and can live some 75 years or more (black mulberry trees more than 500). But the females do make a fruity mess and males do pump out the pollen. And to confuse matters, a mulberry might have both male and female flowers on its branches, or one season might decide to change its gender entirely. What's an urban landscaper to do?

Options include sticking to well-behaved male cultivars or banning mulberry planting altogether. The Tree People of Los Angeles support the former, recommending fruitless white mulberries for big shade. In Sacramento, the same fruitless species makes up about 4 percent of the city's trees. Communities banning mulberries include El Paso, Tex., Pima County, Ariz., and Las Vegas. Imagine Vegas not gambling on this time-honored tree!

THE TREE THAT LINKED CULTURES

Break the leafstalk of a white mulberry and you can see, in the milky sap, the chemical soup that so influenced the course of history. This is the sap that caterpillars of the *Bombyx mori* silk moth mix with their own chemicals to convert into silk. It was white mulberry silk that enriched the Chinese Empire beginning more than 2,000 years ago, that dazzled traders, that prompted the fabled Silk Road across Asia and hastened the meeting of eastern and western cultures. All from that white goo on your fingers.

Silk can be spun from the cocoons of certain other caterpillars feeding off other types of leaves. But no combination has ever proved more successful for China, India, and other Asian producers than the white mulberry leaf and *Bombyx mori* worm, which likes its leaf chopped and wilted just so. In the sixth century, two agents of the Roman emperor smuggled mulberry seeds and silk moth eggs out of China, unleashing a new European tree species and a lucrative industry in Rome and later in France and Spain.

In England in 1608, a royal decree called for local mulberry planting and silk manufacture, but the effort failed for want of the right tree species. Gardeners (apparently including Shakespeare and Milton) cultivated the black mulberry, which took wildly to the land and produced a popular fruit—but did little for the palate of silkworms.

The right tree and worm came to the American colonies in 1631 and made for the beginnings of an industry. (The leaf of the native red mulberry had proved too tough for the silkworm.) A Virginian had raised 70,000 white mulberries by 1664. George Washington, Thomas Jefferson, and Benjamin Franklin planted the tree. To boost the industry, President John Quincy Adams not only brought the worm and the tree to the White House, but put First Lady Louisa to work unreeling the silk filament of the cocoons.

Although the business went well for a few American "sericulturists," as silk cultivators are called, less labor-intensive textile industries promised quicker profits. By 1900, American silk production was dead. All those white mulberry trees now had nothing more to do than feed the birds and propagate. They spread through town and country, often crossbreeding with the native red mulberry to produce vigorous hybrids.

BLOODY BERRIES

The succulent fruit of the black mulberry tree attracts humans as well as wildlife. Hugh Johnson describes its flavor as "searchingly sour and hauntingly sweet." The Romans might have introduced the fruit to Europe as refreshment for its soldiers. Roman citizens gobbled the berries at feasts. Ovid, perhaps energized by the juice, wrote of young lovers Pyramus and Thisbe and their tragic tale of misinformation-under-the-mulberry:

Awaiting Pyramus by a white-fruited mulberry tree, Thisbe was frightened off by a lion and left her veil behind. The lion smeared the veil with blood from a recent kill and moved on. When Pyramus arrived, he deduced that the beast had slain Thisbe and promptly killed himself. Thisbe returned, saw his body, and completed the double suicide. The tree is said to have absorbed their blood to produce, from then on, blood-red berries.

GO BIG RED

"The names of streets are mostly taken from the things that grow in the country, such as . . . Mulberry Street . . . ," wrote William Penn of his young Philadelphia. And the red mulberry did indeed dot the eastern woods, a vigorous native species reaching heights of 70 feet and more. Earlier, the De Soto expedition had encountered the tree and used its fibrous inner bark to make needed ship ropes. The Choctaws fashioned blankets and cloaks from the bark. Though sometimes recommended for urban planting, the red mulberry has infiltrated cities mainly as a park-thicket tree or a natural hybrid with the white mulberry. In Washington, D.C., as in other warm eastern cities, you may occasionally encounter a mulberry whose leaf has a hairy underside. You've found a red. Now watch out for the berries underfoot . . .

BAD PRESS FOR THE BERRY

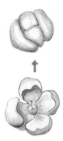

The outer leaves (sepals) of the tiny, fertilized mulberry flower swell and close to make one fruit of the juicy, aggregate berry.

Most urbanites will meet the mulberry fruit on the soles of their shoes, a sorry first impression. So unappreciated is the berry that some property owners go so far as to defruit their trees with hormonal sprays or insecticides. But the virtues of the bountiful berry have been undersold.

The fruit attracts birds and their song to city neighborhoods the way Vegas draws the hopeful. Some gardeners plant mulberries just to detour birds from prime fruit trees such as cherries. Among humans, culinary interest in the fruit began long ago, probably in Asia. Following Rome's lead, all of Europe developed a taste for the black mulberry fruit (see sidebar on page 209). Today, the California Fruit Growers Association cites several cultivated varieties for eating, including the 'Illinois' and 'Kaester'. The berries also have figured in traditional remedies for liver imbalance, poor circulation, weak blood, and constipation.

The berry reveals a secret to the close observer. Examine one of the individual globes that make up the berry's cluster. What appeared to be a smooth ball is actually a complex flower whose petal-like outer leaves (sepals) have swollen into thick and juicy lips that fold over the fertilized seed (see figure above). Botanically speaking, then, the mulberry is not a berry at all, but a collection of tiny fruits.

To birds, this is not an issue.

LINDEN (BASSWOOD)

Tilia cordata, T. americana, and others

IMPORTANCE: A commanding forest tree whose smaller cultivated varieties are darlings of the street landscapers, beloved for their tidy shape and perfumed fragrance. In lore, the tree of conjugal love.

FAMILY: Tiliaceae (Linden). GENUS: *Tilia* (linden or basswood).

COMMON URBAN SPECIES: ❧ Littleleaf linden (*Tilia cordata*) or small-leaved l. ❧ American linden (*Tilia americana*) or American basswood, bee-tree. ❧ Silver linden (*Tilia tomentosa*) or European white l. ❧ Crimean linden (*Tilia euchlora*) or Caucasian l. ❧ Bigleaf linden (*Tilia platyphyllos*) or broadleaf l. ❧ Carolina linden (*Tilia caroliniana*).

TYPICAL CITY LOCATION: Streets, town squares, promenades, yards, parks.

Key features: Small whitish-yellow flowers with 5 petals extend from a tonguelike secondary leaf (*bract*) beside the main leaf (see figure below). Conspicuous even from a distance, the yellow-green bracts are an unmistakable identification feature. Blossoms give off spicy perfumed fragrance. Fertilized flowers produce hard pea-sized fruits on wiry stems extending from bracts.

Tree takes tidy overall shape, ranging from bell to pyramid. Branches start low on trunk. Heavy leafage, solid shade. Suckers (shoots) grow from trunks of untended trees.

Leaf is a lopsided heart, with sharp, even teeth at edges and abruptly pointed tip; top surface is dark green, bottom paler. Length from 1½″ (*littleleaf l.*) to 10″ (*American l.*). In late summer, leaves blacken from aphid infestation, drop sticky honeydew, and curl. Leaves are yellow in fall.

Spring buds are red. Upper bark smoothish, reddish gray-brown.

Average mature size in city: 30–60′ high, 1–3′ thick.

Recent champion: *American:* 78′ height, 100′ spread, 24′ circumf., Montgomery County, Pa.

❧ Sweet Tree of Summer Nights

Scenario one: Strolling on a sultry evening, you are suddenly intoxicated by a floral mist. Something has distilled the sweet fragrance of summer nights and diffused it through the neighborhood. This is the gift of the linden tree in blossom.

Scenario two: In the torpor of a midsummer's night, you have parked your buffed-up automobile beneath a tree with heart-shaped leaves. You drop your heavy lids and give way to dreams and fancies. When you awake, the windows and exterior finish of your vehicle have been caramelized like a candy apple. Thank the sugary droppings from above.

This, too, is the gift of the linden. The sweet offering, called honeydew, has come to you via the digestive tracts of a million or so aphids feeding off the leaves.

As street trees, lindens do have their sticky side. Yet, the beauty of the plant, its perfume, its pugnacity, have made it a city choice for generations—long enough to become an urban fixture throughout much of the United States and Europe. American towns named Linden can be found from the East Coast to Texas. Hundreds of streets and avenues recognize the tree. Unter den Linden, old Berlin's major thoroughfare, celebrated its 350th birthday in 1997, still boasting four rows of linden trees.

For geologic ages, the linden, aka basswood, has reigned as a forest aristocrat, standing as tall as 150 feet among oaks and elms and finding a place in ancient myth. In *Metamorphoses,* Ovid tells of a poor husband and wife who outdid themselves as hosts to a pair of strangers—Zeus and Hermes in disguise. As a reward, the gods

Lindens are distinguished by heart-shaped, pointy-tipped leaves and tonguelike bracts supporting flowers that become pea-sized fruits.

granted the couple's wish to die together, turning the husband, Philemon, into an oak, and his wife, Baucis, into a linden, with their branches intertwined. In the language of folklore, the linden symbolizes conjugal love.

Native tribes used the inner bark of the American linden to make a strong rope, as well as a potent tea that treated lung ailments and heartburn. A calming tea has long been derived from linden blossoms, especially in France, where *tilleul* is sipped with delight. The soft wood of the linden, never wormy, is ideal for sculpting. Native Americans carved false-face masks on the living trunk (not recommended for city dwellers), then removed the carved section to hollow out the backs.

Among varied commercial applications, linden wood has been used for the slats of venetian blinds—perhaps the very slats shadowing Marilyn Monroe in the *noir* film *Niagara.*

EVERYONE'S FAVORITE SWEET

With their abundant flowers and nectar, lindens have long been associated with creation. Pregnant women have hugged them (like elms and ashes) for good luck—though the practice has not quite swept urban America. Here the great linden huggers are bees, which gather the flowers' nectar, and aphids, the tiny, soft-bodied bugs herded by ants for their honeydew.

The pebble-sized linden blossoms are "complete" flowers, having female and pollen-producing male parts. To be fertilized, all the flowers need are pollinators; and for about two weeks, when spring turns to summer, bees are deliriously happy to oblige. They work the trees in such profusion that some observers liken the buzz to an electric power station. Cultivated linden honey, sold as a delicacy and used in liqueurs, gives new meaning to the word "exquisite."

Occasionally, bees are seen tumbling from a linden as if blotto, some not getting up. They are indeed intoxicated, in the sense of having ingested a toxic substance. The phenomenon occurs on certain linden varieties that have been bred for streets and gardens. The silver linden, with its hairy white underleaf, and Crimean linden, whose bright, shiny leaves resist aphids, are two such varieties. While the Crimean KO's both honeybees and bumblebees, only the bumblebees fail to recover. Possibly, they eat toxic pollen while the honeybees stick to the nectar.

Aphids suck the sugary sap manufactured by the leaves as tree food. But an aphid also needs amino acids, which are scant in the sap. As a result, the bug sucks up a great deal more sugar than it can hold. The surplus, to tell it bluntly, shoots out the back door. Some of it lands on your car. Much of it feeds ants, certain flies and moths, and a sooty mold that blackens the leaf. The aphids themselves are dinner to a range of crawling and flying predators. Mites create horn-shaped houses for themselves on the leaf surface. Other visitors include Japanese beetles, caterpillars, lacebugs, and the basswood leaf roller, which makes itself a bedroll from part of the leaf and feeds off it until metamorphosis.

BRED FOR THE STREETS

A tree that hosts so much wildlife, even as it charms humans, deserves its own divine rewards. The linden's potential for longevity may be one of them. A 25-foot-thick linden near Hanover, Germany, was headed for the twenty-first century after some 1,100 years. We mortals have honored lindens with regal stands in parks and on boulevards, with ceremonial plantings—including at the White House by Franklin D. Roosevelt—and painstaking cultivation of street varieties.

Street lindens take varied shapes, but reliably grow bracts by summer.

Native to Europe and the Caucasus, the littleleaf linden has become one of the most popular and feverishly cultivated of all American street trees. It is also called the little-leaved linden, equally fun to say. (The British call it the small-leaved lime.) Its leaves, up to about a finger's length, have tufts of fine brown hairs on the underside. A young tree might be 20 feet tall; eventually, it can reach 50 to 70 feet, spreading some 30 feet wide.

The 'Greenspire' cultivated variety of littleleaf packs its leathery foliage into a neat, slender, oval form. Other common shapes of linden varieties include bell, cone, and pyramid, all with even, symmetrical outlines.

The book on lindens calls for moist, well-drained, silt-loam soil to support the long root structures—this at least for trees that will mature into 15-story towers. Smaller street varieties somehow survive in the impoverished, shallow soil of city plantings. They tolerate average pollution, even moderate drought and salt conditions.

But no tree is a sure thing. In 1997, a New York woman campaigned for the city to replace, with a living tree, the remains of a dead London planetree on her street. The city finally (and for a $450 fee) removed the stump and planted a littleleaf linden in full foliage. Neighbors gathered and cheered the event.

The next day, every last leaf fell off.

Eucalyptus

Eucalyptus ficifolia, E. globulus, E. citriodora, E. gunnii, and others

Left: bluegum eucalyptus. On street: red flowering gum eucalyptus.

IMPORTANCE: California's 150-year experiment with Australian eucalypts has resulted in select urban species with astonishing growth or flowering qualities and unforgettable scent. One species (in Australia) includes the world's tallest individual broadleaf trees. Medicinal source, major reforestation tree.

FAMILY: Myrtaceae (Myrtle). GENUS: *Eucalyptus* (eucalyptus).

COMMON URBAN SPECIES: ❦ Red flowering gum (*Eucalyptus ficifolia*) or flame eucalyptus, scarlet gum. ❦ Bluegum (*E. globulus*) or blue gum, Tasmanian blue gum, fever tree. ❦ Red ironbark (*E. sideroxylon* var. *rosea*) or mugga. ❦ Lemon-scented gum (*E. citriodora*). ❦ Cider gum (*E. gunnii*).

TYPICAL CITY LOCATION: *Red flowering gum, red ironbark:* Streets, yards, small parks, hotel landscapes. *Bluegum, cider gum, lemon-scented gum:* Roadsides, large or wooded parks, coastal windbreaks.

KEY FEATURES: Eucalyptus flowers emerge from an urn-shaped bud whose warty lid drops off as flower opens. Common (but not universal) are long, saber-shaped, aromatic, drooping leaves; bark shredding in long vertical ribbons off smooth trunk; big graceful limbs. Juvenile leaves (preceding slender adult leaves) are often roundish, waxy silver-green, and attached close to stem in opposite pairs.

Bluegum: Narrow irregular crown of stiff, dark leaves on a tall trunk. Heights to 180′ in woods. Leaves 4–10″ by ¾–1¼″. Blue-gray bark shreds to reveal yellow-green trunk, rough at base. Buds top-shaped with warty cap, look sugar-coated. Solitary white flowers to 2″ wide, of many stamens, no petals, November–April. Fruit ½–¾″ long, woody top-shaped capsule with 4–5 seed "slits," October–March.

Flowering red gum: Dense, rounded crown. Leaves 3–7″ long, dark green and leathery. Bark reddish brown, rough, furrowed. Flowers striking crimson (pink or white in some cultivars) in clusters to 12″ wide, January–February, July–October. Fruit ½–1″ greenish-brown, bell-shaped capsules.

Cider gum: Tall, slender tree with bark shredding on smooth brown, greenish-gray, and/or white trunk. Odorless leaves 2–4″ long, 1″ wide, dull gray-green. Creamy white spring flowers in threes. Small (⅓″) fruits.

Red ironbark: Flowers white, pink, or red (*rosea* variety) in large drooping clusters, November–February. Bark rough, red-brown, nonshredding.

Lemon-scented gum: Tall graceful crown. Bark powdery white to pinkish under shredding strips. Leaves to 10″, slim, light green, lemon-scented.

AVERAGE MATURE SIZE IN CITY: *Bluegum, cider gum, lemon-scented gum: 45–75'* high. *Flowering red gum: 20–40'* high. *Red ironbark: 30–60'* high.

RECENT CHAMPION: *Bluegum:* 165' height, 126' spread, 35' circumf., Ft. Ross State Historic Park, Sonoma County, Calif.

❧ HEAVEN-SCENT FROM AUSTRALIA

Whenever this writer visited California from the East or Midwest, the scent of towering, shaggy-barked eucalyptus trees ("eucalypts") stood for everything exotic and enviable in this western paradise. Whether in a Los Angeles park or a Bay Area neighborhood, that piquant smell of good natural medicine for body and soul overwhelmed the air and said "You are not in Kansas." Or Chicago. Or New York.

To swim in such an aroma, most people have to smear eucalyptus preparations on the flesh or fill a room with eucalyptus cuttings from the florist—cuttings of the unique, circular "juvenile" leaves that appear on many eucalypts prior to the narrow adult leaves. But Californians, Arizonians, Hawaiians, and people in a few other warm states can simply walk outside and find the real thing—not just the scent, but the leathery green sabers that form the high foliage of a bluegum, the tallest broadleaf species in North America; or the colorful bark of the cider gum shredding in ribbony tatters from a creamy underbark; or the astonishing crimson blossoms and heavy bell-shaped nuts of the red flowering gum, to mention a few of the 70 or so species in U.S. cultivation.

How shocking it is, then, for visitors to learn that eucalypts—especially the tall, stringy-barked species—mean "weeds" to many Californians. For here, as the antieucalyptans will tell you, are alien trees that grow at warp speed, sometimes 10 feet a year, to dominate and shadow properties, kill undergrowth, block views, and drop a damnable load of brittle limbs, leaves, bark, flowers, nuts, and other detritus year-round. Not to mention their greedy roots, flammability, and pharmaceutical stink. Some municipalities in the eucalyptus-rich north go so far as to brand certain "eucs" as weeds or "unprotected" trees, allowing for their extermination in broad daylight. A statewide monitoring body ranks bluegum as an "exotic pest plant."

On the other hand, California abounds in eucalyptus (or "eukie") lovers who marvel at the trees' features, cultivate and plant urban specimens, and support preservation of woodland species.

Underlying these opposing views is the saga of how eucalyptus entered the Golden State—like almost everything else, in an extreme manner.

AUSTRALIAN TO THE HEARTWOOD

With common names like woollybutt, mugga, mottlecah, and coolibah, where else could eucalypts come from but Australia? And, indeed, that continent is by far the world's primary eucalyptus garden, with some 600 species making up three-quarters of Australia's forest trees and spilling into its parks and avenues. The spread of eucalypts far beyond Australia began in the late 1850s, when the director of Melbourne's Botanical Gardens promoted the powerful leaf oil (a natural insecticide) as a disinfectant in districts where fevers raged.

France planted its Australian seeds in Algiers, where the heat-tolerant, evergreen trees not only thrived but seemed to reveal a quality more significant than their "antiseptic exhalations": mass plantings of eucalypts apparently could dry out marshy, swampy soils, even reduce the malaria-carrying mosquito population. Soon such prodigious trees as the bluegum—with their bonus of therapeutic oils—were put to work for land reclamation in Italy, Sicily, Spain, and other places with mean annual temperatures above 60°F and lows of 20°F or higher.

California was one such place. A San Franciscan nurseryman introduced bluegum eucalyptus there in 1856, and in the 1870s a zealot named Elwood Cooper distributed his eucalyptus seedlings throughout the Santa Barbara region. Cooper wrote a book describing the eucalypts and sang their virtues in public lectures. The trees did their part. Finding the California climate much like home, they established themselves easily and grew with advertised vigor. The University of Califor-

Bluegum eucalyptus leaves, buds, and flowers. When a developing eucalyptus flower is nectar-rich, the unique bud (detail) pops its cap.

nia tested 20 species, and soon varied eucs were everywhere, including on the streets. Among mass plantings was a forest of 190,000 trees near Los Angeles.

Beginning in 1904, the eucalyptus craze became a madness, driven by rumors of an impending hardwood shortage in the States. The remedy: fast-growing, trouble-free eucalyptus. Nurserymen dominating the seed market pushed eucalyptus farming as the easy road to riches: Plant 'em, step back, and enjoy the profits in just 10 years. In 1912, some 50,000 acres were devoted to eucalyptus in southern California alone.

Frost and neglect took their toll on some of the crops. Brittle eucalyptus failed as a wood for railroad ties. And by 1913 the limited market for the lumber petered out. But the big eucalypts were now a part of the California landscape, lining roads, protecting coasts and citrus groves, and naturalizing in the woods. They seemed virtually native to some denizens, invasive to others; rakishly ornamental to some, messy and weedy to others. Few tree critics, however, could demonize the smaller, dramatically blossoming species arriving from Australia to brighten yards and streets, the red flowering gum and red ironbark among them. And, in Arizona, landscapers welcomed the dense, compact coolibah (*E. microtheca*) and some dozen other species as shade and ornamental trees for its arid climate.

EUCS AT WORK

While opinions have been mixed in California, elsewhere the eucalypts and their oils have been revered as near miraculous. And not just by koala bears, whose only diet is eucalyptus leaves. As a fuel, eucalyptus saved the Ethiopian capital in the late nineteenth century by quickly replacing its decimated wood supply. Australia built a timber and pulp industry from its trees (which are now partly protected) and produces oils from several species. Other eucalyptus-growing nations such as Spain and Portugal also extract the oil, which has a dazzling range of medicinal and folk-healing applications.

Woody fruit or "gum nut" of the bluegum eucalyptus.

An antiseptic, fungicide, insecticide, expectorant, and perspirant, it may be most familiar to Americans in decongestant liniments and inhalers. New Age medicine embraces this natural essence, one of the most popular aromatherapeutic oils. A Desert Hot Springs resort offers eucalyptus inhalation rooms for its clients.

Other societies have boiled, chewed, and smoked the leaves to treat everything from wounds to gum disease—though large doses can be toxic. Veterinarians treat horse flu, canine distemper, and other animal infections with eucalyptol compounds. Industry has seized on the extracts, including the citronellal of the lemon-scented gum, for bug-repellent candles and the cleaning and hygienic products that scent the supermarket aisles.

From the bark of several species oozes another useful substance, called eucalyptus gum, red gum, or "kino." Various types of the reddish, saplike kino are used in medicines and in the tanning process.

What more can a tree give? How about sweet nectar that makes for gourmet honey? The bluegum, lemon-scented gum, and others deliver it.

TYPES FOR TOWNS

The tallest broadleaf (nonconifer) species on the planet is *Eucalyptus regnans* or the "mountain ash" of southeastern Australia. There it reaches measured heights of over 300 feet and legendary altitudes of 470 feet. Even at its low end it is 160-ish and no tree for plaza or play-

Scarlet-vermilion flowers make the red flowering gum eucalyptus a flashy street tree. Buds are tubular.

ground. But three of the most popular tall eucalypts in California contain themselves to about 60 to 75 feet in town, about half their forest height. The bluegum, cider gum, and lemon-scented gum are all "stringy bark" types of eucalyptus, with bark forever shredding in long ribbons off a smooth or suedelike underbark. Each has the unique eucalyptus flower bud, a charming miniature urn that protects its developing flower with a sealed cap. When the flower is ready to please its pollinators with sweet nectar, the cap opens and falls away. After fertilization, the remains of the urn and the flower parts shape themselves into a waxy, aromatic fruit or "gum nut" with top slits (valves) containing seeds.

The capped bud inspired the genus name *Eucalyptus,* which comes from the Greek words *eu* (well) and *kalyptos* (covered), or "well covered." And a button worn in France gave the species name *globulus* (Latin for "little button") to the bluegum, whose fruit cap resembled this item.

The bluegum gets its common name from the gray-blue tint of the shredding bark and the blue-green foliage. The leathery adult leaves, narrow and curved liked scimitars or sickles, are models of drought efficiency. They hang downward to drip available rain and fog throughout the tree, and coil inward to expose their edges and not the surfaces to the scorching sun. These habits give a distinctive look to the crown, variously described as a dark curtain suspended from slender branches and leaves that look slept in. A popular 'Compacta' variety brings the foliage closer to the ground.

The bluegum's buds are coated white, like sugared cookies. Its white flowers are sprays of male stamens—no petals—surrounding a spiky female pistil in a well. Flowering is heaviest in February and March. The woody, one-inch, buttonlike fruits that fall to the ground make for precious mementos of eucalyptus country, holding the magical scent for more than a year.

Lemon-scented gum is like a product enhancement of bluegum, featuring added citrus fragrance, greenish-yellow, willow-like, drooping leaves as long as 10 inches, and an airy crown on a slim, straight trunk with powdery white underbark. Its scent perfumes parks and patios from Santa Barbara south, as well as soaps and other aro-

Bell-like fruit of the red flowering gum eucalyptus.

matic products. Flowers (white) and fruits are less conspicuous than those of the bluegum, and the tree is less cold-tolerant than even that cold-hating cousin.

For slightly colder climes, the cider gum is the tall, fast-growing eucalyptus of choice. With sage-green two- to four-inch leaves and a creamy trunk underlying greenish-gray or orangey bark, it is a pretty enough tree and much planted. A favorite in England, it tolerates brief cold spells of 2°F to 13°F, depending on the elevation of the ancestor trees in Tasmania.

With its spectacular blossoms, the relatively small red flowering gum needs neither height nor ornamental bark to make it the most popular of all street eucalypts. Approximately in July and often in January through March, the brushy, scarlet-vermilion flowers erupt in clusters up to a foot across, set against dense clumps of dark green, leathery leaves. Sometimes, depending on variety or chance, the tree produces orange, white, or pink blossoms. But they are never less than brilliant, emerging from colorful tubular buds and formed of bright stamens around a towering pistil.

Not many rough-barked, 30-foot trees could hold their own at the base of San Francisco's Pyramid skyscraper, but red flowering gums have been planted there and elsewhere around town. Eucalypts thrive in these coastal fog zones, but fail when temperatures stay below 25°F.

Farther south, Santa Barbara has some 500 of the trees on the streets, and Buena Ventura honors it as its official tree. As if the red flowering gum needed more garlands, it is regularly adorned by gum nuts shaped like pipe bowls or small goblets. Hanging in clusters, they often end up in flower arrangements and craft creations.

The red ironbark appropriately wraps its trunk in tough, furrowed, nonshredding bark, like other ironbarks in the eucalyptus genus. The "red" may refer to the reddish tint of the bark, or to the pink or red flower clusters that hang from the tree from November into spring. The *rosea* variety grows 40 to 80 feet tall and works well on streets. Hotel entrances seem to be a popular setting for the winter-blossoming tree.

Other popular ornamentals include the small coral gum (*E. torquata*), another winter bloomer with long-pointed red buds and pink blossoms hanging together. Blossoming when just 18 inches high, it can make for a eukie in a pot.

EUC KILLERS

With their natural insecticides, eucalypts are generally pest-resistant, but a weevil known as the eucalyptus snout beetle has been troubling bluegums, red ironbarks, and other eucs in California. A parasitic wasp has been enlisted to control the pest. Another killer of the trees, cold climates, can't be controlled; but a few eucalyptus species can survive dips below 10°F, while the notable snow gum (*E. niphophila*) makes it all the way to 0°F. Typically a crooked, runty 20-footer, it sports a sycamore-like peeling bark of green, gray, tan, and cream, handsome enough to place it in gardens well above the usual eucalyptus belt.

But still not in Kansas, Chicago, or New York.

Acacia

Acacia farnesiana, A. baileyana, A. melanoxylon

Left (of palm), Bailey acacia. Right, sweet acacia.

IMPORTANCE: A vast group of tropical and subtropical trees rich in Mediterranean (Biblical), African, Australian, and American southwestern history and lore. A staple of landscaping in hot, arid climates. Fast-growing, short-lived, drought-tolerant, disease-free.

FAMILY: Leguminosae (Legume). SUBFAMILY: Mimosoideae (Mimosa). GENUS: *Acacia* (acacia).

COMMON URBAN SPECIES: ❀ Sweet acacia (*Acacia farnesiana*) or huisache, cassie, popinac, opopanax. ❀ Bailey a. (*A. baileyana*) or fernleaf a., Cootamundra wattle. ❀ Black acacia (*A. melanoxylon*) or black wood a. ❀ Silver wattle (*A. dealbata*). ❀ Sydney golden wattle (*A. longifolia*).

CLOSE RELATIVES: ❀ Gum arabic (*A. senegal*).

Typical city location: Streets, parking areas, malls, yards, patios.

Key features: Urban species are generally small, with single or multiple trunks. Festooned with puffs or spikes of fragrant yellow flowers in season.

Sweet acacia: Paired thorns on zigzag twigs. Fernlike, 2" leaflets consisting of 10–20 pairs of minute (⅛–¼") subleaflets. Deciduous. Flowers ¾" yellow-orange balls, clustered, deeply fragrant, January–March. Green-pea-type pods, woody, dark purplish, shiny, 2–3", both tips pointed. Flat shiny brown seeds in two rows.

Bailey acacia: No spines. Smooth light gray bark. Evergreen, 1–3" leaflets branch into ⅛" silvery-to-blue-gray subleaflets. Flowers ¼" golden yellow balls in clusters on 3" stalks, late winter to spring. Brown 4" pods.

Black acacia: Larger, pyramidal tree with stout, straight trunk and olive-green, narrow, finger-sized leaves. Small, round, non-showy flowers, yellowish or cream-colored, in spring. Rough dark brown bark. Thin 4" pods in clusters give rusty look to tree in late summer.

Average mature size in city: *Sweet and Bailey acacia:* 15–30' high, 30' wide, 4"–1½' thick. *Black acacia:* 35–60' high, 20' wide, 1–2½' thick.

Recent champion: *Sweet acacia:* 30' height, 46' spread, 13' circumf., Atacosa County Jail, Jourdanton, Tex.

≥ Out of Barrens and Bush

I enclose you some seeds of the Acacia Farnesiana the most delicious flowering shrub in the world.
—Thomas Jefferson, 1792

Picture the African plains and the occasional flat-topped, spreading "thorn trees" casting filmy shade on the savanna. Picture lacy trees among the palms of a Saharan oasis, or silvery ones in the arid stretches of Australia and the drylands of Mexico and the American Southwest.

Picture flowering globes of yellow along the southern California freeways. Ferny shrubs on 15-foot bird legs in a Phoenix parking lot. Gray-green puffs of foliage in a San Francisco fog. Perfumed patio trees in a Texas twilight.

You have only begun to glimpse the world's acacias, a group (genus) of more than a thousand tropical and subtropical species with a long history of service to humankind. Australia, which has acacias to spare, calls them "wattles" and has honored one species (*A. pycnantha,* golden wattle) as its national floral symbol. Great Britain knows them as "mimosas." Of the 20 or so acacia species grown in the United States, about a half dozen or so—including the native sweet acacia— are common in hot or temperate cities of the West and Southwest. The Southeast, too, takes advantage of the acacia's affinity for searing cityscapes.

Some urban acacias may look like boutique creations, but most are as ruggedly acacian as the fabled trees of Africa and the Holy Land. Virtually pest-free and impervious to heat, they send deep taproots after groundwater. They fertilize poor soil by means of nitrogen-fixing bacteria living in special root pods or "nodules." They grow astoundingly fast, often three feet or more a year once established. They blossom from an early age, usually in profusions of small yellow balls or "fingers" that emit a thick, sweet aroma. And, as members of the legume family, they produce bean pods—whose uses have ranged from tanning and dyeing to washing hair and gluing pots.

The bark of many species yields medicinal and industrial gums, none so intriguing as a contraceptive gum in old Egypt, nor so famous as the gum arabic of Africa's Senegal acacia. And, like the acacias (shittimwood) said to be the timber of Noah's ark and the Ark of the Covenant, urban acacias develop hard, heavy, durable wood when not overwatered. Indeed, the urban species do about everything one can ask of a tree but grow old. Most expire after a hyperactive 30 years.

SWEET ACACIA: AMERICA'S OWN

When the Texas and Arizona territories became part of America, America could claim a native acacia tree—namely, the sweet acacia or

Sweet acacia: paired thorns, 10 to 20 pairs of subleaflets, and perfumed, yellow-orange flower balls.

huisache (*weesah-chay*), which also grows in Mexico, Central and South America, and the Caribbean. A small, rounded tree with thorns and feathery leaves, the sweet acacia blooms in late winter, crowning itself with clusters of golden, fuzzy, marble-sized flowers. As garish as yellow punk hair, the blossoms smell infinitely sweeter— like supercharged violets. They attract gardeners in Los Angeles, honeybees in Texas, and perfumers in France.

In about 1611, a sweet acacia probably from the Caribbean caught the nose of the esteemed Cardinal Odoardo Farnese, who cultivated it in his garden in Rome. Described in a 1625 garden catalog, it acquired the scientific name *Acacia farnesiana* (although the name *Acacia smallii* or *minuta* is sometimes applied to what appears to be its frost-hardy version in America).

Within a century, the *farnesiana* blossoms were sweetening the air of Provence and the French Riviera. In time, the French perfume industry seized upon a strain of the tree called "cassie" whose fall blossoms formed the base of a hugely successful perfume group also known as "cassie."

In the American Southwest, sweet acacia is lovingly planted as a native xerophytic or drought-tolerant tree that fits under utility wires, doesn't block mountain views, and whose floral virtues exceed its menace as an allergenic. The flower balls get their fuzziness from scores of radiating stamens,

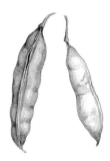

Shiny, purplish sweet acacia pods.

each loaded with pollen. But the pollen grains are relatively heavy and don't wander far from the tree. Nor do the two- to three-inch bean pods, which dangle in groups like shiny purplish ornaments until they release their chestnut-brown seeds.

Landscapers also like the spare desert look of the tree when out of blossom—its whippy, slender branches, thorny twigs, and bright green feathery leaves. Each "feather" is one of four to eight subleaves (pinnae) coming off a central leafstalk, and each subleaf has some 10 to 25 pairs of ¼-inch leaflets of its own. The tiny leaflets drop in autumn, barely qualifying as litter.

BAILEY AND BLACK ACACIAS: AUSTRALIA'S GIFT

California went mad for acacias in the nineteenth century, with some 25 varieties in the trade by 1860. Sweet acacia was part of that craze and is still seen from southern California to Florida; but Australian "wattles" captured the spotlight in urban plantings and dominate the street acacias today. Some of the Bay Area's first wattles were planted by Gold Rush immigrants with seeds from home.

Of the small, flowering Australian wattles, the Bailey acacia, with its gray-blue foliage and golden butterball blossoms, is most popular. It carries its Aussie heritage in its common names—"Bailey" after a Queensland botanist, and "Cootamundra wattle" for its native district in New South Wales. It quickly grows to about 30 feet high and spreads its low, weeping crown some 40 feet wide. Unlike sweet acacia, Bailey acacia is thornless and evergreen, with similar feathery leaves but a fuller look overall. Its abundant, sweet-smelling winter blooms cluster on three-inch stalks; fertilized, they produce four-inch, woody, sometimes twisting seed pods.

In flower lore, the blossoms have been associated with purification, protection, psychic dreams, love, and sexual magic. (It must be the aroma.) As healthy in San Francisco as in southern California and throughout the South, Bailey acacia can give some of its allergic admirers a headache in pollen season. But Australia is still to be thanked for

MESQUITE: OUT OF THE DESERT

To botanists, mesquite is genus *Prosopis*, a cousin of acacia within the same mimosa subfamily of the Legume family. Gourmands know it as the wood that lends piquant flavor to barbecues; ranchers loathe it as the thorny weed with roots far bigger than the surface tree. For indigenous desert people, it was a source of food and indication of groundwater.

Honey mesquite.

Landscapers know mesquite as a feisty drought survivor that, when irrigated, becomes a lovely, lacy, flowering tree for arid urban terrains. Native North American mesquites grow from Texas to southern California and up to Nevada. Trees from Mexico and South America add to the 20 or so favored choices for cultivation.

Landscapers divide the popular South American mesquites into two main types: Argentine mesquites, which are thorny and usually evergreen; and the thornless Chilean or hybrid South American mesquite, usually deciduous. Hardy to about 15°F, the trees shoot up at almost 6 feet a year to form 30- to 40-foot crowns of twisted branches. The ferny leaves create a pastel effect, dense enough for good shade.

American mesquites are slightly smaller and slower-growing as a rule, but the honey or Texas mesquite (*P. glandulosa*) grows to 30 feet high and spreads its bright green, drooping foliage an equal distance. Its greenish-yellow, finger-shaped flowers are more allergenic than ornamental, but they excite the bees that manufacture gourmet mesquite honey.

Southwestern natives, too, welcomed the sight of the honey mesquite and its four- to nine-inch, string bean–like pods. They ate the sourish beans fresh or dried, ground them with the pods into flour, and fermented them for a jolting beverage. They roasted the blossoms. They used gummy mesquite sap for glues, poultices, and snacks, and the heavy reddish wood for fuel and implements.

Mesquites, including the gray-haired velvet mesquite (*P. velutina*), are much seen in urban Xeriscapes, or drought-tolerant landscaping that brings the beauty of the scorching desert to the confines of civilization.

the tree, which in its 15 to 30 years of trouble-free life delivers four-season charm. A cultivated variety, 'Purpurea', adds a touch of purple to its new leaf growth and seed pods.

Other profusely blossoming Australian acacias ornament American landscapes. Two in common use are the silver wattle, whose cuttings wind up in flower shops as "mimosa," and golden wattle, frequently seen along freeways as a good-looking soil binder. But the black acacia, a different type of acacia from Australia, is the one most likely to be encountered on the streets. Shaped more like a conventional, pyramidal shade tree, the black acacia grows about as fast as its smaller relatives but averages some 45 feet in height and lives 40 to 60 years. Its dark, grayish evergreen leaves are spoon-shaped, not feathery, and about two to four inches long. Spring blossoms are cream-colored and sometimes less showy than those of the sweet and Bailey acacias. In late summer, four-inch pods give a rusty look to the tree's dense crown.

Black acacia may have a heartwood of black, but as a street tree, it stands full and erect and serves well, tolerating drought, poor drainage, poor soil, salt air, winds, fog, smog, shade, hot sun, and sudden temperature shifts. Only its rough, somber bark, its aggressive roots, and occasionally rambunctious suckers hint at a dark interior.

Black acacia came to California in about 1860, and within 40 years was well established on the streets. In 1930, it was the most common street tree in San Diego and a favorite in Los Angeles, where acacias made up a fifth of all street species. Having stood the test of time, the tree is still planted where winters (under 20°F) won't kill it. Even such tree-rich cities as Santa Barbara, with 225 species on the streets, hold on to its black acacias. Now and then, when a storm topples an old one, acacia lovers just push it back up.

Southern Magnolia
(and Saucer Magnolia)

Magnolia grandiflora (and *M.* x *soulangiana*)

IMPORTANCE: Native only to the American South, the southern magnolia is lord of the big, blossoming evergreens there and a symbol of southern beauty. It rises languidly to an 80-foot mountain of flashing dark foliage and lotuslike aromatic blossoms. A broad-leaved evergreen, it is planted in warm zones worldwide. Mississippi state tree. Louisiana state flower.

FAMILY: Magnoliaceae (Magnolia). GENUS: *Magnolia* (magnolia).

COMMON URBAN SPECIES: ❦ Southern magnolia (*Magnolia grandiflora*) or magnolia, evergreen m., bull m., bull bay, laurel m., great m., loblolly m.

CLOSE RELATIVES: ❦ Cucumber-tree (*M. acuminata*) or cucumber m. ❦ Sweetbay (*M. virginiana*) or swampbay, beavertree.

Asian hybrid relative: ❧ Saucer magnolia (*M.* x *soulangiana*) or lily tree, common m.

Typical city location: *U.S. South and southern California:* Yards, parks, municipal grounds, broad streets, cemeteries, campuses. *Northern range:* Protected courtyards. *U.K.:* Espaliered on walls.

Key features: Large, creamy, lotuslike flowers framed by big, dark, shiny leaves. Blossoms 8–10″ across, consisting of 9–12 thick, stiff "tepals" (petals and petal-like sepals beneath them) around a cone of female (carpels) and male (stamens) parts. Diffusive lemony fragrance.

Tree grows from youthful pyramidal form to massive, dark, glittering bell-shaped tree in some 75 years. Cultivated varieties are smaller, faster.

Leaves, appearing before flowers, 5–10″ long, 3–5″ wide, dark green with waxy shine above, paler or brownish and rusty-haired (suedelike) below; thick, stiff; oval or football-shaped, tapering to point at both ends, edges smooth and slightly wavy. Yellow midvein; short, fuzzy leafstalk. "Evergreen" leaves may yellow before giving way to new leaves in second year.

Large buds, to 1½″, densely fuzzy. Flowers appear at tips of most branch shoots on mature tree.

Fruit red, hairy, cone- or coblike, consisting of many "follicle" compartments beneath overlapping shingles. In winter, two plump, fire-red seeds extrude from each follicle and dangle from white elastic threads.

Bark smoothish gray, later cracking into scaly plates.

Average mature size in city: 50–80′ high, 30–50′ wide, 2–4′ thick.

Recent champion: 98′ height, 90′ spread, 22′ circumf., Jones County, Miss.

❧ The Anointed One

All across Dixie, the southern magnolia basks pompously in the June sunlight and exudes its heavenly perfume. Its slipper-sized leaves look oiled, its creamy blossoms shaped by cherubs. Only in America's

Southeast does the species grow wild, and there in cultivation it rules the big flowering evergreens. Colder, drier regions envy it. California has planted it with gusto. At least four presidents have enshrined southern magnolias as White House plantings. Magnolia worshipers in 20 nations belong to the Dixie-based Magnolia Society. Even the species' scientific name has a ring of majesty: *Magnolia grandiflora*—*grandiflora* meaning large-flowered, and *Magnolia* after Pierre Magnol, seventeenth-century French botanist *magnifique.*

Other nobles of the southern tree kingdom may be taller (bald cypress), more massive (live oak), or brighter-blossomed (crapemyrtle); but in its claim to royalty, the southern magnolia scores high in these virtues *and* offers lovelier leaves, sweeter-smelling blossoms, more colorful fruit, long life, and amazing resistance to pests, disease, and urban stress.

SEARCH FOR SAFE HAVEN

Some 50 to 100 million years ago, *M. grandiflora* grew far beyond today's natural range (Delaware to Florida, the lower Mississippi region, and east Texas). Fossil evidence shows the magnolia flourishing beyond the then-temperate Arctic Circle. One of the planet's earliest flowering trees, it luxuriated with other great primitives in the toasty forests of Greenland. But the forests cooled. Ice sheets formed and, about a million years ago, began heading south. Tree species either fled before the ice or perished.

Trees could migrate southward only if their seeds were dispersed in that direction to take root in hospitable terrain for thousands of successive generations. In Europe, the east-west mountain ranges halted many migrants and limited the number of species native to the continent today. But North America's largely north-south ranges allowed for the march of trees through temperate passages. And so the *M. grandiflora,* needful of hot summers, mild winters, and soft, moist, slightly acidic earth, found its refuge in the famously hospitable South.

How integral they are to southern culture is clear from the number and placement of full-grown magnolias one sees in town and country.

The big trees require patience—some 75 to 100 years' worth before they approach 60 to 80 feet in height. But as with live oaks, patience is willingly accorded these symbols of old southern grandeur. The trees are ubiquitous, from private estates to corporate campuses—and modest homes and shops, which they seem about to subsume in a nimbus of dark foliage.

Nested among dark, glossy leaves, the southern magnolia's floral cup consists of petals and petal-like sepals, together called tepals.

Often called simply "magnolia" in the Deep South, where the word is drawled with dreamy romanticism, the tree and its blossoms find their way into southern poetry, drama, and, according to one wry observer, every exhibition of watercolors. Realtors offer "The Southern Magnolia" among their custom homes. Mississippi honors the tree as a state emblem and in the Gulf Coast's Miss Southern Magnolia beauty pageant. Ice sheets may have been the best thing ever to happen to *M. grandiflora*.

A TREE OF SENSUAL PARTS

Southern magnolias give pleasure merely viewed from a distance. The big, glistening leaves and extended floral cups are plainly visible. The blossom scent permeates the air. The trees assume a variety of pleasing shapes as they grow, but generally go through a tidy pyramidal stage and then spread into a hulky bell shape in later years.

If left alone, the lower branches usually will rest their foliage on the ground, forming a skirt that obscures the trunk, assuring that nothing will grow beneath the tree. A peek within would reveal a gray, slightly roughened bark, and, on the ground, the "duff" of leaves that fall after about two years to make way for their replacements.

Scales of the ripe, velvety southern magnolia fruit open to release red seeds on strands.

Inspect the trees close-up in spring and summer and enter a realm of sensuality. At each branch tip, the 5- to 12-inch leaves fan out to form a nest for the bud, then the flower, and finally the strange fruit. The top surface of the leaf feels firm and impermeable, like some miracle plastic coating, while the bottom surface is often covered with a rust-brown velvety fuzz. The brown side, which makes a stylish complement to the dark green, is sometimes said to indicate cold-hardiness among southern magnolia varieties. The browner, the hardier. Although high winds can strip magnolia branches, the sturdy leaves hold up well in cuttings for vases and floral bouquets.

Soft brown hairs also appear on the short leafstalk, and the 1- to 1½-inch bud is like a fur-covered bishop's miter. The bonnet-sized blossoms, opening from late May through early June, consist of 9 to 12 creamy petals and sepals. In other flowers, sepals are usually the small green leaflike structures underlying the petals. On magnolias, they imitate the petals in color and texture, and the term "tepals" covers both for convenience. These thick, stiff tepals hold their graceful cupped form, but bruise easily and turn brown in a few days. Under good conditions, new blossoms will appear sporadically through the summer.

Nestled inside the tepals is the flower's reproductive center, with its almost comical crown of curly female styles above a cluster of eager male stamens. The flower's cupped shape reflects its prehistoric accommodation of beetles, before bees and flies were available as pollinators. Some scientists theorize that insect pollination of trees (as opposed to wind pollination) began with beetles and magnolias.

Fertilized, this central crown elongates into a three- to five-inch conical structure with overlapping scales like an artichoke. Its velvety surface will turn bright crimson—another showy spectacle for the tree—before it browns and opens its scale-protected chambers to release the seeds. At this point, science fiction fans will wonder if the aliens are breeding here. From little wombs beneath the scales ooze corpulent seeds as red as Martian skies, each dangling on its own thin white elastic "umbilical" cord. A bizarre sight, but appetizing enough to birds who will eat the fatty seeds and disperse them to other sites, where, in 10 to 20 years, the first blossoms may appear on offspring trees.

Horticulturists, too, collect seeds (or cuttings) of outstanding or unusual magnolias. With these, they will breed and cultivate specialized varieties, some very different from the big, slow-growing species. Among the most popular are such cultivars as 'Edith Bogue', a narrow-leaved *M. grandiflora* cold-hardy enough for Philadelphia; the small and common 'Glen St. Mary', which blossoms young and thrives even in San Francisco fogs; 'Victoria', cultivated in Vancouver and suited to the Pacific Northwest; and 'Bracken's Brown Beauty', with thick orange-brown fur on the leaf underside.

MAGNOLIAS FOR THE NORTH

Although a few *M. grandiflora* specimens are cloistered in Brooklyn, Chicago, and other cold cities, a true "northern" southern mag-nolia remains to be cultivated. But by no means does the North do without the joys of the magnolia genus. Within that genus are some 90 trees and shrubs, about 80 native to Asia and 8 to the United States. Of America's eight, two fine blossoming trees grow in colder zones:

■ The stately cucumber-tree, the only one reaching into Canada, features yellow autumn foliage and drops its thin, three- to eight-inch leaves in winter. In spring, it pro-duces a graceful, bell-shaped blossom, but

Gobletlike flowers of the hardy saucer magnolia appear before the leaves.

MR. MAGNOLIA GOES TO WASHINGTON

President John F. Kennedy and his First Lady planted 'Alexandrina' saucer magnolia cultivars at each corner of the White House Rose Garden. If the one nearest the Oval Office could only talk, what tales it would tell.

But whatever these trees have witnessed, they cannot upstage the great southern magnolias framing the south portico of the White House. The massive pair on the west side were placed there in about 1830 by President Andrew Jackson, according to White House lore. Transplanted from the Tennessee estate he had shared with his wife, Rachel, the trees served to remind him of home and of Rachel—who had died after a pre-election scandal sullying their marriage.

The magnolias have not only lived into the twenty-first century, but they enjoyed a long run on the U.S. 20-dollar bill prior to a redesign in the late 1990s. Jackson's portrait appeared on the front of the bill, and a southern view of the White House on the back, with the magnolias prominent.

A pair of "matching" southern magnolias, planted east of the portico by President Harry S. Truman, does not appear; but the replacement 20-dollar bill dropped the southern vista anyway, favoring the north façade.*

*Melanie Choukas-Bradley includes a treasury of such lore in her Washington, D.C., tree guide and other writings. An American Forests program offers seedlings descended from the Jackson magnolias (see "Resources").

one whose greenish-yellow color blends with the foliage. Its fruit is thought to look more like a cucumber than those of its relatives. Cultivated here since 1746, it has proved an upstanding shade and urban avenue tree.

■ The sweetbay tree is semievergreen in the South, but drops its shiny, narrow, three- to five-inch leaves in its northeastern range. Smaller and airier than *M. grandiflora,* this park favorite is noted for the silvery underside of its foliage, smooth aromatic bark, and intense fragrance of its two-inch white flowers. Its fruit is a compact two inches.

SAUCER MAGNOLIA

From those 80 Asian magnolia species come several that may look delicate, yet adapt naturally—or by cultivation—to colder North American climates. The magnolia most familiar to northern urbanites is a hybrid between two of these Asian trees; it is known as the saucer or common magnolia. Unlike the American magnolias and typical of the Asian species, it opens its blossoms on naked branches, well before the leaves emerge. These are the blossoms that burst from giant fuzzy "pussy" buds in April to stun northerners with their extravagant beauty. The big flowers sit erect on smooth, light gray branches like a thousand porcelain goblets, some 10 inches across, white on the inside and pink, purple, or purple-tinted on the outside. Blossoms on such cultivars as 'Lennei' attain hues in the psychedelic range.

The flowers are transient, and their lovely tepals soon litter the ground in a way that pleases some caretakers and annoys others. The mature tree takes a bushy shape about 20 to 30 feet high and wide—sometimes surprisingly larger. Its leaves are big and robust, broadening toward the tips, but they lack the dark luster of the southern magnolia's; they turn brown and drop in autumn. The four-inch fruit blushes deep pink when ripe.

Southerners, too, treasure the saucer magnolia for its leafless spring display, its relatively fast growth, and blossoming at an early age. Its tolerance for temperatures as low as −30°F is a virtue Dixie can happily ignore.

COMMON HORSE-CHESTNUT (AND THE BUCKEYES)

Aesculus hippocastanum (and *A. glabra*, and others)

IMPORTANCE: One of the showiest big flowering trees of early spring, star of spectacular old stands. Shiny brown seeds known as "conkers" are lovingly collected by children.

FAMILY: Hippocastanaceae (Horse-chestnut). GENUS: *Aesculus* (horse-chestnut).

COMMON URBAN SPECIES: ❀ European horse-chestnut (*Aesculus hippocastanum*) or common h., candle tree.

CLOSE RELATIVES: Native American horse-chestnut or buckeye, including: ❀ Ohio buckeye (*A. glabra*) or fetid b., stinking b. ❀ Texas buckeye (*A. arguta*). ❀ Red buckeye (*A. pavia*). ❀ California buckeye (*A. californica*). ❀ Ruby horse-chestnut hybrid (*Aesculus* x *carnea*).
       ❀ American chestnut (*Castanea dentata*), though unrelated, is discussed here.

TYPICAL CITY LOCATION: Grand boulevards, neighborhood streets. Open spaces such as parks, golf links, campuses, and cemeteries.

KEY FEATURES: Spectacular blossom clusters in 6–12″ upright spires. Dense crown, bell- or head-shaped. Curvy candelabra branch pattern, dipping then rising at ends. Scaly-barked trunk often twisted to the right.
       Huge (to 1″), shiny, sticky winter buds at branch tips.
       Leaf consists of 4–6″ leafstalk bearing clusters of 5–7 stalkless leaflets splayed like a hand (palmate). Each leaflet is 4–9″ long, spatula-shaped with narrow base and pinched point at broad end. Red hairs on underside at base of midrib.
       Fruit a globular capsule with thick green-brown husk, seriously prickled, containing one or more shiny, 1–2″ reddish-brown conkers, toxic to humans.
       (See text for buckeye features.)

AVERAGE MATURE SIZE IN CITY: 45–75′ high, 30–70′ wide, 2–4′ thick.

RECENT CHAMPION: *Horse-chestnut* not in American Forests *Register,* but height of 125′ reported in England. *Ohio buckeye:* 48′ height, 48′ spread, 13′ circumf., Liberty, Ky.

❧ CITY LIGHTS

A horse-chestnut in blossom is a candelabra of the gods. The branches swoop up, then down, then up again at the ends. The sticky, shiny buds—among the largest of any tree buds—look ready to burst even in

The lush flower panicle of the common horse-chestnut and cutaway of husk with shiny seed.

winter. As spring approaches, they virtually explode. In a few short weeks, the terminal buds (those at the branch tips) produce hundreds of upright floral cones, as bright as torches against a massive green background. In cities across the globe, the "candle tree" lights the way for spring's debut.

As a city shade tree, the European or common horse-chestnut is gritty as well as gorgeous. Given these qualities and its quick growth, many urban landscapers tolerate its "dirty" side, a copious litter that includes blossoms, seed husks, and scaly bark. It shines in urban parks and other open spaces such as golf courses and cemeteries, where it can spread itself up and way out.

The mightiest individuals command heights of some 100 feet with trunks as thick as temple columns. The branches form a broad crown and sometimes an almost perfect bell-shaped body with rim close to the ground. Runtier or tightly pruned versions are more typical of city streets and yards.

Growing wild in Greece, Albania, and Bulgaria, the horse-chestnut caught the eye of the northern Europeans in the sixteenth century. Soon this flowering beauty adorned the great continental gardens and boulevards. It reached North America in the eighteenth century. Asia, too, knew this tree and its close relatives in the *Aesculus* genus.

The Turks used an extract of its seed as a medicine for equine wind (wind from which end of the horse is unclear) and were first to name the tree horse-chestnut (*at-kastan*). However, the name might have derived from other associations with horses—the horseshoe-shaped scar left on the twig by a fallen leafstalk; the large brown seed with its irislike scar (hilum), resembling the eye of a horse (and buck, thus "buckeye").

The horse-chestnuts of Paris are the grand stuff of romance, the very "chestnuts in blossom" of the heartrending ballad "April in Paris." They line the Champs-Élysées. Near London, visitors flock to the spectacular horse-chestnuts of Bushey Park. There the trees form a mile-long avenue of five spacious rows, ending in a circle around a pond. Sir Christopher Wren began the grove in 1699; some of the original trees still thrive amid the towering canyons of blossoms seen each spring.

The tree is a good urban survivor, but certainly not invulnerable. In 1996, for example, hundreds of horse-chestnuts (and maples) were cut down in Brooklyn, N.Y., to limit an Asian longhorn beetle infestation. The beetle reached Chicago (and this writer's neighborhood) in 1998. Enjoy this great performer while it still thrives.

WATCHING THE SPRING SHOW

The horse-chestnut's spring extravaganza is a must-see for any urbanite, especially in areas without tropical blooms. Start by watching the lipstick-sized, resin-coated buds as they bust open in late winter. The bud scales part and give way to fuzzy white bundles, which over the next few weeks will progress into gawky miniature versions of the floral spires and big leaves to come. (A budding branchlet put in water will open similarly.) Then one mild day, look up and shield your eyes: Standing proud at the tip of almost every branchlet will be a seven- to eight-inch spire (panicle) of dazzling blossoms. Beneath these spires hang clusters of tender young leaflets.

The days grow warmer. Now the spires have stretched another inch or two. The hanging leaves have stiffened and splayed their five to nine leaflets like fingers on giant hands. These uniquely shaped leaflets are widest near the tips, dark green on top, with soft red hair on the lighter underside.

Each panicle bears some 100 to 200 blossoms in a cotton-candy fluff. Like tiny orchids, the flowers roll out their petals with tips curled

Leaflets of horse-chestnut trees fan out from one point on the leafstalk (palmately compound). Left, Ohio buckeye; right, European horse-chestnut.

down to ease the entry of bees. From deep within comes a soapy summery aroma. The petals are white with splashes of bridesmaid yellow and deep pink.

To produce its famous shiny seed or conker, the horse-chestnut does what nature requires of insect-pollinated plants. It induces the visitor to come and stay awhile, bringing (male) pollen from another tree and touching (female) stigma. Pollen gathered here in the process will, ideally, fertilize another horse-chestnut. The tree carries out such inducement with a flair that has inspired not only billions of insects but also generations of humans on four continents—lovers, songwriters, and naturalists among them.

The individual flowers could not be more gracefully structured or inviting. Examine them closely. Pollen sacs are extended on long wiry filaments. A sweet nectar lures pollen spreaders along the female parts. Color markings on the petals provide "honey guides" for the clueless. And when the sweet stuff is used up, the petals undergo color changes from yellow to orange and carmine, signaling, MISSION ACCOMPLISHED. VISIT OUR OTHER FINE BLOSSOMS.

Once fertilized, the flowers' ovaries develop into seed fruits that take over the flower stalks. The panicles become spikes of prickly, pea-sized capsules—golf-ball-sized by maturity. By autumn, most of these green prickled balls are off the tree thanks to nature, squirrels, and kids with sticks. The proper use of the seed within the husk is to make more horse-chestnuts. Unfortunately, the caramel-brown conker looks good enough to eat. But in humans it can cause vomiting, paralysis, and sometimes death. The edible chestnut belongs to another tree type entirely (see sidebar).

The seeds of common horse-chestnuts and the related native American buckeyes contain esculin, a substance that destroys red blood cells. Native tribes managed to boil and leach out the bitter toxin and put buckeye seeds on the menu, a substitute for acorns. In Eastern Europe, a detoxified horse-chestnut fodder works for cattle, although pigs take a pass on it.

Esculin has been used as a stupefying agent, mainly for elusive fish. Squirrels, however, devour the stuff all year without a sign of slowing down. Nonsquirrels exploit the seed in other ways. British youngsters play a dexterous game of "conkers" with it. Every year, an English club sponsors a dotty if

THE TRAGIC AMERICAN CHESTNUT

Attention, please: Your life may depend on knowing that the horse-chestnut is *not* the native American chestnut (*Castanea dentata*), the tree that ruled the forests and graced the eastern U.S. towns until the early twentieth century.

"It was very exciting at that season to roam the then boundless chestnut woods," Henry Thoreau wrote in *Walden* after some of his local Massachusetts woods had been cleared. "Occasionally I climbed and shook the trees. They grew also behind my house, and one large tree, which almost overshadowed it, was, when in flower, a bouquet which scented the whole neighborhood."

The American chestnut and the European horse-chestnut are both seductive trees, efflorescent and aromatic. Both spawn lustrous brown fruit in a burred capsule. But how do the two differ?

First, the American chestnut is of another family, the beeches. Its flower is no spire, but a long thin catkin or tassel.

The American chestnut's five- to nine-inch leaf.

(continued on p. 246)

(continued from p. 245)

Second, the American chestnut, once a majestic spreading tree with trunks as thick as 11 feet, is now history. Between about 1904 and the late 1930s, a fungal blight from Asia brought cankered, suppurating extinction to virtually every tree. Believed to have been around for 40 million years, the species is now kaput except for doomed sprouts that rise from stumps and a few struggling cultivated hybrids.

Finally, American chestnuts (or, today, seeds of the European Spanish or sweet chestnut) are the savory "chestnuts roasting on an open fire"; the sweet and nutty nuts of street vendors, of holiday stuffings and extravagant gourmet concoctions. *But a horse-chestnut seed is the kiss of death* (see main text).

There are probably no American chestnuts in your neighborhood. Yet the wood of this near-extinct species was used so widely for its rot-resistant quality that here and there an old post, a railroad tie, remains. Telephone poles were often made of chestnut. If in your neighborhood there's an old brown pole, older than anyone can remember, give it a hug. It's an American legend.

charitable World Conker Championship. Bookbinders have used horse-chestnut mush in a vermin-repellent paste. Believers carry conkers in their pockets to prevent attacks of rheumatism. A modern study has found dried-seed extract to be as safe and effective as compression stockings for treating limbs swollen by vein problems.

For landscapers who find the conkers simply a nuisance, the Swiss have cultivated a tidy, sterile variety named Baumann, which produces luxuriant double flowers but no chestnuts—a "chestnothing" tree to squirrels.

THE BUCKEYES

Horse-chestnuts native to America are known as buckeyes and thrive in the nation's urban spaces. The state tree of Ohio—the "Buckeye State"—is commonly called Ohio buckeye, though its region spreads from the Canadian prairies to the American South. A medium-to-large shade tree, it flowers like the European horse-chestnut, but with duller, greenish-yellow flower panicles. Dry—not sticky—terminal buds help identify the Ohio buckeye and the smaller, closely related Texas buckeye.

The Ohio's fruit capsule is tan with weak prickles, and the seed a purplish brown. The leaves and twigs emit a telltale stink when bruised. With its yellow or orange autumn foliage, the Ohio buckeye easily beats the dry brown European horse-chestnut for fall color. Its flowers, however, are usually not as yellow as those of the yellow buckeye, a similar tree that can flourish in the same urban areas. The yellow buckeye better resists the leaf infections and infestations that plague its relatives.

Distinctive pear-shaped seed capsule of the California buckeye.

Color is the strong suit of the red buckeye of the southern states. The tree rises only to some 25 feet, but its carmine panicles, up to a foot long, dazzle the eye and attract hummingbirds and butterflies. Crossbreeding of red buckeye with the European horse-chestnut has yielded the magnificent red or ruby horse-chestnut, a good-sized tree whose flowers are rose-red or, on the 'Briotii' variety, crimson. Unlike most hybrids, the ruby reproduces itself from its own seeds, not reverting to one of the parents. Red buckeye capsules are smooth; those of the red horse-chestnut prickled.

Sorting out these species and their hybrids can cause buckeye vertigo, but the California buckeye is easier. You find it in California, especially in coastal areas, a small tree with smooth, light gray bark and sticky buds. Its seed capsules are smooth and distinctively pear-shaped. Topping out at about 40 feet, the tree can produce pinkish-white spires of blossoms when only 10 to 12 feet tall. Often sculpted by sea winds, the California buckeye is "an oddly lovely little tree," in the words of naturalist Donald Culross Peattie.

CATALPA

Catalpa speciosa, C. bignonioides (and *Paulownia tomentosa*)

IMPORTANCE: Tenacious trees widely admired in cities for their jumbo heart-shaped leaves, showy late-spring blossoms, and long, dangling seed capsules. Fast growth and pollution tolerance are urban pluses; messy litter a minus.

FAMILY: Bignoniaceae (Trumpet creeper). GENUS: *Catalpa* (catalpa).

COMMON URBAN SPECIES: ❧ Northern catalpa (*Catalpa speciosa*) or western c., hardy c., cawtawba tree, cigar tree, Indian bean tree. ❧ Southern catalpa (*C. bignonioides*) or common c., catalfa, catawba, smoke bean tree, Indian bean tree, caterpillar tree, fish-bait tree.

CLOSE RELATIVES: ❧ Paulownia (*Paulownia tomentosa*) or foxglove tree, empress tree, princess tree.

TYPICAL CITY LOCATION: Residential streets, parks, cemeteries, rail routes, undeveloped areas with moist soil.

KEY FEATURES: *Northern catalpa:* Grows tall, with medium-stout trunk and large angular limbs, a Halloweenish look in winter.

Big, down-pointing heart- or spade-shaped leaves, tropical look; 7–12″ long, fuzzy undersides, largest on young trees.

Flowers appear late in spring. Trumpet-shaped blossoms form pyramidal clusters up to 1′ tall. Each blossom roughly 2″ wide, ruffled, white with yellow and purple speckles inside.

Dangling fruit capsules are 10–24″ long "string beans," green, ripening to brown in fall. Inside are many thin flat seeds with "beards" at each end.

Southern catalpa: Leaves are smaller, emit strong odor when crushed. Tree achieves less height, to 60′ or so. Blossoms more profuse, more purple-spotted. Seed "beards" are pointed; northern c.'s are rounded.

AVERAGE MATURE SIZE IN CITY: 40–70′ high, 1½–3½′ thick.

RECENT CHAMPION: *Northern:* 107′ height, 85′ spread, 20′ circumf., Lansing, Mich. *Southern:* 69′ height, 71′ spread, 18′ circumf., Palestine, Tex.

❧ RICH BOUQUET, BAD CIGAR

For all its beauty, the catalpa finds itself rebuffed by the more fastidious landscapers. They consider it a high-maintenance slob, throwing off copious litter during three seasons. Yet, with its big heart-shaped leaves

"String bean" capsules up to two feet long dangle from catalpas in fall.

and towers of ruffled blossoms, it wins aficionados in almost every town where it can grow.

Dangling brown seed pods give it the nickname "cigar tree," but a good cigar is decidedly not one of the catalpa's virtues. Up to two feet long, the pods looks more like giant string beans than Havanas. Those who have puffed a pod are sorry for it.

The pods (actually capsules) do make for wonderful sights. In summer they dangle like exotic jade pendants. In winter they fringe the branches. But even without them, the catalpa would stand proudly in urban settings. It is a fast-growing, husky tree, thick enough to support heavy limbs. In less than 10 years it can shade a house. Mature trees commonly reach 50 feet and now and then surpass 100. A 107-footer rises on the Michigan State Capitol grounds.

The catalpa is a lush tree, displaying cascades of big green valentine-heart leaves, wide end up. Given space, the tree can spread its canopy outward and cast cellar-dark shade as broad as its height. It is the catalpa's floral display, however, that brings a tropical touch to northern cities and a late rush of beauty after magnolia, apple, and other early blossoms have disappeared.

Around June, the flowers rise in vertical, conelike clusters called panicles, sometimes towering 10 to 12 inches above the twig (as large as horse-chestnut panicles, though not so prettily mounted on candelabra-like branches). Making up each panicle are trumpet-shaped blossoms up to 2½ inches wide at their ruffled, scalloped mouths. Within the white petals, lavender and gold speckles and trails attract pollinators. A ripe (some say cloying) aroma also draws the nectar crowd. Individual blossoms resemble small orchids. The full flowering tree becomes a gown of velvety green festooned with white corsages.

NORTH VS. SOUTH

Most of the catalpas seen in North America are of two species: northern catalpa and southern catalpa, each with a host of other popular names (see summary data). They overlap broadly in their growing regions and to casual viewers look and act more or less the same. The southern catalpa, however, is likely to have a smaller, thicker leaf with a shorter point and considerably more blossoms on each panicle, with more lavender or purple coloring. The

ROYAL LOOK-ALIKE: THE PAULOWNIA OR PRINCESS TREE

There is no "cigar" on this catalpa look-alike, but the fragrant deep purple flowers of the royal Paulownia (*Paulownia tomentosa*) have won it a place in eastern America, where it appears in gardens and as an escapee to roadsides. A fountain at Philadelphia's Logan Square is ringed by these beauties.

Introduced from China and named after a Dutch princess, the tree also goes by the common names princess, empress, cotton, karri, and foxglove tree. One of the most vigorous deciduous trees, it grows rapidly and as high as 40 to 50 feet. Botanists differ on its family classification—some place it with the figwort family, others with the trumpet creepers as a cousin of the catalpas. The flowers are similar in shape (not color) to the catalpa's, but the leaves are slightly more angular and the seed capsules entirely different. Rather than long, dangling string beans, the capsules look like clusters of small castanets. Each capsule contains some 2,000 winged seeds ready to take flight to a roadside near you.

northern catalpa can grow considerably taller than the southern, although neither species gets much beyond 40 to 60 feet high in cities.

To distinguish the trees, a scratch-and-sniff test is conclusive. Crush a leaf (ideally, a freshly fallen leaf) and smell it. If it emits a strong, unlovely odor, the tree is a southern catalpa or part southern. Another determinant: Open one of the fallen pods in autumn and examine its pa-

Big, heart-shaped leaves set off the catalpa's showy summer blossoms.

pery seeds, which are bearded at the tips. On southern catalpas, these silvery beards come to a point. On northerns, they are blunt or rounded, like Abe Lincoln's.

Which is the more impressive tree, northern or southern? That depends on one's tastes. For massiveness, northern has the edge. For flowers, southern is more seductive—discounting the unsavory leaf. For adaptability, although northern has survived −30°C winters in Montreal, southern may still win out: Not only can it crossbreed with certain other species, but it has flourished far beyond its south-central U.S. origins. First cultivated in 1726, it is planted from Seattle to New York, as well as in southern Europe. An observer with the Brooklyn (N.Y.) Botanic Gardens reports that 95 percent of the catalpas she finds appear to be southerns.

'Aurea', a golden-leafed cultivar of the southern catalpa, has been called "the nearest thing to a permanently sunlit hill" (Hugh Johnson). A cross with a Chinese catalpa has created the 'Purpurea', whose burgundy spring leaves are often seen around town before they fade to green in summer.

Northern or southern, it makes no difference to one particular catalpa lover as long as the tree is there for dinner. The caterpillar larva of the catalpa sphinx moth feeds on catalpa and only catalpa, often defoliating the branches in its frenzy. The tree may not be happy to see these black and yellow pests, but many a fishing enthusiast prizes "catalpa worms" as bait. In some communities, the catalpas may be raised primarily to host the bait, though not every tree is infested. Most catalpas can survive a defoliation or two, but a succession of attacks can be fatal. Nor does the infested tree benefit from stick beatings, reportedly administered to shake the worms loose.

ROMANCE OF THE GENUS

Catalpa species, native also to China and the West Indies, have enjoyed some high moments in civilization. As one of four primary trees of the Chinese gods, catalpas were planted in strategic temple sites to please divinities. Today, the yellow flowers and long, thin fruit of a Chinese species sometimes enjoy the honor of being eaten.

The name "catalpa" —pure music when drawled in the American South—came to English from the Creek tribal language, where it meant "head" plus "wing," possibly in relation to the flower. (Some sources credit the Cherokees for the name.) Native Americans derived a poultice from the leaves and a purgative from leaves and bark, neither extract making medical history.

A one-man campaign put the tree on the U.S. map in modern times. Around 1900, an Indiana engineer became a near-fanatical proponent of northern ("hardy") catalpa power. Secretary of the International Society of Arboriculture, he boosted the easy-to-grow tree at the 1904 Louisiana Purchase Exposition in St. Louis, promoting what he believed were its rotproof qualities and industrial uses. Soon a number of railroads were creating catalpa plantations along their rights-of-way, hoping to use the timber for ties, telegraph poles, and fence posts. Farmers planted catalpas as windbreaks and commercial orchards.

Then troubles came: poor soil, mixing of species, catalpa worms, fungus, root rot, and a rot that could destroy even the resistant heartwood if it found its way in. The commercial projects failed, but an army of plantation workers had enjoyed a stretch of employment, and the tree had established itself around the country.

With some pruning and maintenance, the catalpa will deliver on its promise as a dramatic, shade-giving, sturdy ornamental for urban landscapes. Some city forestry departments, such as Chicago's, continue to recommend it as a durable street tree where space allows. And one respected Website—of *This Old House*—named it as one of "Twenty-one Trees for the Next Millennium."

You'll be seeing it around for a while.

'KWANZAN' CHERRY (AND YOSHINO)

Prunus 'Kwanzan' (or 'Kanzan'), Sato Zakura cultivated cherries

IMPORTANCE: In North America, 'Kwanzan' is the most popular and one of the healthiest breeds of "Sato Zakura"—a fanatically cultivated group of flowering cherry trees from Japan. Its unparalleled masses of deep pink fluffy blossoms brighten urban settings and draw millions to spring festivals in Washington, D.C., Brooklyn, N.Y., and elsewhere. (The white-blossomed Yoshino cherry is a co-star of many annual spectacles.)

FAMILY: Rosaceae (Rose). GENUS: *Prunus*.

COMMON URBAN SPECIES: Note: 'Kwanzan' and other Sato Zakura cherries were long classed as offspring of the species *Prunus serrulata*—the double Chinese cherry. But owing to uncertain parentage, these cultivated varieties are now named without species, as the following two: ❀ 'Kwanzan' cherry (*Prunus* 'Kwanzan') or 'Kanzan' c., Sekiyama c., Sek Yoma c.   ❀   White column cherry (*P.* 'Amanogawa') or apple blossom cherry.

CLOSE RELATIVES: ❀   Yoshino cherry (*Prunus* x *yedoensis*) or Potomac c., Somei-yoshino c.

TYPICAL CITY LOCATION: Parks, gardens, campuses, entryways, mall containers, suburban streets.

KEY FEATURES: Flowers bloom late, cover branches in pendulous clusters of 3–5 blossoms, each blossom 2½" across, carnation-like in density with some 30 ruffled, hot bubble-gum pink petals. Faint scent, no fruit. (Cherry fruits are normally drupes, with a single "stone" or pit.)

Stiff ascending branches create V-shape in youth, spreading with age to roundish low-branching tree. Bark is thin, purple- or red-gray, with thick horizontal lines or lenticels (breathing pores).

Young bronze leaves emerge with flowers, grow lustrous green and 3–5" long (up to 7.5") after petal drop. Boat-shaped with long tapering point and fine saw-toothed edges. Fall color yellow to bronze to orange-brown.

(See text for Yoshino features.)

AVERAGE MATURE SIZE IN CITY: 20–30' high, 15–25' wide.

RECENT CHAMPION: 'Kwanzans' have reached heights of over 50'. (The American Forests *Register* lists only native U.S. cherries, the tallest being a black cherry of 134' height, 70' spread, and 18' circumf., Great Smoky Mountains National Park, Tenn.)

❧ One Brief, Dazzling Blush

The cherry trees
Heedless of this tearful world
Have burst into flower . . .
    —Anonymous Japanese poet, ca. 1400

Don't those Japanese flowering cherries read the papers? Each spring, whatever the bad news, they light up Washington, D.C., New York, Tuscaloosa, Vancouver, and a thousand other cities as if nothing mattered but the color of happiness. The famous 'Kwanzan' and Yoshino trees that draw millions to the U.S. capital ignore the crises of the day, even controversies over their own preservation. But that's how it is when trees are cultivated to focus on one thing: a week or two of earth-stopping floral perfection.

For a millennium or more, several Asian cultures have contributed to the breeding of wild cherry trees into showy garden ornaments. The Japanese have raised the activity to an institution, with exuberant April celebrations and an elite group of intensely bred, mostly fruitless cherry trees called Sato Zakura, meaning domestic, garden, or village cherries. Since the early twentieth century, Europe and North America have embraced and perpetuated some 50 to 75 of these Sato Zakura cultivated varieties (cultivars).

One very special Sato Zakura takes its name from a Chi-

'Kwanzan' cherry blossoms: bubblegum pink, thick with ruffled petals.

nese sacred mountain. Though averaging only some 35 feet in height and 25 years' longevity, the tree is one of the most voluminous and enduring of the group. A favorite in Japan itself, the 'Kanzan' or Sekiyama cherry wins the popularity prize in the United States, where it is known as 'Kwanzan', with a *w*.

And so when spring comes to cities and suburbs across temperate America, the 'Kwanzan' does its thing whatever scandals and troubles taint the atmosphere—as long as pollution doesn't cloud it. All along the dark branches that radiate upward from a short trunk, clusters of pale pink buds explode—seemingly at once—into thousands of luxuriantly pink fluffs, a cloud of dense blossoms with some 30 ruffled petals per flower. And big flowers, as wide as

Some five inches of lustrous green blade— the 'Kwanzan' cherry leaf.

tennis balls, pile up like wadded tissues in clusters of three to five.

The 'Kwanzan' leaves emerge at about the same time, a youthful reddish bronze that will turn to lustrous dark green as the blades mature. Eventually, a vigorous 'Kwanzan' leaf will measure about five inches from its U-shaped bottom to the end of the long pointed tip. Its edges are finely saw-toothed.

Describing America's native black cherry tree in blossom, writer Charlotte Green spoke of young leaves "like a rose-hued undergarment beneath a white lace dress." But the bronzy underwear of the 'Kwanzan'—if there at all—is barely visible under the fleecy pink adornment on every overloaded branch. The pinkness itself is overwhelming, variously described as a deep rose, carmine, piercing, gaudy, neon, hot, or bubble-gum pink. With that much presence, the tree is best seen as a single specimen in a spacious green (or urban-gray) setting, or as one of a group of cherries set off by some large unifying something—like a monument or body of water. "The Jefferson Memorial is a good thing to put up to enhance the cherry trees, but difficult of attainment in the usual town garden," cracks gardener Henry Mitchell.

According to Mitchell, the flowering cherry has two strikes against it anyway as a yard ornament: greedy roots, and the speed at which the blossoms disappear to leave an "ignorable" tree the rest of the year. Others find more lasting pleasures in the 'Kwanzan': long graceful leaves, which often color orange-brown in autumn; and the dark gray bark, tinted red or blue and striped by thick horizontal lines of breathing pores (lenticels). Even the bare 'Kwanzan' can be interesting in its later years, with bowed branches remembering their happy spring burden.

BRIEF IS BEAUTIFUL

The very brevity of the Sato Zakura blossoming is a virtue of the trees, at least to the early Asian poets and to contemporary Asians celebrating spring rites in Tokyo, Kyoto, and other cherry capitals. The flowering symbolizes the rarity and preciousness of beauty, to be savored with all one's soul (and film) while extant, and to be remembered with lyric heartache when gone. As tenth-century poet Ki No Tsurayuki felt it,

The wind is not cold
that blows the cherry petals free—
And what better snow
*   have the skies ever known?*

At America's major cherry festivals, that brevity may be more headache than heartache. Planners must prepare for hundreds of thousands of visitors to blossomings whose dates they cannot guarantee and to settings more suited to contemplation than stampeding tourists. With trees (Yoshino and 'Kwanzan') that blossom in a staggered sequence, Washington, D.C., can stretch its world-renowned festival (see sidebar on page 260) a few weeks, even if the site remains a hazard for agoraphobics. The Brooklyn (N.Y.) Botanic Garden draws multitudes in late April or early May to 'Kwanzan' trees lining its Cherry Esplanade. One borough over, the 'Kwanzan's bloom along Cherry Circle Lawn in Queens Botanical Garden. In Branch Brook Park, in Newark,

N.J., half a million people watch some 2,700 Japanese cherry trees in bloom over a three-week period.

YOSHINO AND THE STREET CHERRIES

One enormous festival takes to the streets—the neighborhood streets of Macon, Ga., where under warm skies the city's cherry trees bloom early, about the third week of March. Macon claims to have some 200,000 Yoshino cherry trees—almost twice its human population and vastly more than the famous Yoshinos of Washington, D.C.

Though not part of the Sato Zakura group, the Yoshino is greatly revered in Japan and the rest of the cherry-blossom-loving world. Of unknown ancestry, it was first cultivated in 1872 in Tokyo, where today it reigns as the most popular type. The Arnold Arboretum introduced it to North America in 1902. A rounded, widespreading tree, it produces "single"

White or pale pink, Yoshino cherry blossoms are lightweight but profuse.

blossoms of fewer petals than the double-blossomed 'Kwanzan', but in profuse clusters of two to five blooms. The flowers measure an inch or so in diameter, roughly half the size of those of the 'Kwanzan'. Their color is white or pale pink, sometimes fading to white, creating a lighter feel overall.

Yoshino petals are clearly notched at the tips. Blooming two weeks earlier than the 'Kwanzan's, the Yoshino flowers give off a scent of almonds. There is no mistaking the two trees during blossom season, and afterward only the Yoshino bears fruit—half-inch, bitter black cherries. Yoshino leaves are smaller, but with coarser, two-pointed teeth.

THE CAPITAL'S FLOWERING CHERRY TREES

Spring of 1912 would turn out to be a tragic one, with the sinking of the *Titanic* in mid-April. But solace was already taking root in Washington, D.C., where the first of 3,020 flowering cherry trees given to the United States by Tokyo had been planted on March 27.

Some 2,000 trees given in 1909 had been destroyed when found to be infested. But the new trees were healthy, all 12 varieties of them, including the 'Kwanzan' and Yoshino cherries that would dominate Washington's dazzling annual displays. (The United States later thanked Japan with a modest gift of flowering dogwoods.)

Today, visitors from around the world find some 3,700 cherry trees in three major locations: The circular Tidal Basin (site of the Jefferson Memorial) features the early-blooming Yoshinos; more Yoshinos ornament the Washington Monument grounds; 'Kwanzan' cherries, whose massive pink flowers erupt about two weeks after the Yoshino's white blossoms, fill in at the Tidal Basin and abound in spacious East Potomac Park.

April 5 is the average peak time for viewing the trees (and hordes), but first blossoming ranges from mid-March to mid-April.

As far as officials can determine, about 150 of the original 'Kwanzan's remain, which is extraordinary for a tree considered old at 25. A few original Yoshinos also stand. Saplings related to the early trees can be purchased from American Forests (see "Resources"). As for replacement trees on these near-holy sites, there have been two schools of thought: nursery-grown trees that look like the originals, vs. the more costly and laborious use of genetic descendants. For the awestruck April crowds, it hardly matters.

If it lives long enough, the mature Yoshino tree can grow tall—60-footers have been reported—making it a risky tree under utility wires. The 'Akebono' cherry, a smaller, pinker, and cold-hardier Yoshino cultivar, is more likely to serve as a street tree. But street placement is always risky with cherries, which stress out in heavy pollution. In quiet suburbs or away from city traffic, they make good if short-lived urban trees, transplanting easily, tolerating heat, drought, and sea air, and fighting off the aphids, scales, borers, and viruses that assail them. With

human intervention, they can rid themselves
of uglifying black knot—dark swellings on
branches—and tent caterpillar nests.

Humans do intervene painstakingly in
the life of ornamental cherries, undaunted
by the oh-so-brief payoff. Most new trees
must be hand-cloned from the cultivated
parent, because the parent's seeds, if any,
carry unknown and possibly unlovely ancestral traits. Much of this cloning is done
by grafting (see "Crabapple" for a descrip-
tion of the technique), attaching a parental
bud to a vigorous rootstock such as the
wild sweet or mazzard cherry (*Prunus
avium*).

Glossy bark of 'Kwanzan'
cherry with rows of
breathing pores.

For all the effort, risk, and poignancy of planting flowering cherries around town, urban landscapers seem happy to do it. The 'Kwanzan' and its narrow cultivar 'Amanogawa', for example, brave the San
Francisco fog and the cold of Quincy, Mass., Buffalo, N.Y., and
Toronto. The double weeping Higan cherries (*Prunus pendula* 'Pendula Plena Rosea') hunch low and hang their boughs in Philadelphia
and Chicago. The big, robust Sargent cherry (*P. sargentii*), with its red
autumn leaves, or the bushy, early-blooming 'Okamé' cherry (*P.*
'Okamé') make their urban stands in both Europe and North America.
And so on, with scores of cultivars.

As with other large groups of cultivated trees, precise identification
of flowering cherries can be maddening, especially after the blossoms
have fallen. Rather, take pleasure in recognizing such common features
as the horizontally lined and often lustrous bark of cherry trees. And,
of course, revel in spring's ultimate extravaganza. For almost as fast as
A. E. Housman could write,

> *Loveliest of trees, the cherry now*
> *Is hung with bloom along the bough . . .*

it is memory.

CRAPEMYRTLE

Lagerstroemia indica

IMPORTANCE: An icon of the American South, where it is used every-where, this small, sinuous tree from Asia produces brilliant flower clusters from July into September. Other features offer year-round interest. Also popular in California. Northern landscapers are plant-ing cold-hardier cultivated varieties and the related copper crape-myrtle.

FAMILY: Lythraceae (Loosestrife). GENUS:*Lagerstroemia* (crapemyrtle).

COMMON URBAN SPECIES: ❀ Crapemyrtle (*Lagerstroemia indica*) or crape-myrtle, crepe myrtle, ladies' streamer, flower of the South. ❀ (Hybrid) 'Natchez' crapemyrtle (*L.* 'Natchez', from *L. indica* 'Near East' x *L. fauriei*).

CLOSE RELATIVES: ❀ Copperbark crapemyrtle (*L. fauriei*) or Japa-nese c.

TYPICAL CITY LOCATION: Streets, street containers, small parks, plazas, parking lots, medians, yards, patios, campuses, borders.

KEY FEATURES: Spindly trunk or multiple trunks, often angled, fluted, rippled. Arching, vase-shaped crown. Gray-brown bark, flaking off to reveal pinkish new bark and bone-smooth surfaces.

Profusion of 1–1½" frilly, orchidlike flowers in 4–15" cone-shaped clusters (panicles) at branch tips. Usually 6 crinkled petals per flower. Blossoms in wide color range from white, pink, and lavender to purple and blue.

Leaves mouse-ear-shaped, 1–3" long, glossy, slightly leathery, smooth-edged. Fall colors gold, orange, and red. Leaves in both opposite and alternate positions on shoots. Leafstalks minute or absent. Twig grows 4 "tracks" along its length.

Fruit ½" round woody capsules, like sleigh bells, brown, splitting into sections to release many winged seeds.

AVERAGE MATURE SIZE IN CITY: 15–35' high, 15–35' wide, ⅓–¾' thick (per trunk).

RECENT CHAMPION: Not listed in American Forests *Register*. Trees 60' high have been recorded elsewhere.

⁀ THE ENDLESS STUNNER

A tree beloved by emperors in its native China and ubiquitous in the American South should be rich in lore. But the crapemyrtle goes about its summerlong blossoming devoid of legend.

Its less-than-myth-making size may be partly responsible; the species is no oak or beech. It grudgingly transcends shrubbiness to become a spindly 20- to 30-footer. Or maybe the legends have been lost in transit from Japan, China, Korea, and India, where the tree has long flourished.

The crapemyrtle arrived in America unheralded in the eighteenth century, a robust, heat-loving bloom for southern gardens. Soon it was under cultivation and proving its mettle in public spaces. By the twentieth century, it was to the South what the omnipresent dooryard lilac was to the North, even if Walt Whitman never immortalized the south-

Crinkled, crepe-paper-like petals and cleft seed capsules identify the crapemyrtle in late summer.

ern beauty. California towns embraced it. And after the National Arboretum developed a series of super-disease-resistant hybrids in the 1960s, the crapemyrtle gained new attention as a four-season ornamental. Northern planters discovered the improved tree. In Brooklyn, N.Y., for example, hybrid crapemyrtles brighten a southern-facing hillside in the Botanic Garden each summer, and the garden recommends plantings even in lower New England.

A tree so commonplace could become a wallpaper plant in southern cities—if its blossoms were any less prolonged and pyrotechnical. Whether shrubby runt or gangly spreading tree, a happy crapemyrtle is one of the longest-blooming trees in the world, up to 120 days from June or July into September or October. Even dull blossoms would stand out during that span, when most other showy trees have closed shop. But crapemyrtle blossoms form giant pink or red or lavender clusters, erect at the tips of slender radiating branches like torches held by a mob or a burst of fireworks against a green background. Up to hundreds of ruffled flowers make up the conelike clusters (panicles). Each flower measures 1 to 1½ inches across. Crinkled petals give the tree its crepe paper texture and name. ("Crepe" or "crape" is from the Latin *crispus*—curled or wrinkled—via the French *crêpe.* As for "myrtle," it refers to a likeness between the crapemyrtle leaf and that of the common myrtle shrub, a true member of the Myrtle family.)

Summerlong blossoming helps compensate for the most common problems of crapemyrtles: hordes of leaf-blackening, honeydew-excreting crapemyrtle aphids, and powdery mildew, a talcum-powder-like fungus that feeds on the honeydew. Both tarnish the tree's little mouse-ear leaves, which can be lustrous green and part of the crape-myrtle's charm; but neither seriously damages the tree. Various chemicals can control the problems, or the aphids can be tolerated. Specialized critters with the exotic name of *Tinocallis kahawaluokalani,* the aphids earn their place ecologically by attracting beneficial insects to the environment.

LEGGY BEAUTY

Although crapemyrtles are now part of the southern European landscape, they apparently arrived too late for the Greco-Roman myth makers who imagined a godly or human transformation in every tree. If poplars, lindens, and mulberries could embody souls (see profiles of those trees), why not the crapemyrtles, with their anatomically leggy trunks and skeletal limbs? These features at least make for winter and spring interest, just as the tree's bright yellow, red, and orange autumn foliage rounds out a yearlong performance.

Unless pruned into a single bole, crapemyrtles grow multiple trunks, five or six of them angling outward from the shallow roots. They have a coltish look, slender and jointed, knobby where branches have been pruned. The much-admired bark is smooth, light, and mottled, as if applied in thin, sometimes peeling patches. On the natural species, gray bark gives way to bone-smooth pinkish surfaces. Hybrids with the copperbark crapemyrtle (see below) flake to greenish and luscious cinnamon layers.

A vest-pocket park in Atlanta's lively Buckhead section features a group of leggy crapemyrtles opposite a fanciful sculpture of a human figure with a stag's head. Pausing in the park one recent winter, this writer felt intimations of a crapemyrtle myth at last—but just what was it? The clue lay in the crapemyrtle's tawny "forelegs," amazingly deer-like. Suddenly (perhaps because the park faces a movie theater) the myth emerged: *The gods, witnessing a hunter's cruel wounding of a doe, transformed the doe into an eternally blossoming crapemyrtle—and the hunter into a buck-headed nude forever exposed to the elements.* Mystery solved, myth in place.

COPPERBARK CRAPEMYRTLE
AND THE HYBRIDS

Elsewhere in Atlanta—and much of the nation—one encounters the cinnamon-patched bark of the crapemyrtle hybrids, which are cross-breeds between the crapemyrtle species, *Lagerstroemia indica,* and the copperbark crapemyrtle species, *Lagerstroemia fauriei.* (The *Lager-stroemia* genus was named for Magnus von Lagerström, an influential pal of the great Swedish plant namer Carolus Linnaeus.) Brought to the United States in 1956, the copperbark crapemyrtle comes from a Japanese island where cooler temperatures have made it hardier than its Chinese cousin. That strength plus a resistance to powdery mildew add to its virtues: ample size, white blossoms (smaller and earlier than the crapemyrtle's), and the lovely peeling layers of bark.

The U.S. National Arboretum saw copperbark crapemyrtle as a perfect breeding partner for cultivated crapemyrtles with their multi-colored blossoms. The vigor to be gained through hybridization also figured in the arboretum's goals when in 1962 it started crossbreeding the two species. The best results included a group of hybrids that were given Native American tribal names—and which today get raves from horticulturists. Most popular of these is the 'Natchez' crapemyrtle, a 25-footer with profuse white flowers that bloom early and often during the summer. Among the most mildew-resistant (owing to short hairs on the leaves) are the pink-flowered 'Osage' and 'Choctaw' and the lavender 'Apalachee'. The 'Apalachee', one of the few crapemyrtles with a light floral scent, also ranks high for density and upright form.

OF PODS AND PRUNING

In winter, airy bouquets of seed pods decorate the crapemyrtle's branch tips, where fertilized blossoms bobbed during the summer. Each pod is a woody round capsule, cleft like a sleigh bell when the capsule splits to release its small winged seeds. Gardeners prune these spent bouquets to promote continued or larger blossoming. The common practice of pruning the whole season's growth may encourage summer flowering, but at the cost of an arching tree structure. Recent advice says prune only to remove suckers (new shoots from the ground) and dead and crowding branches. A crapemyrtle that gets full sun, warmth, halfway decent soil, water, drainage, and air circulation will serve many years with a smile.

CRAPEMYRTLES ON THE TOWN

Queen crapemyrtle, Indian nanan tree, and other tropical members of the crapemyrtle family provide industrial wood. The North American crapemyrtle is for ornament. Tolerant of most city stresses except sea winds, it gussies up urban sites from coast to coast. Common in Los Angeles and recommended by L.A.'s TreePeople, it enhances such special sites as the Japanese American National Museum garden in Little Tokyo. It rules the late-summer blossom scene in Washington, D.C., and thrives as far north as Baltimore.

Houston, Dallas, Abilene, Natchez, and New Orleans love the crapemyrtle. Charleston, S.C., alternates it with larger street trees. Raleigh and Chapel Hill, N.C., run crapemyrtle festivals. In Florida, no decorative tree may be more common. In Jacksonville alone, the city and Electric Authority recently donated some 70,000 crapemyrtles for local beautification.

Robert E. Lee, who planted a crapemyrtle at his Virginia birthplace, suffered defeat in the War Between the States. But his tree lived to see the resurrected South. And one day, given the eagerness of its cultivators, crapemyrtle may yet march triumphant through the North.

Dogwood

Cornus florida, C. kuosa, C. nuttallii

IMPORTANCE: Small, stunning ornamental trees of early spring, with long-lasting summer beauty and red fall color. Their unique blossoms inspire myths, festivals, and vandalism. Flowering dogwood is the Virginia and Missouri state tree and North Carolina state flower. Pacific dogwood is the British Columbia floral emblem.

FAMILY: Cornaceae (Dogwood). GENUS: *Cornus* (dogwood).

COMMON URBAN SPECIES: ❀ Flowering dogwood (*Cornus florida*) or eastern flowering d., white cornel, American boxwood. ❀ Kuosa dogwood (*C. kuosa*) or Japanese d., Korean d., Chinese d., Japanese strawberry tree. ❀ Pacific dogwood (*C. nuttallii*) or western d., western flowering d., mountain d.

CLOSE RELATIVES: ❀ Pagoda dogwood (*C. alternifolia*) or alternate-leaf d. ❀ Giant dogwood (*C. controversa*) or table d. ❀ Evergreen dogwood (*C. capitata*). ❀ Cornelian cherry (*C. mas*) or cherry d.

TYPICAL CITY LOCATION: Parks, gardens, yards, campuses, foundation plantings, entryways, southern residential streets.

KEY FEATURES: The three species below bear leaves in opposite pairs (unlike the alternate-leaved pagoda and giant dogwoods). Leaf veins echo curve of leaf edges in "arcuate" pattern. Petals (actually petal-like bracts) with soft parallel veins surround core clusters of ¼" flowers or "florets."

Flowering dogwood: Four bracts with notched tips, 15–20 florets in cluster. Leaves 3–5" long, pointed, dark green on top, silvery pale below. Flower buds onion-shaped on extended twigs. Bark broken into small raised plates like alligator hide. Reddish twigs. Fruit clusters of 5–6 shiny berries.

Kuosa dogwood: Four bracts in pinwheel-like formation, with sharply tapered and pointed, often colored tips. Leaves 2–4" long, crinkled edges. Peeling, mosaic-patterned bark. Brown twigs. Fruit a round, mulberry-like compound berry, dull red and bumpy.

Pacific dogwood: From 4 to 8 (often 6) large bracts, 3" long by 2" wide, with abrupt pinched points. 30–40 florets in flower cluster. Shiny green leaves, 2½–4½" long, short-tipped. Thin bark, smooth or scaly. Purplish twigs. Crowded fruit clusters of 20-plus red berries.

AVERAGE MATURE SIZE IN CITY: *Flowering and kuosa dogwood:* 15–25' high, 20–30' wide, 1' thick. *Pacific dogwood:* 30–50' high, 20–35' wide, 2' thick.

RECENT CHAMPION: *Flowering dogwood:* 31' height, 48' spread, 10' circumf., Clinton, N.C. *Pacific dogwood:* 60' height, 58' spread, 14' circumf., Clatskanie, Oreg.

❧ GROOMED FOR URBAN LIFE

Sensitive to downtown stress, North America's native dogwood trees have no business in cities. Their natural role is lighting up the forest understory with spring blossoms and fall blaze, feeding dozens of wildlife species with their bitter, mealy berries. People catch glimpses of wild dogwood along scenic highways, where the small trees glow white or pink or red against dark conifers at the forest's edge. Their branches spread wide, forming horizontal tiers that extend every blossom to the light.

Trees so distinctively beautiful cannot hide from urban planters, who crave them for the sparkle they bring to a city's niches and green spaces. After some three centuries of grooming by cultivators, native dogwoods still struggle in civilization; but along with tougher Asian species, they make their stand. Dogwood trees have entered the urban forest to stay.

THE FLOWER THAT ISN'T

In America's eastern half, the flowering dogwood is often one of the first trees introduced to children, thanks to its pervasiveness and to a fable attached to its (so-called) flower: "See how the four petals represent the cross? How the tips are stained with Jesus Christ's blood? And the crown of thorns at the center?" The fable has it that the dogwood was once a straight and mighty tree whose wood was the obvious choice for the crucifixion of Jesus. Condemned to this fate, the dogwood was so anguished that Jesus, in the midst of his own suffering, promised the tree that henceforth it would have an inconspicuous shape—small, slender, and twisted—never again to serve as a cross. But its flowers would forever symbolize the crucifixion.

The story needs one botanical footnote: Technically, the stained "petals" are neither true petals nor part of the true flower. Called "bracts," they originate as the four outer scales of a flower bud. These bud scales are joined at their tips to enclose a bundle of tiny developing flowers. When the flowers are ready to emerge, the scales pull apart, each bearing the characteristic "stained" and puckered notch at its tip.

Bud scales often drop away, but on flowering dogwoods and related species, they now elongate into the beautiful, petal-*like* bracts that surround a buttonlike flower cluster. Bracts and cluster together look like one big flower—and for convenience we call it a blossom in this

Dogwood blossoms, from left: Flowering d., kuosa d., Pacific d. The petal-like structures are actually bracts that develop from bud scales. The true flowers are the tiny florets clustered at each center.

profile. But within the cluster are a dozen or more of the true—if flea-sized—dogwood flowers. Each has the requisite parts for reproduction, including minute petals to accommodate pollinators. (The so-called petals of daisies and many other familiar plants are also protective bracts surrounding a cluster of miniflowers or "florets.")

ACT I: THE THREE-DOGWOOD SHOW

So much for the botany lesson. Let us now take a sightseer's swing to Seattle, a town as blessed with flora as it is with cafés. Not only has its climate fostered a tree lover's paradise, but one of those tree lovers—Arthur Lee Jacobson—has energetically chronicled the city's tree life, street to street (see "Resources"). His work leads us to imagine a three-act spectacular of blooming dogwoods each year, because all three of the nation's most popular dogwoods thrive in the region.

So imagine: Come mid-April and the first of the three trees to flower is the Pacific dogwood, largest of the North American dogwoods with blossoms to match. Native to cool terrain from British Columbia to southern California, it is the big western version of eastern flowering dogwood. It towers up to 80 feet in some Seattle parks, putting out bract-type blossoms as large as six inches across.

From four to eight (most often six) of these glowing bracts surround a yellow-green cluster of florets (30 to 40 florets compared to the flowering dogwood's 15 to 20). The tip of each bract ends in a pinched point, rather than a "stained" notch. The crucifixion symbolism may be lost, but the tree has its own lore. An extract of its bark, substituting for quinine, is said to have cured two Cowlitz Indian children of malarial fever and shakes in three days when administered by ornithologist John K. Townsend in about 1834. British Columbia honors the tree as its floral emblem and forbids its unauthorized digging up or cutting down.

Setting off the tree's cream-colored and pink-tinted bracts are lustrous, elliptical, dark green leaves with long tips. The sunken leaf veins, as on other dogwood leaves, follow the curve of the leaf edge toward the leaf tip. As with all dogwood leaves, the blades curl up at the edges when sun-scorched. Pacific dogwood bark is relatively smooth, developing small, shallow plates with age.

ACT II: FLOWERING DOGWOOD

With one tree already in bloom, Seattle's next dogwood act opens between late April and mid-May. Now the smaller eastern flowering dogwoods hoist their blossoms, each with four notched bracts angled to the sun. Seattle favors cultivated varieties with pink bracts—'Cherokee Chief' among them.

Flowering dogwood trees grow to about 30 feet high and wide, with long, slender branches in horizontal layers. The bark builds up into a stylish alligator hide of small squarish blocks.

Over winter, the tree's flower buds give a silver-gray cast to the crown. The buds, shaped like little onion domes, are held aloft on erect reddish or greenish twigs. The blossoms emerge before the leaves. Bracts, often white, are gracefully curved and etched with parallel lines. The true flowers (in the central cluster) are fewer and the bracts slightly smaller than those of the Pacific dogwood, but the tree is no less distinguished as an American treasure. So treasured is it that people still flout protective laws and snap off boughs to stick in vases or flog as bouquets.

Presidents from George Washington to Bill Clinton have admired and planted the tree. One of Washington's Mount Vernon dogwoods was still alive in the 1970s, hollow-trunked but blooming. At the Arkansas state capitol, a variety of flowering dogwood served Governor Clinton as a harbinger of spring.* The Clintons planted a dogwood at the White House in April 1996, honoring Commerce Secretary Ron Brown and other victims of the tragic plane crash in Croatia.

Flowering dogwood has been cultivated since about 1680, but even in its native territory, from Maine and Toronto to Florida and Texas, the species has been suffering from dogwood anthracnose fungus (*Discula destructiva*) that seems only to get worse. Purple-edged blotches on shriveled leaves mark the infection, which spreads to twigs and branches and sometimes kills the tree. Experts are working feverishly to control the disease and cultivate resistant hybrids, especially in Tennessee, which claims to produce 75 percent of the nation's dogwoods for nurseries. In the late 1990s, a Dogwood Anthracnose Team at the University of Tennessee Agricultural Experimental Station was taking a SWAT approach, with specialists from several fields on the case. Meanwhile, landscapers are generally advised to plant only regionally cultivated trees, in well-drained, acidic soil, on sites that get both sun and shade and good air circulation. A tall order for many urban planters.

ACT III: KUOSA DOGWOOD

In June, just when Seattle's dogwood spectacle seems to be winding down, out pop the creamy, profuse blossoms of the kuosa dogwood, the flowering dogwood's Asian cousin. While there are scores of cultivated kuosa varieties, the species can be recognized by the sharp-tipped

---

*Descendants of this cultivated variety, the 'Clinton Pink Flowering Dogwood', are available from American Forests. See "Resources."

From fertilized florets at the center of the dogwood blossoms come these berries, from left: Flowering d., kuosa d., Pacific d.

pinwheel shape of its four bracts. (The pointed bracts develop from the *inner* bud scales.) The bract tips are often stroked with intense color. An attractive jigsaw-puzzle pattern distinguishes the reddish-brown, peeling bark.

Native to Japan, Korea, and China, the kuosa (Japanese for "dogwood") tree came to America in 1861. In many ways, it has proved tougher than the native tree, which, some believe, it will eventually displace or subjugate to hybrid partnership. Bushier and a touch smaller than the flowering dogwood in overall size and parts, it may not have quite the grace of its American cousin. But it resists the disfiguring anthracnose disease, tolerates full sun, and holds its blossoms longer. The flowers remain for five or six weeks as their bracts fade from white to pinkish. Leaves turn rich purple and red in fall.

DOGWOOD FRUIT AND WOOD

Sometimes as summer turns to fall, Seattle and other West Coast cities enjoy yet one more dogwood blossoming. The Pacific dogwood (which fails in eastern plantings) may feel vigorous enough to offer a second serving of blossoms at this time. But the season always delivers two other dogwood charms: colorful berry fruit produced by the small fertilized flowers, and vivid autumn foliage in shades of red.

By their berries, one can distinguish the three bract-bearing dogwoods (as well as other dogwood species), but one has to beat ravenous birds to the site. The half-inch, orange-red Pacific dogwood berries form a profuse cluster, like 30 elongated balloons in a vendor's bundle. Flowering dogwood berries are similar in size and color, but the clusters consist of only five or six shiny red fruits, loosely packed.

The kuosa dogwood binds its little berries into one dangling, dull-red ball, a bumpy compound fruit on the order of mulberries but one that looks like W. C. Fields's nose on a bad morning. A theory holds that as the evolving tree developed its fruit, one form appealed to Asian monkeys, which dispersed its seeds in their dung. That form won out. Similarly, Pacific and flowering dogwoods developed berries more suited to the local feeders and dispersers, namely, birds.

Humans, who can eat if not stomach some dogwood fruit, have chosen other ways to interact with the trees. The name "dogwood" probably comes from old European words for dagger or skewer, and not from the mangy dogs once bathed in a dogwood bark decoction or from an inversion of "Godwood." The hard, shock-resistant wood of Europe's hedgerow dogwoods made fine skewers and cattle goads, perhaps daggers as well. From the American trees came hard, heavy wood that took a high polish, ideal for the shuttles and spools of cotton mills and the cogwheels of big clocks. As a club head for golfers, the wood could blast mighty hooks and slices without breaking. Dogwood slingshots were formidable. Piano keys of dogwood took endless abuse.

Dogwood extracts served as colic and diarrhea treatments as well as a quinine substitute. Berries soaked in brandy were prescribed for acid stomach. American Indians, slaves, and pioneers used the fibrous ends of chewed dogwood twigs as effective (if sometimes gum-damaging) tooth polishers.

But today's dogwoods are for brightening landscapes, and some American towns are lit from end to end when the trees blossom. An 18-mile Dogwood Trail highlights the annual Fayetteville (N.C.) Dogwood Festival. Other dogwood celebrations take place in Atlanta, Charlottesville (Va.), and Knoxville (Tenn.). Dogwood-rich cities include

Washington, D.C., and Philadelphia—where a giant old specimen in Longwood Gardens dazzles visitors.

DOGWOODS FOR ALL

Some 40 to 50 species of dogwood trees and shrubs grow in the world's northern temperate zones. Among the tree-sized dogwoods are varieties for almost every taste and need. Choices include species and cultivars with broad flat heads of flowers instead of bract-type blossoms. The North American pagoda or alternate-leaf dogwood is one such species, dramatically tiered and producing unclustered blue berries on red stalks.

A notable marriage of eastern flowering dogwood with Pacific dogwood has yielded 'Eddie's White Wonder', a cultivar whose giant leaves turn luscious red, orange, and purple in fall. Cultivators also have produced a group of "double flowered dogwoods" featuring fluffier blossoms made up of extra bracts. In the early 1990s, Rutgers University introduced a series of vigorous crosses between the flowering and kuosa dogwoods, blending some of the best traits of each species.

But monkeys, birds, and berry-decoction drinkers be advised: As gorgeous and hardy as these well-bred cultivars may be, many are without fruit, or, as nurseries might declare, they are tidily sterile.

CRABAPPLE (AND APPLE)

Malus hybrids

IMPORTANCE: Beloved for showy blossoms and bright fruit, crabapples are the most common group of ornamental trees in cities with cold winters. Cultivated in warmer cities as well. No better example of cultivator's art (and frustrations) than variable, disease-prone crabapples.

FAMILY: Rosaceae (Rose). GENUS: *Malus* (apple).

COMMON URBAN SPECIES: ❀ Japanese crabapple (*Malus floribunda*) or showy c. ❀ Siberian crabapple (*M. baccata*). ❀ Prairifire (*M. 'Prairifire'*, hybrid) or 'Prairie Fire'. (See end of profile for extended list.)

CLOSE RELATIVES: ❀ Common apple (*M.* x *domestica*) or orchard apple, edible apple, apple tree.

TYPICAL CITY LOCATION: Parks, yards, gardens, foundation plantings, malls, plazas, streets, highways.

KEY FEATURES: Much variation in some 800 types, but in general: Small rounded or spreading trees, below utility wires. (Also weeping, narrow, and mushroom-shaped types.) Short trunk, often divided. Bark flaky, mottled, gray and brown, with knobby scars. Pointy buds (leaf and flower) grow from stubby, ringed twigs. Thorns are uncommon.

Leaves are alternate (not opposite each other) on twigs, 2–4" long, often spoon-shaped with pointed tip and finely toothed edges, sometimes smooth-edged, sometimes lobed. Color dark to pale green. Surface often hairy, scruffy by summer. A few types achieve fall color.

Flowers emerge in abundant clusters from (often) deep pink or red buds. Some trees bloom every other year. Individual flowers have 5 petals (more in some cultivated varieties), 5 pistils, and many pollen-bearing stamens. About 1½–2" across, mostly white, often pink-tinged, sometimes pink to deep red or purple-red. Often fragrant. Last about three weeks in spring.

Fruit is a "pome," with seeds enclosed in papery ovary wall surrounded by fleshy pulp. By definition, crabapple fruit is about 2" wide or smaller. Often less than ¾". Apple, olive, or berry shape. Small "crown" of sepal remnants usually on end of fruit opposite stem. Color often bright red, orange- or yellow-red. Several gold varieties, some maroon. On selected varieties, fruit remains on tree into early winter and beyond.

AVERAGE MATURE SIZE IN CITY: 15–30' high, 20–30' wide, 1' thick.

RECENT CHAMPION: American Forests *Register* lists only the four native American species, uncommon in urban use: *Sweet crab:* 37' height, 35' spread, 6' circumf., Hampstead, Va. *Southern crab:* 47' height, 60' spread, 8' circumf. *Prairie crab:* 46' height, 68' spread, 3' circumf. *Oregon crab:* 79' height, 47' spread, 6' circumf., Nisqually Nature Reserve, Wash. Tall introduced urban species include pillar crabapple (*M. tschonoskii*), 59' record height, Westonbirt, England.

❧ TREE OF KNOWING, OR NOT

I saw apples with the hue and heft of olives or cherries, next to glowing yellow Ping-Pong balls and dusky purple berries. . . .
  —Michael Pollan, viewing some 2,500 apple varieties at an experimental orchard, *The New York Times*, November 5, 1998

For such a friendly little tree, the crabapple can throw would-be experts for a mean loop. The dizzying varieties! The genealogies! The scientific and common names!

Take, for example, *Malus sieversii* 'Niedzwetzkyana'. Can you say that? Be thankful you don't have to. Without mouthing a syllable, you still can be dazzled by the magenta blossoms of this distinguished crabapple.

Nor do you have to know the tree's pedigree to appreciate its bronzy foliage and purple fruit. Yes, the 'Niedzwetzkyana' descends directly from the *Malus sieversii* species of Central Asia, possibly the original parent of every scrumptious orchard apple. And, yes, the cultivated 'Niedzwetzkyana' was the first of the "Rosybloom" crabapples to enchant gardeners with their deep-pink flowers. But you needn't know all that, or even the tree's common names—Turkestan apple, redvein crabapple, Russian purple crabapple—to rejoice in the natural and horticultural miracles that have brought stupendously flowering crabapple trees into everyday urban life.

To lose yourself in a sweet-smelling, billion-petal cloud of unknowing crabapple bliss, take a spring drive through The Morton Arboretum near Chicago or along the Merritt Parkway in Connecticut. Or join the annual Celebration of the Trees in Delaware. Or simply plunge into any one of a thousand public gardens and parks at blossomtime.

APPLES AND CRABAPPLES

What your analytical left brain might want to know, however, is the difference between a crabapple tree and a plain old apple tree. Botanically, there is none, except possibly in the way of ancient ancestry. The sim-

Buds and blossoms of the wide-spreading Japanese crabapple.

plest answer is that the crabapple—as opposed to the apple—is the blossoming tree you see around town and which produces either no fruit or fruit smaller than two inches. Some 35 species considered crabapples (including four native North American species) exist in the wild, while about 800 variations (at this writing) have been cultivated mainly for ornamental traits and/or disease resistance.

The plain old apple tree—also known as the "common," "orchard," or "edible" apple—is one that has been bred to produce bigger, less-blemished, more-palatable fruit. About 7,500 types have been cultivated mainly from strains of two Eurasian species (*M. sylvestris* and *M. pumila*), with centuries of crossbreeding focused on the fruit. Orchards and rural yards are their usual haunt. The general botanical handle for the common apple tree is *Malus* x *domestica,* but you don't have to know that to sink your teeth into a Red Delicious, Golden Delicious, McIntosh, or Fuji fruit.

Not based on structural differences, the dividing line between apples and crabapples gets fuzzy if you look too close. Edible vs. inedible can be misleading. Consider Shakespeare's mischievous sprite Puck, whose disguises include that of a cooked crabapple:

> *And sometime lurk I in a gossip's bowl,*
> *In very likeness of a roasted crab,*
> *And when she drinks, against her lips I bob*
> *And on her wither'd dewlap pour the ale.*

An edible crabapple? Yes—all crabapple fruit is fit for human consumption, but most types are so sour as to be judged "spitters" by those who taste them. Many, however, are consumed as jams, jellies, ciders, and vinegars. To further blur the dividing line, some common apple trees grow small fruit, and some escape to the woods (often via apple cores tossed by humans) to join the wild crabapples in spring blossom.

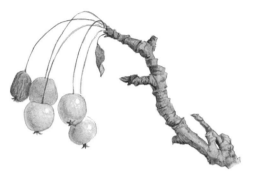

Late fall reveals persistent crabapples and stubby spurs on twigs.

But for the urban observer, here's a functional distinction:

■ Crabapple trees are the blossoming, fruiting beauties planted to decorate the town and feed our eyes. The birds and squirrels get the fruit.

■ Common apple trees are the ones out in the commercial orchards, sometimes seen in fall when we (mostly northerners) take a weekend drive to "pick our own."

AN APPLE IS A ROSE BY ANY NAME

All apple and crabapple trees are members of the larger Rose family (Rosaceae), whose approximately 2,000 species include the roses themselves and a huge range of trees grown for fruit and ornamental blossoms. A big Delicious apple may seem unroselike, but the family resemblance is clear between small crabapples and rosehips (the rose fruit), both with little crowns of leaflike sepals at the tips. Like other members of the Rose clan, the crabapple trees contain both male and female reproductive parts in their ("perfect") flowers, usually showy five-petal flowers one to two inches across.

Crabapple trees share another Rose family trait: They attract a juggernaut of plant diseases. Until modern crabapple arboriculture produced resistant trees, a corridor of blooming crabapples in spring could mean a ward of festering trees the rest of the year. In Washington, D.C., where springtime crabapples once rivaled the famous cherry blossoms, the city held an annual crabapple parade and crowned a Crabapple Queen. The event died in the 1950s, perhaps because once the blossoms fell, no one wanted to be queen of scab, rust, mildew, fireblight, canker, scales, borers, and aphids.

Washington is still rich in crabapples, and like most cities can take advantage of the healthier, hardier breeds in constant development. The march of improved crabapple trees owes much to the ways of *Malus* genes.

BREEDING, CLONING, AND HONEST GRAFT

While the apple group won't mix its genes with plum or hawthorn or other close-seeming relatives in the Rose family, in sexual reproduction it combines and mutates its own genes in ways that produce frequent varied offspring. Cultivators then select and breed variations with such desirable traits as bigger fruit, doubled blossoms, and tough constitutions. When new breeds test out over the years—and often they don't—they can be abundantly cloned for sale and distribution.

Much cloning is accomplished by an amazing asexual process called grafting, which works exceedingly well on apples and crabapples. A scion—a mere bud and its attached bark—is taken from the tree to be cloned. A young host tree (rootstock), which can be any number of hospitable *Malus* species, is cut down to a bit of trunk above the roots. The scion is then worked into this rootstock trunk and firmly attached. The resulting tree takes on all the genetic traits of the scion and none of the rootstock, which affects only size and vigor.

In nature, of course, a crabapple tree reproduces by seed, the end product of fertilization by pollen from another tree. This blending of parent genes and survival of the fittest offspring are good for a plant group, keeping it in step with evolving enemies. But apple growers shun combinations of unknown genes. Seeds of the fanciest orchard apple can and often do produce a tree that reverts to wild ancestral traits. So orchard apples and ornamental crabapples are cloned or pollinated under controlled conditions to produce known or experimental hybrids.

EVOLUTION OF THE URBAN CRABS

No one knows when apple cultivation began. Carbonized fragments of apples found in prehistoric Swiss lake dwellings suggest early domestication of the tree. The Bible does not specify apple or any other type of fruit on the Tree of Knowledge. Elsewhere in the Bible, what translators have called "apple" are thought to be apricots and other warm-climate fruits. (The word "apple" itself is from the German *Apfel,* which referred to any fruit. "Crab" is possibly derived from a Celtic term for "sour" or from the Scandinavian *skrub* for brushwood.)

A thousand years ago, the Romans were avidly cultivating apples and may have brought the techniques to Britain, where *M. sylvestris,* one of the fundamental crabapple species, grows in the wild. A fifteenth-century monk wrote of apple (and crabapple) trees as "gracious in syght and in taste and vertuous in medecyne," some bearing "sourysh fruyte and hard, and some ryght soure and some ryght swete with a good savoure." Early medical uses included laxative preparations and a skin ointment made from apple pulp, swine's grease, and rose water.

Through the seventeenth century, cultivators in the Western world still concerned themselves with improving the apple fruit, whether sweet or sour, for food and drink. As early as about 1650, America had a cultivated and named orchard apple, the 'Yellow Sweetening' (later renamed 'Sweet Rhode Island Greening'). In time, freak seedlings appearing in orchards would be nurtured into such famous eating apples as Baldwin and McIntosh. And a zealous nurseryman called Johnny Appleseed (John Chapman, 1774–1845) would rove the Midwest selling and giving away seeds that launched orchard trees by the thousands.*

---

*American Forests sells apple seedlings descended from Johnny Appleseed trees. See "Resources."

Savoring a Crabapple Tree

To one writer, winter crabapple trees looked like crabs scurrying across the parks. Upside-down crabs or whatever, they do suggest critters with knobby bottoms and widespread limbs. Close-up, they offer nature lovers much more for observation.

Late winter is a good time to examine the trunk's flaky, mottled bark and lumpy pruning scars. Branch bark displays stripelike lines of breathing pores (lenticels). Sharp little leaf and flower buds grow off stubby twigs (spurs) along the shoots and branches. Short stubs better support the weight of fruit. Notice the twigs' crowded annual rings, indicating slow growth.

Spring buds may turn dramatically red before the first leaves appear. Blossoms and leaves come in quick succession, but in April and May, the flowers can blanket the tree. Five is the key number for crabapple flowers—five sepals at the base, five petals, and five "female" pistils in the center, leading to five ovules deep in the flower that will become five seed chambers after fertilization. Many more petals may appear on certain cultivated trees, but the pistil count remains five. Observe the cupping of the petals and their fragrance and coloration, all varied according to cultivated type.

(continued on p. 285)

In the late eighteenth century, however, England's Kew Gardens received a Siberian crabapple species (*M. baccata*) with only pea-sized fruit but fetching, fragrant white flowers. The species blossomed early and profusely, survived cold weather, and grew tall. With this and such other majestically blossoming species as the Japanese crabapple (*M. floribunda*), Western cultivation of ornamental crabapples was under way.

To this day, the Siberian crabapple strain runs through some of the finest cultivars on the city streets, including the upright, disease-resistant Jack crabapple (*M. baccata* 'Jackii'). The wide-spreading Japanese crabapple remains a star in its own right and serves as breeding stock for a number of cultivars.

Around the dawn of the twentieth century,

crabapple cultivation got a boost from Charles Sprague Sargent and Ernest H. Wilson, the legendary arboriculturists and first leaders of Harvard's Arnold Arboretum near Boston. They introduced many an Asian species to North America through that challengingly cold New England portal. Among them was the Sargent crabapple (*M. sargentii*), named after Charles himself. It remains popular coast to coast as a wide, shrubby tree with cupped white flowers and red berrylike crabapples that hang in fall against yellow leaves. Often it appears in urban containers, which it overflows with blossom- or fruit-laden branches.

Crabapples were naturally tolerant of urban stresses, but cultivators worked toward an ideal tree that would grow neatly and bear pretty buds that exploded each year into brilliant, abun-

(continued from p. 284)

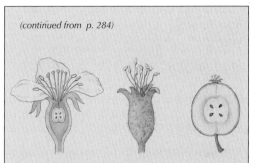

After fertilization, crabapple flower parts change radically to become the fleshy fruit.

Notice the green structure in which the flower sits. This is the calyx, whose leaflike sepals will by summer's end transform themselves into the outer flesh of the crabapple fruit. You can watch it happening in stages, and finally observe the shriveled tips of sepals and flower parts protruding (usually) at the end of the fruit.

Before the leaves exhaust themselves fighting pests and diseases, note their characteristics: Shade of green? Sawtooth or smooth edges? Lobes? Hairs? Texture? Your notes can help you distinguish one tree from the next.

In fall, enjoy the look and feel and aroma of the mature fruit. Examine its pulp and seed chambers. Though the taste may have you spitting fragments like a wood chipper, know that crabapples have made some of the most respectable jams and formidable ciders.

dant, and long-lasting flowers. Its contrasting-green foliage would stay healthy and turn a fall color. Fruit would be small and exciting, persistent into winter, and either nonmessy or scant. The tree would endure temperature extremes and poor soil conditions and resist the worst diseases.

As lovely as North America's four native crabapples could be when blossoming in the wild, they fell short of the ideals for ornamental crabapples, especially in the disease department. Yet, from natural variations in these natives, cultivators developed some of the most successful ornamentals. To name just three:

■ The Bechtel crabapple, one of the most-planted in America until the 1970s, was cultivated from a freak native *M. ioensis* (prairie crabapple) found in 1840. Its late, sweet-smelling blossoms have double petals—up to 33 per flower—which has become another desirable trait in modern cultivars.

■ The extremely common *M. coronaria* 'Klehm's Improved Bechtel' descends from the American or wild sweet crabapple native to the Midwest. Cloned from a Chicago park tree, it stays healthy and bears large aromatic flowers as well as leaves that turn orange in fall.

■ From seeds of the native southeastern *M. angustifolia* (southern or narrowleaf crabapple), cultivators developed the *M.* 'Prince Georges', long popular for its thick rosy-pink blossoms—with up to 50 petals!—glossy, narrow, and long-lasting leaves, fall color, and tendency not to fruit.

TOP OF THE BARREL

Does any crabapple measure up to the ideal? Some of the trees flower and fruit only in alternate years, though with great profusion. Many of the popular cultivars are flawed in some respect, often disease-prone, yet planters keep them around for some overriding charm—the edible fruit of 'Dolgo', the purple-red flowers of 'Lemoinei', the showy yellow fruit of 'Golden Hornet'.

The perfect tree may not yet exist, but a substantial number of high-scoring cultivars form a core of near-ideal crabapples for urban use. Here are 10 disease-resistant trees (unranked) that various landscape experts favor, pending the Next Great Crabapple. (All have fruits about a half inch wide that hang on into winter.)

M. 'Adams'—Round. Deep pink profuse flowers. Leaves green with red tint, orange-red in fall. Abundant glossy deep red fruit with red pulp.

M. 'Adirondack'—Compact, columnar shape. Waxy-white flowers, heavy petals. Late-fall tree hung with bright orange-red fruit.

M. 'Centzam'—Column-shaped, widening at top. Quick grower, rosy-red flowers, cherry-red fruit, fall color.

M. 'Donald Wyman'—Round shape. Dark green leaves, carmine buds, abundant white flowers and glossy bright red fruit.

M. 'Hargozam'—Upright, with dark green leaves and golden fruit.

M. 'Molazam'—Broad, weeping shape. Rosebuds become white flowers. Yellow fall leaves. Abundant orange-red fruit persists into winter.

M. 'Prairifire'—Oval, spreading shape. Crimson buds, pink-red flowers, shiny orange-red fruit. Leaves orange-gold in fall.

M. 'Sentinel'—Narrow, good street tree in youth, widens with age. Dark glossy leaves, white flowers brushed with pink, showy dark red fruit with yellow pulp.

M. 'Sutyzam'—Round shape. Fragrant white flowers, bright red fruit.

M. x *zumi* 'Calocarpa'—"Redbud crabapple." Wide, dense tree. White flowers blanket branches. Profusion of bright red fruit.

Hawthorn

Crataegus phaenopyrum, C. crus-galli, and others

IMPORTANCE: A venerable group of tough, small, thorny trees that brighten urban spaces with profuse, applelike spring blossoms and colorful little fall/winter fruits called haws. Downy hawthorn is Missouri state flower.

FAMILY: Rosaceae (Rose). GENUS: *Crataegus* (hawthorn).

COMMON URBAN SPECIES: ❀ Washington hawthorn (*Crataegus phaenopyrum*) or Virginia h. ❀ Cockspur hawthorn (*C. crus-galli*) or cock's spur h. ❀ Common hawthorn (*C. monogyna*) or English h., May tree, Maythorn, oneseed h., whitethorn. ❀ English Midland hawthorn (*C. laevigata*) or English woodland h. ❀ Downy hawthorn (*C. mollis*) or red haw. ❀ 'Winter King' green hawthorn (*C. viridis* 'Winter King'). ❀ Lavallé hawthorn, hybrid (*C.* x. *Lavallei*). ❀

CLOSE RELATIVES: ❀ Black hawthorn (*C. douglassi*) or western black h. ❀ Blueberry hawthorn (*C. brachyacantha*).

TYPICAL CITY LOCATION: Sunny yards, streets, campuses, malls, parking lots, foundation landscaping. Singly or grouped in parks, golf courses, cemeteries.

KEY FEATURES: Features shared by most of the 1,000-plus types of hawthorn include: compact height and dense horizontal branching; thin flaky strips of bark on a fluted (sinewy) trunk or multiple trunks; toothed leaves with at least some lobing; crooked branches and zigzagging twigs, with thorns ¾–4"; profuse blanketing clusters of white or sometimes pink or red blossoms, each flower with 5 petals.

Most distinctive is the abundant fruit, ripening in fall to colorful "pomes," olive-sized and applelike with a tuft of withered petals (calyx) at the tip and one or more hard seed-stones inside. Fruit often remains on tree after leaves have fallen.

(See sidebar on page 292 for species features.)

AVERAGE MATURE SIZE IN CITY: 20–35' high, 20–35' wide.

RECENT CHAMPION: *Washington:* 36' height, 38' spread, 4½' circumf., Abingdon, Va. *Cockspur:* 40' height, 48' spread, 5' circumf., Manassas, Va., *Common:* 37' height, 58' spread, 9' circumf., Mount Vernon, Wash. *Downy:* 52' height, 62' spread, 9' circumf., Grosse Ile, Mich.

❧ GLORIOUS RUNT

"Every shepherd tells his tale/Under the hawthorn in the dale," wrote English poet Edmund Spenser (1552–1599). Let's hope the shepherds were sitting, not jumping up to meet the spike-hard thorns of such trees.

A member of the vast Rose family, which includes roses and familiar orchard trees, the hawthorn made its name in England as a border-hedge plant. "Haw" derives from Germanic words for hedge—and what a hedge the hawthorn gave old Europe. It grew in interlocking thickets between pastures, and the low, dense, wide-spreading branches presented a hostile bramble to any man or beast with a notion to cross boundaries.

Hawthorn leaves and fruit. From left, cockspur h., downy h., common or English h.

Once rooted, these formidable runts will stake their claim in spite of drought, heat, poor soil, and salt spray. But hawthorns have another side that has made them one of the most beloved garden trees and a fixture in urban landscaping where conditions allow. Twice a year, they put on ornamental garb as glorious as any downtown finery.

In spring they virtually cover themselves with white (sometimes pink or red) blossoms. Their small, five-petaled flowers cluster into tea-saucer-sized corymbs, or flat-topped groups whose outer blossoms open first. The tree is blanketed in flowers all along the branchlets, almost covering the leaves. In folklore hawthorns symbolize hope, perhaps because folks waited with considerable hope for the flowers to appear on May 1 and usher in spring. Whether such hope was fulfilled or not, the word "May" attached itself to several common names.

The sweet May fragrances of some hawthorns are recalled with rapture by Marcel Proust and others. But two weeks of putrid stench mark the blossoming of certain other species, such as the widely planted cockspur and Washington hawthorns. To pollinating flies, the scent is the bouquet of fine dining. In England, some blossoms were said to remind country villagers of the Great Plague of London. But most people overlook the aroma in light of the trees' seasonal glories.

GOOD HAWS

The second of those glories, after flowers, are the fruits (also called "haws") produced by the fertilized blossoms. Looking like bunches of miniature green apples at first, they range in size from pearls to marbles and ripen into such colors as carmine-red, fiery yellow-orange, purple, and even a frosty blue (blueberry hawthorn or *pommette bleu* of south-central United States). Often dotted like certain tasty apples, the munchkin fruit begs to be tasted; but the edible flesh usually turns out to be mealy and sour, better suited to the birds and other wildlife that gobble it with gusto. Aside from the decent preserves and liqueurs made from some varieties, the haws please us most as bright baubles against a dense green foliage.

For many species, the fruiting glory extends into winter, after the leaves have dropped. The uneaten haws remain ("persist") on the zigzag branches, making for bursts of color and texture in the bleak urban landscape. On other species such as the downy hawthorn, the haws drop from the tree in autumn and form a pretty circle around the base—until nature and city life turn the bright marbles to mush.

Like the apple and pear, the haw is a "pome," or fruit with a fleshy outer tissue surrounding a papery seed wall and seeds. Pull apart a ripe haw and you'll find a few small seed stones among the flesh, about like grape pits. If you find only one seed, you have probably come upon one of the more notable of the hawthorns, the English or oneseed, also known as the common hawthorn, May tree, and whitethorn. A European native that grows to about 30 feet tall and wide, it is the white-blossomed May hawthorn of English lore and legend.

With its varieties, the English hawthorn also stars in American urban settings. A Glastonbury thorn variety or 'Biflora' was planted in Washington, D.C., in 1901. The Glastonbury originated, so the story goes, when Joseph of Arimathaea thrust his staff into the ground as he sought to convert Britons to Christianity. It is supposed to bloom at Christmas as well as May, but usually misses the holiday by several weeks. In Washington, the tree was reputed to bloom whenever royalty appeared, but it has actually blossomed several times a year in that city's ambitious atmosphere.

Hawthorns: A Starter Set

How many species of hawthorn are there? (How long do you have for an answer?) Short-lived variations in off-spring and rampant interbreeding have played havoc with estimates, which have ranged from some 1,100 (in 1910) to a more exacting 200 or so today (with a ton of named varieties). Esteemed botanist Robert A. Vines spent five years just trying to sort out expert opinion. But here are identification clues for five popular hawthorns to be found in eastern and other, scattered U.S. urban areas. Their variations abound.

Cockspur: To 20–25′ high, flat-topped, very wide-spreading. Highly glossy stiff leaves, 1½–4″ long × 1½″ wide, spatula shape, angling away from twig, wine red in fall. If thorned, bone-hard spikes up to 4″ (thus banned in some communities). White foul-smelling late May or June flowers. Fruits ¾″, deep red, stay into winter.

Washington: To about 20–25′ high and wide, dense rounded crown, often single-trunked. Leaf about 2 × 2″, dark green glossy top, duller bottom, two opposite winglike lobes at base, subtler lobes higher up, large pointed end lobe, all with jagged teeth. Red, orange, burgundy in fall. Peeling brown-gray bark reveals red-

(continued on p. 293)

Upstaged by blossoms and haws, the hawthorn's foliage, bark, and trunk offer good sideshows for the observer. Leaf shape varies, but several types are distinctive (see sidebar). Most of the hawthorns around town bear leaves of dark green color, thickish texture, sharp teeth, and lobes (extensions) that may be slight or fingerlike but very charming as a pattern.

Ancient Athenians found hawthorn leaves charming enough to wear as wedding crowns. Pliny of Rome mixed them with wine as a lockjaw remedy. Canada's Kwakiutl people smoked them. New Age medicine promotes them (with cautions) for congestive heart failure.

Often the leaf will have orange spots on it by midsummer, a sign of cedar rust. (A similar cedar-quince rust attacks the fruits, covering them with angel-hair-pasta-like stubs.) Rusts are among the legions of pests that torment but rarely kill hawthorns. Some trees, such as Washington, cockspur, and Lavallé, resist rust, and their leaves make it into fall to turn lush shades of orange, coppery red, and burgundy.

Hawthorn twigs and young bark are frequently a snappy light gray. Older bark often roughens into shaggy, ticketlike flakes, some of which peel away to uncover an orange-tan layer and give the trunk a stylish motley tone.

Some writers mention the "fluted" or "muscular" look of hawthorn trunks, but the look is even more dramatic on many trees. The trunks suggest anatomical studies, with sinews stretched and joints bulging and tibia and fibula revealed. Cankered old trees are grotesquely beautiful. The slender multiple trunks of numerous species twist and wrap around each other in public displays

(continued from p. 292)

orange bark. Abundant white June flowers with putrid smell. In fall, bedecked with small (¼") persistent red fruits.

Downy: A bigger hawthorn, to 30–40', taller trunk, wide-spreading, lower branches may droop. Large, fuzzy medium-green leaves, 4" long × 3" wide, more or less spade-shaped, saw-toothed all around. First to bloom in May, flowers 1" wide. Fruit ¾–1" thick, ripens to scarlet in September, sweet and not bad-tasting, falls quickly.

Common: To 25–30' high, dense rounded crown. Leaves glossy green upper surface; pair of long winglike lobes at base and "paw" of 3–5 jagged lobes above. White flowers becoming pinkish with 20 red pollen heads inside. Fruit elongated, to ½" thick, purple to bright red; only species with 1 nutlet instead of 2–5 inside fruit. Much planted, but disperses easily to open and waste spaces.

'Winter King' green (a variety of green hawthorn): To 25–30' high, vase-shaped branching pattern. Young bark gray-green or silver, trunk fluted. Few thorns. Leaves 1–3", spoon-shaped with slight lobes, dark glossy green turning to lovely scarlet, bronze, gold, orange, or purple. Flat 2"-wide white flower clusters. Fruit ¼" thick, abundant, orange-red or yellow, stays to winter.

Fantastic forms emerge from cankered trunks of old hawthorns.

that would lead to arrest among humans.

STREET-THORNS

For almost four centuries, the glorious runts have been selected and cultivated from wild hedges into trees that stand up to the demands of urban landscapers. You will still see bushy thickets as park stands or property borders; but also hawthorns as mall centerpieces or proud residential-street trees (in Cleveland, for example) that do not threaten utility lines. Some cultivated breeds are low-thorn/high-blossom: the 'Crimson Cloud' English Midland hawthorn features bright red jumbo flowers with a white star at the center. Some varieties raise their branches in a vase shape, while others droop them in weeping forms. And a few hawthorns—among them a 64-foot whitethorn in Seattle—just keep growing, as if to lose that runty reputation once and for all.

'Bradford' Callery Pear (and Siblings)

Pyrus calleryana 'Bradford'

IMPORTANCE: A charming, widely used, and controversial street tree, cultivated from a hardy Asian species and embraced by urban landscapers for the last half of the twentieth century. Inspiration for many successful varieties.

FAMILY: Rosaceae (Rose). GENUS: *Pyrus* (pear).

COMMON URBAN SPECIES: ❧ 'Bradford' pear (*Pyrus calleryana* 'Bradford', cultivated variety of *Pyrus calleryana* or Callery species).

CLOSE RELATIVES (OTHER COMMON CULTIVATED VARIETIES OF *P. CALLERYANA* INCLUDE): ❧ 'Chanticleer' pear (*P. c.* 'Chanticleer') or 'Cleveland Select', 'Select', 'Glen's Form' p. ❧ 'Autumn Blaze'

pear (*P. c.* 'Autumn Blaze'). ❦ 'Aristocrat' pear (*P. c.* 'Aristocrat').
❦ 'Whitehouse' pear (*P. c.* 'Whitehouse').

Typical city location: Streets, plazas, parking lots, subdivisions, malls, gardens, industrial parks.

Key features: A small-to-medium tree with a neat, dense, egg-shaped crown, glossy leaves, profuse white spring blossoms, and marble-sized fruit.

Blossoms appear before or with leaves. Flowers ½–1" across, in clusters; 5 broad, white petals and many stamens tipped with distinctively dark anthers. Slightly acrid aroma.

Leaves are rich glossy green, alternate (not opposite each other on shoots), 1½–4" long, tear-shaped, leathery, with small, rounded teeth. Green into late fall, then mixed autumn colors (including orange) on individual leaves, eventually dominated by crimson or burgundy.

Fruit a round, fleshy pome (with core), ½–¾" wide, russet-colored with white dots. Attached to stubby "spur" twig by slender stem.

Trunk branches into many weakly attached vertical "leaders" that tend to break off in storms if not pruned when tree is young. All branches sweep upward. Bark pale gray, slightly fissured and cracked with age.

Average mature size in city: 25–40' high, 15–35' wide.

Recent champion: The American Forests *Register* lists only the common or orchard pear tree (see sidebar): 59' height, 56' spread, 15' circumf., Waitsburg, Wash. Arthur Lee Jacobson cites a 'Bradford' pear tree 59' high × 62' wide in 1990, Bowie, Md.

﴾ Egg-Shaped Icon

For a week in early spring, it may turn your head with its cloak of white blossoms. But in summer you pass this modest tree along streets, malls, and parking lots, barely noticing its neat, egg-shaped crown of shiny foliage. A row of such trees is as regular as lampposts and as easy to tune out.

The dense foliage remains green until midautumn, when a unique dappling of orange, crimson, and yellow on individual leaves may catch your eye. Eventually, the foliage turns burgundy red overall. Those who look close enough will see fall fruits with russet, white-dotted skin. The fruits are actually pears, but only mothball-sized, nothing to make people think that an orchard has risen on Main Street.

The tree that millions of urbanites perceive as background is the 'Bradford' Callery pear—Bradford, for short—cultivated in America from an Asian species called the Callery pear.*

Glossy, leathery leaves of the Callery group turn multiple colors in fall.

From about 1950 to 1990, urban and suburban landscapers and nurseries had a love affair with the Bradford. Here was a flowering tree that could live in traffic, fluttering its glossy, leathery green leaves all summer. Dense as a hedge, it housed nesting birds for nature lovers. It progressed through a rainbow of fall colors. Adaptable and easily obtained, it made for instant landscaping in subdivisions.

Sometimes, the love was strained, as commonality bred contempt, or nesting birds made a mess, or older trees flew apart in a stiff wind. But the multitude of planters who greened America's downtown streets and outlying crescents with these promising new trees formed a Bradford generation. And in much of urban America, the Bradford legacy goes on.

Cherry-sized fruit of the 'Bradford' Callery pear.

*If not the Bradford itself, it is likely a variety cultivated from Bradford or other Callery stock.

BRADFORD PEAR: THE MOVIE

All that revolution, all that turbulent street action in the decades 1950 to 1990—replayed in a hundred documentary films. But what about the tree so often in the background? Where is the 'Bradford' Callery pear story?

To inspire tree watchers (and producers), we offer this abridged, true-to-the-facts scenario:

Opening (documentary footage): February 1998—A downbeat neighborhood of Venice, Calif., west of Los Angeles. Gang members and upscale Venice residents work side by side in a project to plant Bradford pear trees donated by the L.A. Conservation Corps. Some 90 of these new trees will soon blossom along a scruffy stretch of Broadway—a symbol of hope for the drug-ridden community (as reported by Julia Scheeres in the *Los Angeles Times*).

Tight shot on hands planting saplings. Zoom out.

Cut to (reenactment): 1858—central China. The French missionary Joseph Maxine Marie Callery, wandering swamps and highlands, comes upon a shrubby tree with minute pears. He gathers seeds and other plant parts for stock that—beyond his knowing—will carry his name into thousands of New World gardens, parks, and avenues.

Dissolve to (reenactment): 1908—central China. The intrepid Ernest H. "Chinese" Wilson, on one of his celebrated plant-collecting trips, poses formally with the Callery pear species he will bring back to the Arnold Arboretum near Boston. By crossbreeding the disease-resistant Callery with orchard pears, he hopes to protect orchards from a devastating "fire blight" disease.

Actor's voice: "Yes, the *Pyrus calleryana* is already achieving prominence as the most resistant to the dreaded pear blight of all the species, and in consequence is a valuable stock on which to work our garden pears."—Ernest H. Wilson, 1920.

Narrator: In spite of these and later efforts, the Callery stock fails to bolster orchard pears against fire blight. Nevertheless—

(Cut to low aerial pan of 300 blossoming Bradford pears along 12 miles of Tara Boulevard in today's greater Atlanta.)

—this disease-resistant, urban-tolerant strain would inspire U.S. government agriculturists under Frederick Charles Bradford to develop a brilliant ornamental variety of the Callery. And a generation of nursery people and landscapers would make this flowering 'Bradford' Callery pear one of the most successful, most urban-tolerant street trees of modern times.

Theme music . . .

In a full treatment, our documentary portrays the post–World War II plantings of the parent Callery species, which enjoyed a good run before the improved Bradford variety began to displace it. It shows the original cultivation of the Bradford pear at the U.S. Department of Agriculture Plant Introduction Station in Glenn Dale, Md., where Callery pear seeds sent from Nanjing in 1918 resulted, some 32 years later, in a superior flowering tree that handled drought, heat, pollution, salt, poor soil, pests, and fire blight disease. (The "Bradford" name honoring the station's director was attached to the variety in 1963.)

Callery-type pear blossoms with their dark-tipped stamens, though lovely, emit an unlovely aroma.

Finally, the documentary underscores the Bradford's rise to glory with street scenes coast-to-coast—with shots of trees shimmering white or green or burgundy in New York's Greenwich Village and along Philadelphia's Chestnut Street and New Orleans's DeBouchel Boulevard. With more trees in Toronto, Cincinnati, Cleveland, Milwaukee, Denver, Salt Lake City, and back in Los Angeles. It fades out on a still of Lady Bird Johnson planting Bradfords on the Washington Mall. . . .

PYRUS COMMUNIS: THE PEAR YOU EAT

There are ornamental pears such as the 'Bradford' Callery, and there are orchard pears, bred over the centuries from Eurasian wild pears with edible fruit. Among the world's tree crops, pears are second only to apples in popularity. Asia, cultivating pears for perhaps 3,000 years, has its sand pear (*Pyrus pyrifolia*), with a round apple-shaped fruit, and many sand pear cultivars. The Western world has derived its eating pears from an old hybrid named *Pyrus communis,* known in English as the common, domestic, orchard, or European pear.

A big, thorny, long-lived tree in the wild, the common pear yields top-shaped ("turbinate") fruit up to six inches long. Determining that characteristic "pear shape" is the distance from stem to ovary (the core), greater in pears than in apples. The developing pear fruit swells less around the long base than over its seed-bearing ovary. Pear flesh contains "grit" or "sand" cells—squarish, juicy cells with tough woody walls—that give the fruit its distinctive texture.

Pear blossoms can be distinguished from apple blossoms by their dark anthers—the pollen heads at the tips of the stamens. These deep red or purple tips stand out against the five white petals. And while apple blossoms are usually fragrant, pear flowers are considered "malodorous"— although not by everyone. "The scent . . . which reminds some of a dirty fish and chips shop, is to me attractive," says garden writer Henry Mitchell.

Outside of Asia, breeding for superior fruit and a cider called "perry" has been Europe's specialty, historically in France ('Anjou'), Belgium ('Bosc'), and England ('Bartlett'). North America boasts orchards second to none and many choice cultivars ('Rescue'). Unfortunately, North America also contributed fire blight to pears of the Western Hemisphere, a disease that continues to maim or kill orchard and ornamental trees. "But then," says writer Mitchell, "we all die of something."

A TRAGIC FLAW

The Callery and Bradford pears have suffered reversals of fortune, too, perhaps another story. Seeing too much of the trees, horticultural writers soon began to resent their seeming perfection, calling them plastic, short-lived, "engineered" substitutes for the great unruly elms, ashes, and maples. And when the Bradford started to show the same flaw that ran many Callery pears off the streets, some critics and urban foresters moved in for the kill.

That flaw is what is known as poor or weak branching structure—meaning the tree's excessive vertical branching above the bole (lower trunk). Perhaps the cultivation of a wild shrubby tree into an erect street ornamental had forced the issue. Instead of growing one or two strong vertical "leaders" to carry lateral branches, the tree sends up many verticals attached to one another at such narrow angles that a good wind, snow load, or vandal's tug can strip them off. Sometimes the brittle tree simply splits in half under trauma.

Older, bigger trees are more vulnerable to breakage, and Callerys or Bradfords that have survived 25 years to grow to 45 to 50 feet constitute a real hazard. A 1986 article in *American Nurseryman* sounded the alarm on Callery pears, and many planters either abandoned the species or saw to it that the vertical branching was thinned early and regularly as a safeguard against breakage.

Today, nursery-thinned trees are mitigating the problem for the Bradford pears in particular. But Bradfords were drawing flak by the 1970s for being overplanted, and frequent minor breakage and some major incidents have battered their reputation. For example, six 40-footers lining a Washington, D.C., road went down in a 1995 snowstorm. In 1996, Hurricane Bertha wiped out more than a quarter of the 273 Bradford pears that had been planted at Camp Lejeune to honor Marines killed in the 1983 Beirut barracks bombing.

Maybe these scenes belong in the film.

BEYOND THE BRADFORD

While (pruned) Bradford pears continue to hold their own among new street plantings, many pear-loving landscapers have turned to other Callery cultivars that show stronger or more columnlike branching habits or both. Some communities have abandoned their Bradfords with a vengeance: Cambridge, Md., just 40 miles from the very plant introduction station that developed the variety, has downed an avenue's worth of mature, debris-shedding, sidewalk-heaving Bradfords to replace them with other trees.

Some of the "improved" Callery cultivars have proved less resistant to fire blight than the Bradford. Fire blight is an insidious bacterium that loves pear trees, wet springs, and humid summers. It enters through flowers or wounds and finds its way to twigs and branches, leaving a trail of destruction that looks like fire scorch. For the newer cultivated pears, most of the fire blight problem occurs in the South. For example, the Callery 'Aristocrat' suffers badly there, but thrives in the North as an ample, well-structured urban tree with narrow, cupped leaves and yellow-orange to purple-red fall brilliance.

One of today's most promising cultivars originated with an unusually narrow, vigorous Callery pear tree growing on a Cleveland street in the late 1950s. Ohio's legendary Scanlon nursery would propagate and develop the tree into its 1965 'Chanticleer' variety, also known as 'Cleveland Select' and 'Select'. At maturity, the 'Chanticleer' is only about 16 feet wide, half the width of the mature Bradford and better suited to tight urban spaces. It is disease-resistant, exceptionally cold-hardy, heavily flowered, and richly colored in autumn. Reportedly, it even offers a few bonus flowers in fall.

The 'Whitehouse' Callery that came from the U.S. National Arboretum in 1981 is another attractive, narrow variety popular among urban landscapers. Even narrower is the 'Capital', a Bradford offspring developed in the 1960s at the Glenn Dale, Md., plant station.

Cultivated in Oregon and introduced in 1980, the Callery 'Autumn Blaze' gets highest marks for the stability of its horizontal branching pattern. It is also the most cold-tolerant Callery and one of the most disease-resistant. It limits its fruit drop to an untroubling few minipears.

'Autumn Blaze' turns red early in fall. But most of the Callery family holds its green into cold weather, risking a freeze that will kiss any fall coloring good-bye. They also blossom early, in the dangerous frost weeks. At The Morton Arboretum near Chicago, researchers are cross-breeding superior Callery strains to create hybrids that better align themselves with the seasons. If they succeed, the world will have an ornamental pear even closer to perfection, one that the antiperfectionists will just have to live with.

PART II

Trees with Cones and Needlelike or Tightly Scaled Leaves

AUSTRIAN (EUROPEAN BLACK) AND SCOTS PINE

Pinus nigra and *Pinus sylvestris*

Austrian pine.

IMPORTANCE: These two beautiful pines are among the most common urban evergreens throughout much of North America. Introduced here for their hardiness as well as good looks, they are now disease-threatened. Both species—but especially Scots—are grown as tidy Christmas trees, but older living trees are ruggedly picturesque. Scots pines are the world's most widely naturally distributed pines.

FAMILY: Pinaceae (Pine). GENUS: *Pinus* (pine).

Common urban species: ❧ Austrian pine (*Pinus nigra*) or European black p., Corsican p., Crimean p., Pyrenees p. ❧ Scots pine (*P. sylvestris*) or Scotch p.

Close relatives: ❧ Red pine (*P. resinosa*) or Norway p.

Typical city location: Landscaped properties, highways, and parking areas; yards, campuses, fairways, parks, shorelines.

Key features: Both species are "two-needle" pines, with needles in bunches of two enclosed at the base by a short papery sheath.

Austrian: Shape changes from pyramid to umbrella during life of tree. Foliage in dense, globular tufts; abundant throughout crown on younger trees. Needles 4–6" long, firm, slightly curved, dark military green; they fold but do not snap when bent in half, stay on twigs some 3 years. Twigs dark, jaggedly rough. Older bark broken into picturesque rounded plates of gray, brown, and pinkish gray. Cones 2–3" long, 2" wide when scales open; scales tan, with snouty tips topped with small prickle. Cones cluster at right angles.

Scots: Progresses from plump pyramid (à la Christmas trees) to elongated, handsomely irregular tree with bluish-green foliage arranged in widely spaced horizontal layers. Needles 1½–3½" long, sharp, and twisted 360 degrees. In older trees, the orange upper bark peels in papery flakes. Cones smallish, to 2½"; young closed cones are dark green with humpy reptilian scales. Usually no prickles at tip.

Average mature size in city: *Austrian:* 40–70' high, 20–40' wide. *Scots:* 30–60' high, 30–40' wide.

Recent champion: *Austrian:* 114' height, 49' spread, 10' circumf., Tacoma, Wash. *Scots:* 64' height, 76' spread, 16' circumf., Lenawee County, Mich.

❧ A Couple of Two-Needle Troupers

You may have noticed them as small Yule trees or mere yard ornaments in much of North America; but the very common Austrian and Scots pines are as rich in heritage and botanical interest as any of the great pines. They offer a handy entry point to the *Pinus* or pine genus, which numbers some 110 species, including about 40 in North America.

Invited immigrants from Eurasia, the two trees have performed like troupers against the stresses and toxins of our big cities and have been rewarded with zealous planting. But now they face their biggest challenge: epidemic attacks by insidious microbes.

LOOKING AT PINES

The closer one examines the parts of a pine tree, the faster a Christmas-tree level of interest gives way to a state of wonder. Pines in their forest settings may be the most wondrous of all, rising 100 feet or more and humming with wildlife; but the maturing cones may be too high to observe, and in the sunless understory the trunks often lose their lower branches. Urban pines may be less grand, but the whole tree can be seen and their low branches usually reached. The leaves can be touched and examined.

"Leaves," did we say, instead of "needles"? Yes, because needles *are* the main leaves of these evergreens. They may not flutter, but for some 170 million years they have served as foliage for this tree type, which evolved long before broadleaf trees ap-

Scots pine.

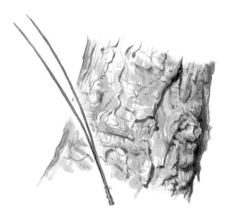

The four- to seven-inch, paired needles of Austrian pine, shown against plated, multihued bark of older tree.

peared. They have worked well enough to stay as thin and waxy as they please. Like all leaves, they take in water, carbon dioxide, and light, and with their photosynthesizing gear convert them to sugar for the tree and oxygen for us. They feed a host of leaf pests in the process. And like broad evergreen leaves, they cool the summers and green the winter landscapes for us.

Still, pine leaves differ from broad leaves in ways both obvious and subtle. An obvious one is their fragrance, the delightful aroma of their essential oils. And here is a subtle one: Like a puzzle piece, each needle is part of a group (bundle or fascicle) that would form a cylinder if brought together. Thus, the two needles of the Austrian pine bundle are the two halves of the cylinder. You can join them together to see, or cut one of the needles crosswise and note that it is a half circle. On a three-needle pine, each cross section would be like a third of a pie, and so on.

The number of needles in a bundle—though it can vary on some trees—has much to do with identifying and classifying pines, the look of a tree, and the nature of its wood (see sidebar). Even the sheath—the papery wrapping at the bottom of a bundle—is a telling feature and unique to pines. It always clads new growth, like a bootie.

Scots pine needles, in twos, are up to 3½ inches long and twisted. Upper tree bark peels, flakes, glows orange.

LOVE AMONG THE STROBILES

Like all pines, the Austrian and Scots species have male and female reproductive parts on the same tree, but they seek romance with other trees so as not to interbreed weak stock. Small cone-like structures called *strobiles* are the pine's flowers. Female conelets display tender, usually bright scales; the smaller male conelets are more catkinlike, clustered, and often yellow.

The love life of strobiles, though not as cinematic as that of ovary-based flowers, does not lack for action and intimacy. In spring, if a tree has built up the en-

THE HARD AND SOFT OF IT

In North America, most pines with two or three needles in a bundle are so-called "hard" pines, rich in gummy resin that heals tree wounds and is processed into medicines and turpentine products. Austrian and Scots pines are classified as hard. The continent's "soft" pines, with five needles in a bundle, include the Eastern white pine (see profile). Light of resin, strong of wood fiber, soft pines are a joy to the lumber industry.

The sure way to distinguish between the hard and soft is to view a magnified cross section of a living needle. If two groups of water-carrying ducts are visible in the center, the tree is a hard pine; if one group, it's a softie. Lacking a magnifying glass, one can see if a tree's older needles (away from the growing tips) lack sheaths. Soft pine needles drop their sheaths in a year. Needles of hard pines die with their booties on, so to speak, maintaining their sheath even as they drop off the tree after two or more years.

ergy for the 1½-year reproduction cycle, the female conelets develop two ovules—egg cells—on each scale. Meanwhile, the male catkins produce vast amounts of pollen grains, each buoyed by tiny air sacs that will ride on a breeze.

After such a ride, a lucky grain (ideally from another tree) finds a sugary droplet awaiting it between slightly opened scales on the female conelet. Touching the liquid, the grain breaks the surface tension and is pulled into the conelet. Within the soft tissue, the grain grows an inseminating tube but waits until the next spring or summer to fertilize

Left, Scots pine cone with scales closed. Right, Austrian pine cone scales have opened to release seeds.

an egg. By the end of that summer, the fertilized conelet becomes a full-size cone consisting of woody scales around a central stem.

Under each scale of the fertilized cones are a pair of bare seeds. These are termed *naked seeds* or *gymnosperms,* the botanical term for pines and other trees that do not encase their seeds in ovaries (as do *angiosperms*). But the cones do keep their scales tightly closed until a propitious time for seed dispersal. For Austrian and Scots pines, that time could be between October and March, depending on regional climate.

The opening scales change the shape of the cone—from compact teardrop to rough oval in the case of the Scots pine—and expose the winged seeds to wind, wildlife, and the tenacious observer. All or most of the seeds are gone by the time a cone drops from the tree, but their outlines at least can be seen on the undersides of the scales. The imprint resembles a deer track, a cloven hoof. The Austrian pine seed looks like a grape seed at the narrow end of a wasp wing; the Scots pine seed is about half that size.

DARK AUSTRIAN

The puffy, pyramidal pine that frames parking lots or greens industrial parks is likely the same species worshiped in Cybelian revels some 2,200 years ago in Rome. Most of America's Austrian or "European black" pines descend from Austrian trees, but the species' full native range reads like an exotic itinerary: Italy, Sicily, Corsica, Morocco, France, Spain, Turkey, Cypress, and the Crimea on the Black Sea. Members of the Roman cult of Cybele would have buried an Austrian pine at one of Cybele's sanctuaries, resurrected it three days later, and partied madly into the night. Today, the urban-tolerant tree serves so many prosaic landscaping functions it is rarely thought of as festive—unless its occasional use as a Christmas tree qualifies.

Landscapers often use the dense and dark Austrian pine as a backdrop for showier plants. Yet, as a featured specimen, it has much to admire if not revel in. From a distance its globular tufts of needles are like soft pastel strokes. Up close, the long, lustrous needles look stylishly coiffed.

Austrian pine cones cluster at right angles on dark, rough shoots.

In its first few decades, the tree evolves from a jolly triangle to an imposing pyramid on a short trunk. Then, into its seventh or eighth decade, it does what many people do: goes eccentric, picturesque. It angles one way or the other, it grows quirky flat-topped branches and loses its lower ones until it becomes umbrella-like or leaning-figure-with-arm-shading-eyes-like. Meanwhile, its bark develops one of those exquisite ornamental textures gardeners love—swirling plates of pink and pearly gray broken by dark fissures—a mantle worthy of Cybele herself.

To otherwise identify the Austrian pine, make sure the needles are two to a bundle, four to seven inches long, sharp-pointed, and not spiraled, and that they fold but do not snap when bent in half. If they snap, they are probably the thinner needles of the red pine (*Pinus resinosa*), a similar, native North American species that occasionally turns up around town. The cone of the Austrian pine usually has small prickles on each scale; the red-pine cone has none.

Sadly, another identifying feature of the Austrian pine these days might be tufts of stunted resiny needles on pale deteriorated shoots. Say good-bye to such trees and hello to the *Diplodia* twig blight fungus (*Sphaeropsis sapniea*), now the most menacing of the pests attacking Austrian pine. And here was a tree that hung tough in America for some 230 years: the first tree of 217 million planted in the nation's great dust bowl shelterbelt project. A tree that was considered indomitable as it weathered the wind and sleet, stood up to city drought and salt spray, coped with the heat of rooftops and pavement, and flourished around such frenetic, disturbed-soil sites as New York's Kennedy Airport. Stress has taken its toll and opened the door for opportunistic bugs, but the battle goes on. Even as towns cut back on Austrian pine plantings, botanical gardens are exploring whether some timely babying of at-risk trees will give them the muscle to beat the blight.

UNRULY SCOTS

Not long ago, a Chicago developer planted young Scots pines in each postage stamp of a front yard along a row of pint-sized attached town houses. Perhaps he was influenced by the Scots pines seen in every other Christmas-tree lot, those bushy six-footers characterized by their stiff two- to four-inch twisted needles in bunches of two and their blotter-green to blue-green color (often enhanced by a spray). But the developer should have known that his particular Scots were no dwarf variety. At about six years old, the trees are already blocking the upper windows and getting a bit unruly.

Enjoying good light, these hardy pines could well grow six stories high and wildly irregular, as is the nature of the species. (Its scientific name, *sylvestris,* means wild, of the woods, or not cultivated.) In 15 years, the town houses will look mean in comparison, but, oh, what glorious features will greet the tenants if and when they open their blinds. Tree connoisseur Hugh Johnson finds the beauty of the Scots pine "unrivalled." He lauds the distinctive papery upper bark of mature trees, "flaking in butterfly wings," its cinnamon-orange color glowing "with the warmth of a fire in the sky." To handle a heavy resinous spray of foliage with its young jade-colored cones, says Johnson, "is an intoxication."

Although Scots pine is the world's most widely distributed pine, with a native range across Asia, Scandinavia (except Denmark), and most of Europe, only a relatively few survived ice and ax in Scotland itself. But since these were Great Britain's only survivors, Scotland's magnificent few inspired the species' common English name. "Scotch" pine is also heard in North America, but not appreciated by the Scots. Scotch is for booze, period.

Trees with fiery bark, shapes like thunderbolts, and life spans up to 1,000 years (in Sweden) accumulate their share of worshipers. Even into the twentieth century, societies in east Siberia viewed Scots pines as sacred, adorning them with ribbons, talismans, and sacrificial sheepskins. Victorian painters adored the tree. String musicians treasured Scots pine rosin for their bows. Eurasian lumber industries still bless the Scots pines that feed their mills.

North Americans imported the species for reforestation and Christmas-tree plantations (some 30 percent of America's Yule trees are Scots pines); it has spread to forests by natural seed dispersion and into urban landscapes via nurseries. Appearing from the East Coast to San Francisco and Seattle, it tolerates smoke, drought, cold, and a little salt, but not shade. It is a sociable tree, known to network with the roots of other Scots pines and even to partner with some 40 kinds of root-dwelling fungi to boost its nutrients. But some of the same pests assailing Austrian pines, including *Diplodia* and pine wood nematode, are wearing down the stressed Scots pines.

Will they prevail? A species that survived the last Ice Age may well find the winning strategies, with some help from plant scientists. For sure, it will be around when those Chicago town houses are returned to dust.

(Eastern) White Pine

Pinus strobus

IMPORTANCE: Now hoisting its tiered foliage over urban spaces, this native pine was one of the most important commercial and political trees in American history. Tallest North American native tree east of the Rockies. State tree of Maine and Michigan. Provincial tree of Ontario.

FAMILY: Pinaceae (Pine). GENUS: *Pinus* (pine).

COMMON URBAN SPECIES: ✤ White pine (*Pinus strobus*) or eastern white p., soft p.

CLOSE RELATIVES: ✤ Western white pine (*P. monticola*) or silver pine, Idaho white p.

TYPICAL CITY LOCATION: Parks and ample yards, campuses, fairways, cemeteries.

KEY FEATURES: Branches grow in platformlike tiers, separated by 1–3′ of branchless trunk. Young trees medium green and pyramidal; older trees blue-green and mastlike with foliage in off-balance, horizontal tiers. Young top branches form flamelike crown that veers away from prevailing winds.

Needles thin, flexible, to 4″ long in bundles of 5, with papery sheath at base until first summer. Only 5-needle pine east of the Rockies.

Cones 5–8″ long, slender, slightly curved, conspicuous stem both ends; 50–80 toelike scales "sugar-coated" with resin, opening wide in second year to release ¾″ winged seeds.

Bark divided into flat, gray-brown-and-pinkish plates surrounded by deepening furrows as tree ages.

Western white pine: A towering 5-needle pine of the American West and Northwest. Cones to 12″ long, 90–160 scales. Darker, denser, and narrower tree than eastern white pine, more like bottlebrush in form when mature. Bark broken into small blocks.

AVERAGE MATURE SIZE IN CITY: *Eastern:* 50–80′ high, 30–50′ wide, 2–3′ thick.

RECENT CHAMPION: *Eastern:* 201′ height, 52′ spread, 16′ circumf., Marquette, Mich. (*Western:* 151′ height, 52′ spread, 33′ circumf., El Dorado National Forest, Calif.)

❧ A GIANT SAILS INTO TOWN

No pines rise more dramatically in urban settings than the eastern white pines, with foliage in horizontal platforms on a straight trunk. Like ship masts crossed by blue-green furls, they tower over gardens, parks, and yards.

One could view such white pines as memorials—to the most pre-

cious and plentiful forest species ever to be felled in eastern America—
or as survivors seeking haven and new glory as landscape trees.

Not that cities are the safest haven for white pines. Sensitive to
ozone pollution, salt, and poor soil conditions, the trees favor well-
tended green spaces away from traffic. There, given plenty of sun and
well-drained acidic earth, they can reward their caretakers with monu-
mentally beautiful specimens.

One sees such specimens in towns like Evanston, Ill., a busy, tree-
loving suburb abutting Chicago. In winter especially, one is struck by
an armada of these 60- to 80-foot evergreens along a ridge of private
properties. The oldest trees are missing some cross "spars" on one side
or the other as if they were blasted away in battle, giving the trees a
heroically lopsided look. Even in cramped Chicago spaces, an occasional white pine struggles to 30 to 40 feet, softening the cityscape with
outstretched layers of delicate needle foliage. To the delight of urban
naturalists, mature trees produce lovely hanging five- to eight-inch
cones, green at first, becoming brown, slightly curved, and sticky with
white resin deposits on their long toelike scales.

Thus has the eastern white pine, besieged for 300 years by ax and
buzzsaw, earned its way into towns of eastern and central North America—and not just within its 25 native states and 6 Canadian provinces.
Urban landscapers elsewhere crave the striking effect of its layered
branches. In the nation's capital, eastern white pines ornament the Jefferson Monument, Lincoln Memorial, and White House, among other
sites. Atlanta plants this cool-forest tree. Even some western towns
grow it as a companion to their local related species, the equally majestic western white or silver pine (also known as Idaho white pine, state
tree of Idaho).

A FRIENDLY FIVE NEEDLES

Not every white pine loves the city. An urban tree may be spared the
sawmill and the darkness, fires, and pests of forests; but it meets with
new stresses that set it up for fatal diseases. It must also overcome transplant shock and find its balance of nutrients. Failure can result in

stunted trees with oozing sap and yellow or brown dying needles.

Sick foliage alone will sadden anyone who has fondled the needles of a healthy white pine, whether on a fresh-cut Christmas tree or a live specimen. Wire-thin, flexible, and about four inches long, the needles grow in graceful bundles (fascicles) of five—the only five-needled bundle on any eastern pine tree and a reliable identification feature. A magnifying glass reveals two or three white "racing" stripes on each needle. Made up of breathing pores, the stripes make for a silvery blush on wind-tossed foliage.

A five-needle pine, the eastern white pine produces five- to eight-inch cones daubed with white resin.

In spring, a small papery sheath encloses each new bundle at its base. The sheath falls away in summer, but the needles remain at least another year, until the next crop of needles is in place to sustain the tree. This "evergreen" cycle assures the tree of density and color year round. (See "Austrian and Scots Pine" for more about pine needles and pines in general.)

The bundles cluster in pretty brushlike formations at the tips of spindly, purplish-brown twigs. Those familiar with wire brushes for drum playing will appreciate the resemblance. These slightly drooping, plumy clusters give the foliage a distinct look, just as the stepped "whorls" of branches distinguish the whole tree.

In botany a whorl refers to a circle of three or more parts growing out of a cylinder like a stem or trunk. The white pine follows "the rule of five"—each year, five branches-to-be whorl out from the trunk at the same height. The baby branches (shoots) develop from five buds surrounding the leader bud, which is the trunk's growing tip. As the five shoots head outward, the leader shoot raises the height of the trunk another one to three feet or so. The process is repeated each year, so that the whorls form horizontal layers separated by one to three feet of clean trunk.

When blue sky or sunset fills the open spaces between 60 feet of whorls, when prevailing winds sculpt the young top boughs into leaning flames, the white pine achieves a glory to compete with its legendary past.

A TREE TOO EXCELLENT

The eastern white pine made too many innocent mistakes to endure in its forests: It grew in seemingly inexhaustible numbers in a New World that was looked to for raw products. It achieved prodigious mass, up to 250 feet of height with straight trunks 8 to 10 feet thick and free of branches for several stories. And it formed wood that was clean, light-weight, workable, and strong enough for a thousand uses from ship's figureheads to shingles. Largely free of the resin that gums up wood-working equipment, the tree was what lumber merchants call, with a gleam in their eye, a "soft" pine.

A limitless crop of perfect wood. The American colonists, the Canadian settlers, and the British Royal Navy licked their chops, and the harvest began. In 1623, a Maine sawmill chewed into its first white pine log. The following centuries saw financial empires built on white pine; murder-ous battles over white pine ownership; the bravado and folklore of white pine lumberjacking—of cutting and mov-ing and floating whole pine forests to the mills; and, ultimately, the destruc-tion of the last magnificent virgin stands. Farmers, too, cleared their lands of centuries-old trees, trees ca-pable of living some 400 or 500 years.

Bundles of white pine needles form plumy clusters at twig tips. Furrows divide chunky bark plates.

Colonial America's march toward revolution was hastened by white pine fever. England imported white pine seeds from Maine to raise what are called "Weymouth" pines. But the superior native American white pines were still needed as masts for the British Royal Navy. To claim them, England had such pines marked with a blaze known as the King's Broad Arrow. Despising these blazes, homesteaders and rebels cut the trees for domestic use or to be shipped to England's enemies. England sent spies to identify the cutters. Spies met with violence. In the spirit of this defiance, a white-pinish pine appeared on the first flag of the revolutionary forces.

In 1912, some 72 million board feet of the noble eastern white pine

---

WHITE PINE, HEAL THYSELF

Herbal healers used compounds of white pine to loosen mucus or soothe mucous membranes. The needles, strong in vitamins C and K (which aids blood coagulation), could be steeped as a tea to treat coughs, colds, and scurvy. Whiskey was added to calm arthritis pain.

These medicinal and other properties protect white pine against pests. But an epidemic fungus called white pine blister rust has a way around the defenses. Growing alternately on the white pines and any nearby gooseberry or currant bushes (called ribes), it uses one species as a biological launching pad for its assault on the other. When the white pine's turn comes up, the fungus enters the bark through the needles and chokes off the tree's conduits.

Cities are hardly fields of currants and gooseberries, and some communities even ban white pine and ribes in proximity. But now and again, the rust spores somehow get to town and into the pines. An afflicted tree cannot heal itself, but tree doctors often work miracles by cutting away the icky blistered areas of infection.

---

were chopped into matchsticks. For all such sadly trivial uses, at least much of the forest was transformed into the houses, barns, bridges, and churches of America. Even today, white pine pervades national life in the form of such lightweight, nonwarping wood products as window sashes and doors.

Happily, white pine reseeds itself vigorously, so that managed second-growth forests exist for both cutting and recreation. But only in the Allegheny National Forest can one find a hint of America's great virgin growths.

COFFINS AND CATHEDRALS

Some of the white pines planted by settlers on their own lands survived as twentieth-century landmarks. Among these are the "coffin" trees that pioneer couples raised as wood for their own burial boxes when the time came. Where regional trees were unsuitable for woodworking, midwestern settlers would obtain white pine seedlings from the East for "his and hers" coffin trees. Some of these trees, as in Union County, Ill., lived on and became local sights.

Charles Edgar Randall and Henry Clepper, the great compilers of landmark trees, also describe the "cathedral" of white pines planted by a utopian community in Brentwood, Long Island, N.Y. Called Modern Times, the group operated only nine years, until 1862, but the trees remained to reflect the superior tastes of these artists and intellectuals.

PONDEROSA PINE (WESTERN YELLOW PINE)

Pinus ponderosa

IMPORTANCE: A big pine that "defines" the American West geographically and in popular lore. In its three natural varieties, ponderosa is the most common and widely distributed pine in North America. State tree of Montana.

FAMILY: Pinaceae (Pine). GENUS: *Pinus* (pine).

COMMON URBAN SPECIES: ❧ Ponderosa pine (*Pinus ponderosa,* var. *ponderosa*) or western yellow p., bull p.; blackjack, Pacific ponderosa p.

Other varieties: ❧ Arizona pine (var. *arizonica*). ❧ Rocky Mountain pine (var. *scopulorum*) or interior ponderosa p., Black Hills ponderosa p.

CLOSE RELATIVES: ❧ Jeffrey pine (*P. jeffreyi* or *P. ponderosa* var. *jeffreyi*).

Typical city location: Parks, spacious grounds and gardens, road embankments, mall landscaping.

Key features: A highly variable pine species, usually straight-trunked with spire-shaped crown, rounded at top (or flattened on older trees). Long, sharp needles form dense tufts at the ends of branchlets. Bark of mature trees divided into large orange- or reddish-brown plates separated by dark grooves and made up of jigsaw-puzzle-like flakes.

Usual features of three regional types include:

Western yellow (Pacific): 90–130′ tall, needles dark green or yellow-green, firm and glossy, 5–11″ long, in bundles of 3 with sheath at base. Cones 3–6″ long, shiny reddish brown, hooked prickle on tip of each scale; part of base remains on tree when cone falls. Elongated, ¾″ wing on seeds.

Arizona: 80–100′ tall, needles 5–10″ long, 5 to a bundle; cones 2–4″ long, less prickly than *ponderosa's*.

Rocky Mountain: 60–125′ tall; dark needles, 3–6″ long, 2–3 per bundle.

Average mature size in city: 60–100′ high, 25–30′ wide, 2–4′ thick.

Recent champion: (var. *ponderosa*) 227′ height, 68′ spread, 24′ circumf., Plumas County, Calif.

❧ Western Soul Tree

Under the yaller pines I house,
When sunshine makes 'em all sweet scented,
An' hear among their furry boughs
The baskin' west-wind purr contented.
　　—James Russell Lowell, *Biglow Papers*

Its tall, orangy patchwork trunk supports a spire of glistening green. Call it ponderosa or western yellow pine, but call it western *soul* in the towns that count it among their flora. In North America, the ponderosa favors the lower montane zone, which includes some of the most romantic stretches of the scenic West. To landscape with ponderosa is to bring some of that romance, that western soul, into town.

Rugged-looking, lean, and enduring, a Clint Eastwood of a tree, the ponderosa grows from British Columbia to Mexico, from the Black Hills of South Dakota to western Texas. No conifer claims a larger or more storied native territory in America. With three regional varieties, it appears in every western state, on soils rich to rocky, at altitudes of 300 to 10,000 feet.

Its kingdom and character—not to mention its high-grade lumber—make the ponderosa a star among North American pines. There are bigger pines (such as the sugar pine) and more stylish ones (Monterey pine), but ponderosas are heavyweights by any measure. The intrepid Scottish botanist David Douglas had good reason to call the species *ponderosa* (Latin for "ponderous" or "weighty") when he came upon it in about 1825 along the Columbia River. Some of the specimens he saw would have been more than 20 stories high and as thick as brewing tanks.

Douglas (of Douglas fir fame) was scouting American species for the Royal Horticultural Society of London, and British gardeners were soon cultivating ponderosas as a result of his trek through the hazardous wilds. Early settlers of the American Northwest had their own name for the hulking conifer. They called it the bull pine—a name tinged with irony considering the fate of the adventurous Douglas: At age 35 in Hawaii, he fell into a pit for trapping animals and was mauled to death by a bull.

BARKING UP THE RIGHT TREE

Sometimes ponderosas can be raised to respectable heights outside the West, as garden specimens demonstrate in Pennsylvania, New York, Ohio, Illinois, Ottawa, and elsewhere, as well as in Europe. But for the authentic ponderosa experience, go West, young (or old) tree lover, to where the trees border the grasslands. Go to the western heights, to the lower forests, or to such ponderosa-rich urban settings as Flagstaff,

The big, orangish plates and jigsaw-puzzle-like flakes (detail) of ponderosa pine bark.

Denver, Vancouver, Seattle, and Portland.

Once out West, you will know the ponderosa by—if no other feature—its mature bark. The bark of the adolescent tree is usually a dark and flaky affair, dark enough for the tree to be nicknamed "blackjack" in the lumber industry. But by the time the ponderosa has matured, at about age 70, the bark has developed its most distinctive features.

Approaching the tree, one sees a pattern of colorful flat plates, each at least several inches wide and sometimes three or four feet tall, each outlined as if by a black paintbrush. The surface colors vary according to region, age of tree, quality of light, and the eyes of the beholder. Orange-brown seems to be most observed (including by this writer), with cinnamon-red, reddish brown, grayish pink, and yellow-gray vying for second place.

A close look at the bark reveals what may be its most distinctive feature. Each plate is made up of layers of brittle scales or flakes, some of which fall off and accumulate at the base of the tree. In size and shape, the flakes suggest jigsaw-puzzle pieces. Nature writer Rutherford Platt saw them as "whimsical animals—little dogs barking . . . skunks with huge tails, wild geese . . ."

To observe these features, one can cruise right up to a tree in towns like Flagstaff, where landscape ponderosas are found in the parking lots of shopping malls. But if one happens to be in Flagstaff—which was named after a flag-flying ponderosa pine—one is in reach of the

Usually in threes, ponderosa pine needles measure up to 11 inches.

Grand Canyon. There ponderosas play second fiddle only to the great gorge itself.

At the canyon's peaceful North Rim, a high-spirited park ranger introduced this writer and others to the trees by asking us to pick one out, hug it, and experience its scent. Why not? Warmed by a June sun, the flaky bark all but spoke to us with its sweet, resiny breath. Many a delicate scent has been attributed to the ponderosa, including vanilla to the bark and mandarin orange to the needles and broken twigs. In what might have been a form of aromatherapy, northwestern Native Americans applied ponderosa resin salve to treat backaches, rheumatism—and even dandruff.

Ponderosa pine cone: burnished red-brown with a prickle on each scale.

Our hugging session over, the ranger admonished our group to respect all forest denizens, never to "bankrupt their energy" by causing them stress. For us gentle visitors it was hard to imagine draining such energy as the ponderosas showed here, even on the harsh and windy roof of the canyon.

Ponderosas appear to begin life with a whimper, taking up to a decade to grow two feet. But meanwhile their roots are digging in for years of massive growth. In ideal settings such as Oregon's Siskiyou Valley, the trees can grow to 120 feet in 50 years, sometimes achieving twice that height and 10 feet of thickness within a life span of 300 to 400 years. Throughout the tree's range are legendary 200-plus-footers, among them a giant that marked the Gold Rush trail in California's El Dorado County.

Consisting of stout, sharp needles up to 11 inches long, ponderosa foliage also hints at the tree's awesome energy. Most commonly in bundles of three, the needles cluster at the tips of their branchlets to form thousands of green daubs, like brushes painting the sky. (See "Austrian and Scots Pine" for more on needles and pines in general.) Ponderosas also pad themselves with some four inches and more of fire-resistant bark, the better to survive forest fires while competing trees—those that would put them in shade—burn down.

Only the size of the cones, hand-grenade-shaped and three to six inches long, seem disproportionate to the ponderosa's might. But they are handsomely burnished to a reddish brown. Each scale sports a rigid prickle at its tip, a little outcurving horn. A medium-sized crop of ponderosa cones appears at about two- to three-year intervals, when the tree throws its energy into reproduction. (Bumper crops come at longer intervals.) The cones open up a season or two after fertilization and release a pair of winged seeds from under each scale.

The great naturalist John Muir seemed to draw uncanny energy from giant ponderosas without bankrupting them in the least. Not only did he write about them with gusto—". . . *waving its bright plumes in the hot winds undaunted . . .*"—but he found the stamina to scramble some 200 feet up their trunks:

> Climbing these grand trees, especially when they are waving and singing in worship in windstorms, is a glorious experience. Ascending from the lowest branch to the topmost is like stepping up stairs through a blaze of white light, every needle thrilling and shining as if with religious ecstasy.

If anything will bankrupt the ponderosa species, it may be the oxidant air pollutants of population centers, which have already drifted into western forests with apparently devastating effects. The trees do tolerate some urban toxins, such as moderate salt spray, but seem to stress out when ozone-charged. Weakened defenses open the door to some 200 damaging insect species as well as such ghastly-sounding diseases as "white stringy root rot." On one front, conservationists are fighting for more aggressive control of the devil smog.

THE FAMILY PONDEROSA

For the 400 million people in 87 nations who watched the television series *Bonanza* (1959–1973), the name "Ponderosa" forever evoked the Ponderosa Ranch, a Nevada spread beloved and protected by its owners, the Cartwrights. The ranch may have been fictional, but its name was apt: Nevada has its share of western yellow (Pacific ponderosa) pine, the most typical of the species' three natural types and the most cultivated (and the type on which much of this profile is based).

Like the three Cartwright sons, each of the ponderosa types shows distinct character traits, but at heart is made of the same good, reliable stuff. Pacific ponderosa, the westernmost variety, usually has three needles to a bundle. Interior (Rocky Mountain) ponderosa, with both two- and three-needle bundles, stretches from Montana through Colorado, Arizona, and New Mexico. The token rebel of the family is the Arizona pine, viewed by some taxonomists as a separate species. Native to southeast Arizona and southwest New Mexico, it tends to bundle its needles in fives.

There are other small differences between types; but each has a family resemblance, and each can draw itself up into a pillar of brawn when, so to speak, the chips are down and the ranch needs saving.

Spruce: Colorado (Blue) and Norway

Picea pungens (*P. pungens* f. *glauca*) and *P. abies*

Left, Norway spruce. Right, Colorado spruce.

IMPORTANCE: The two most commonly planted spruces in North America. Their classic conical shape, grace, and symmetry have won them fame as big Christmas trees. Colorado spruce is state tree of Colorado and Utah.

FAMILY: Pinaceae (Pine). GENUS: *Picea* (spruce).

COMMON URBAN SPECIES: ❀ Colorado spruce (*Picea pungens*) or Colorado blue s., blue s., silver s., including cultivated variety blue s. (*P. pungens* f. *glauca*). ❀ Norway spruce (*P. abies*) or common s., spruce fir.

TYPICAL CITY LOCATION: Parks, plazas, yards, cemeteries, and landscaped areas other than street parkways.

KEY FEATURES: Four-sided needles (in cross section) distinguish most spruces from other conifers. The spruce needles sprout singly from woody pegs on all sides of a twig. Needles are *not* flat (like fir), nor in scaly groups (cypress), nor in tufts of 2 or more (pine). Fertilized cones hang down (fir cones are erect); they eventually drop off the tree whole, not in pieces (firs). Like all conifers, spruces have flowerlike strobiles of both sexes on same tree. Female strobiles become cones.

    Colorado: Needles stiff and prickly sharp, to 1½", curved, usually of powdery blue color on cultivated trees, stay up to 9 years on twig. Cones (mostly at treetop) 2–4", light fawn color, scales like stiff paper, jagged-edged. Trees are cone- or pyramid-shaped, limbs horizontal and dense but droop and thin out with age. Many dwarf cultivated varieties.

    Norway: Needles angled toward tip of twig, softer and less prickly than Colorado's. To 1" long, medium to dark green, stay 3–7 years on twig. Cones commonly 5–6" (to 9"), largest among spruces, dark tan, scales broad, woody, and wavy-edged. Trees are cone- or pyramid-shaped, mature limbs swoop downward, then up at the tips. Older trees also have branchlets (skirts) dangling straight down along the branches. Many dwarf cultivated varieties.

AVERAGE MATURE SIZE IN CITY: *Colorado:* 30–65' high, 15–20' wide, 2–3' thick. *Norway:* 40–80' high, 20–30' wide, 2–3' thick.

RECENT CHAMPION: *Colorado:* 122′ height, 36′ spread, 16′ circumf., Ashley National Forest., Utah. *Norway:* 120′ height, 66′ spread, 15′ circumf., Clinton, N.Y.

❧ YEAR-ROUND YULE TREES

When the season for huge, crowd-pleasing Yule trees comes around, urban fancies turn to Colorado and Norway spruces: spruces for their classic conical shape, their branches whorled around the trunk in annual layers; Colorado and Norway spruces for their color, density, and the availability of tall, stately specimens.

Both species start their limbs low on the trunk, but on forest trees these lower boughs tend to die for lack of sunlight. Searching for full-bodied Christmas specimens, the big-tree hunters gravitate toward sunny sites, often on private property. For its annual Yule tree, New York's Rockefeller Center seeks specimens at least 65 feet tall with boughs to support some 26,000 lights. In 1996, landscapers took a seven-ton, 90-foot Norway spruce (with permission) from a family's yard in Armonk, N.Y., and trucked it some 45 miles south to the Center's skating rink.

In 1924, seven years before Rockefeller Center launched its Yule tradition, President Coolidge planted a Norway spruce near a White House entrance. The American Forestry Association had presented it as a living Christmas tree for the nation. Half a century later, a big Colorado spruce transplanted to the public Ellipse (south of the White House) became the national Yule tree. A gift from the National Arborist Association, it died in about one presidential term—a pitiful fraction of the species' 600-year potential under ideal conditions.

A replacement Colorado spruce, given by the same association to President Carter in 1978, dug in its deep roots and survived the transplant. In 1993, before a crowd of some 9,000, First Lady Hillary Rodham Clinton rode a lift to the treetop and crowned the spruce with a fiber-optic starburst ornament.

ATOP THE COLORADO

The First Lady's ascent was a fine opportunity—unrealized, no doubt—to study the top third of a Colorado spruce. For here most of the cones cluster. Matured by Christmas, the cones would have been fertilized in spring when they were erect, flowerlike, and exposed to the pollen of other trees. Summer would have seen them turn green and rotate on the twigs as their weight pulled them downward. Now, at maturity, they would be light tan and two to four inches long, loaded with some 100 fertilized seeds beneath their ragged, stiff-paper-like scales.

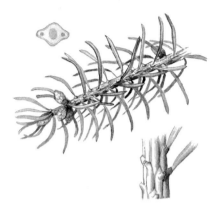

Colorado spruce needles are four-sided (cross-section), sharp and curved, and attached to woody pegs.

With the approach of winter, some of the cones would be lifting their scales to release the winged seeds to the wind. Other cones would wait a year or two.

SPRUCE VS. FIR

No ascent is necessary to distinguish a spruce tree from a fir (genus *Abies*), which can resemble a spruce at first glance. If mature cones are seen sitting upright on top of the branchlets, then the tree is a fir (or a cedar—see "Deodar Cedar"). Spruce cones hang downward and fall to the ground in one piece; fir cones disintegrate first. Also, spruce foliage is prickly and whorled all around the rough twig, while fir foliage is made up of friendlier needles—flat, rounded at the tip, and usually in two thick ranks, springy and pleasant to the touch. Colorado spruce is one of the prickliest, with saber-shaped needles up to 1½ inches long and sharp enough to pierce the skin. (*Pungens,* the species' Latin name, means "piercing.")

A close look at a spruce needle reveals other identifying features. The needle is four-sided, diamond-shaped in cross section. The fir needle is essentially flat, though its surfaces curve slightly, like an airplane wing. Each spruce needle grows from a short woody peg, which usually comes off the twig with a shred of wood when the needle is yanked. If the needles drop naturally (after staying "evergreen" for three to nine years), they leave the pegs behind. The stout Colorado twigs are distinctively marked by these peg stubs, which sprout from pleatlike ribs. Fir needles come off cleanly, leaving just a circular scar on the relatively smooth twig. "F is for flat, friendly firs," goes the standard mnemonic. "S is for square [needles], sharp spruce."

COLORADO SPRUCE:
AN UNCOMFORTABLE TREE

Writer Hugh Johnson calls the spruce an "uncomfortable" tree—spiny foliage, rough twigs, scaly bark, "gaunt and gappy" with age. And true, it may not be a tree hugger's favorite squeeze or the easiest border shrub to penetrate. ("Impossible to lob a cat through," cracks horticulturist Michael Dirr.) But as a landscaping specimen, spruce is as comfortable as silk pajamas or it would not be ornamenting millions of urban yards in its hundreds of cultivated varieties. The tree name "spruce," after all, is from the same source as "spruce" meaning stylishly smart: from an Old French word (*Pruce*) for Prussia, the nation that supplied both England's spruce wood and pruce leather for stylish sleeveless jackets.

The Colorado or blue spruce is probably the most cultivated of all spruces in North America, happiest where cool air and water are plentiful, yet fairly adaptable to drier regions. Native to America's mountain states, it can grow from Canada to Georgia and northern Texas. In muggy Washington, D.C., it has shaded the Frederick Douglass home, among other historic sites. New York City has grown it in tubs.

As if to compensate for its unfriendly handshake, the tree has produced offspring (f. *glauca*) with soft blue or silver-blue colors, and since 1865, cultivators have bred the bluest specimens for the nursery trade. In its natural settings, Colorado spruce is a tousled olive-green tree showing lots of pinkish-gray trunk. Forest lovers like to scorn the cultivated varieties, especially the shrubby, symmetrical dwarfs that Johnson describes as "bluer and stiffer than God had ever intended." After all, detractors point out, the blue is nothing more than a waxy or powdery deposit that can be rubbed off the needle. But whatever its composition, the coating helps protect the tree against urban pollution, notably salt, and gives rise to cultivars blue enough to be called 'Bizon blue', 'Baby Blueyes', and 'Ice Blue'. (One of the bluest, however, has the flapperish name of 'Hoopsi', after the German Hoops nursery.)

Naturalists may belittle the dwarfs and such semidwarfs as the rotund 'Fat Albert', but home gardeners (and Yule-tree buyers) have had a 100-year love affair with such spruce shrubs. Spruces are relatively slow growers; a tree takes some 40 years to reach as many feet. But shrubs can be bought ready to fold into a garden landscape, where they will remain shrubby with a little trimming. They fetch good prices as well, thanks to lengthy growing time at the nursery and heavy demand.

Tree-sized Colorado spruces, third-rate as lumber, find greater worth as urban fixtures. Just ask the Colorado driver who ran into one not long ago. A medium-sized median tree, the spruce was assessed at $1,240.27.

NORWEGIAN WOOD

Standing side by side as they sometimes do in city landscapes, Norway and Colorado spruces are easily distinguished. The Norway spruce is darker. Its boughs extend more gracefully, curving gently, some of them sloping, then rising like ski jumps. Often the branches are hung with pendant shoots (skirts), creating a weepy effect. The Colorado spruce has no such skirts.

The Norway spruce cone is larger—largest among the spruces—commonly five or six inches and sometimes up to nine. The scales are

Left, woody cone of Norway spruce, larger than the papery Colorado spruce cone at right. Seed is also larger.

much broader, woodier, not as ragged-edged as the Colorado spruce cones. The single-winged Norway seed is bee-length compared to the gnat-sized Colorado seed.

Unlike the aggressively upright needles of the Colorado spruce, Norway spruce needles bow toward the front of the twig so that a grasp encounters their smooth sides and not their tips. The points are duller, and the needle is only about ½ to 1 inch long. The overall look is softer than the stiff and puffy Colorado foliage.

Should a violent storm hit the two species, the trees most likely to go down are the shallow-rooted Norway spruces. But otherwise this introduced tree from Scandinavia, Russia, and the European Alps is a staunch urban survivor that transplants well and handles most pollution, some drought, snow loads, resident pests, and arctic cold. It is also the taller-growing of the two species, rising to over 200 feet in its forests and 60 to 80 feet in cultivation. But unlike such long-living spruces as Colorado and Sitka, and more like humans, it struggles to exceed a century and loses its best shape after age 60 or so. Norway spruces planted in New York's Central Park in about 1860 are now mummies at best.

Eagerly grown across North America for ornament, windbreaks, and land reclamation, the Norway spruce has escaped to various woodlands and become naturalized to some extent. But in Eurasia, it is one of the great and historic trees of the cold forests, the dark evergreen of the Black Forest, with origins in ancient Russia and Siberia. Not until about 500 B.C. did it spread to its namesake country, Norway, where today it makes up most of the forest (which, in turn, covers some 37 percent of the nation). In Norwegian legend it was the tree of life, a leafy paradisal plant that tempted Eve with succulent fruit—and paid for it by becoming hard-needled and woody-fruited.

Cultivated for some five centuries, the Norway spruce is used for landscaping, lumber, pulp, turpentine, varnishes, medicines—and, of course, for Christmas trees, though its needles quickly drop from cut trees that are not watered. Nurseries often use Norway spruce as an "understock" for propagating other spruces—including Colorado—by grafting techniques.

As a cemetery tree, the dark-skirted Norway spruce and its weeping cultivars (*P. abies* f. *pendula*) mourn the dead, while its spirelike cultivars (e.g., *P. abies* 'Pyramidata') honor them. Norway spruces in Bishop Hill, Ill., marked the mass graves of pioneers who died of cholera in 1849. In Newman, Ill., a young tree memorialized a child who died when the family came through by covered wagon in about 1855. That tree was still standing tall 120 years later.

The world's Norway spruces have another special victim to mourn: their own species, said to be dying by the millions from Eurasia's acid rain. A sad thank-you, indeed, for a tree that brings holiday cheer to half the industrial nations on earth.

Deodar Cedar
(and Cedar-of-Lebanon)
Cedrus deodara (and *Cedrus libani*)

Left (background), cedar-of-Lebanon. Right, deodar cedar.

IMPORTANCE: A member of the venerated "true" cedars—four majestic conifers from the Himalayas and mountains of the Mediterranean region. Deodar cedar prized as ornamental in cities of warmer U.S. states, especially Pacific Coast. Related cedar-of-Lebanon an upscale ornamental tree with many Biblical associations, including Solomon's Temple.

FAMILY: Pinaceae (Pine). GENUS: *Cedrus* (cedar).

COMMON URBAN SPECIES: 🕮 Deodar cedar (*Cedrus deodara*) or deodar, Himalayan c., Indian c., California Christmas tree.

CLOSE RELATIVES: 🕮 Cedar-of-Lebanon (*C. libani*) or Lebanon c. 🕮 Atlas cedar (*C. atlantica*) or Atlas mountain c., African c. 🕮 Cyprian cedar (*C. brevifolia*).

TYPICAL CITY LOCATION: Parks, large gardens, estates, churchyards, cemeteries, golf courses.

KEY FEATURES: *Deodar:* Conical and wide-spreading evergreen, with horizontal branches that droop gracefully toward the ends, cascading in layers. Usually strong central trunk, may lean at top. Older trees picturesquely open and slightly irregular. Needles stiff, very sharp, 1–2″ long, light green to blue-green, in bunches of 15–20 at tips of stubby side twigs (spurs) or arranged singly in spirals along shoots. Shoots reddish and very hairy.

Mature seed cones grenade-shaped, 3–5″ long, 2–3″ wide, cinnamon-brown, resiny, erect and upright on stem. Scales hard, wide, and shallow. Cone deteriorates after releasing seed.

Lebanon: On mature tree, horizontal branches are spaced out, level (not drooping), massive, with dark foliage. Treetop is table-flat. Shoots are mostly hairless. Cone barrel-shaped, 3–4″.

Atlas: Like Lebanon, except branches often ascending. Foliage usually more silvery blue. Cones smaller at 2–3″.

AVERAGE MATURE SIZE IN CITY: 40–70′ high, 30–50′ wide, 2–3′ thick.

RECENT CHAMPION: Not in American Forests *Register.* Reported deodar cedars include: 121′ height, 13′ circumf., Hampshire, England; 114′ height, 10′ circumf., Seattle, Wash.

ɘ̃ TIMBER OF THE GODS

How else could they regard it but as godly, this fragrant evergreen of the Himalayas? This broad-winged eagle of a tree? This wood that lasted forever? Sanskrit-speaking people of India named it *devadaru,* "timber of the gods." The Hindus called it *deodar.*

And deodar or deodar cedar it has remained through the centuries:

through massive exploitation of the trees in India under British rule; through its march into nineteenth-century gardens of Europe and America; through its damage from modern-day skirmishes along the India-Pakistan border; and through its adoration in towns of the American West Coast.

Deodar cedars love the California climate in particular, and Californians love their deodars in return. In the town of La Canada Flintridge, one man so revered his neighbor's 113-foot deodar that he opposed its removal even when root rot indicated it would fall on his own garage. And fall it did, all 12 tons of it.

Altadena, just outside Los Angeles, is blessed with an avenue of some 140 deodars, including almost 100 surviving giants planted in 1882 for an estate never completed. Each year, volunteers festoon the deodars—many 90 feet high—with holiday lights, and the stretch of trees along Santa Rosa Avenue has become a crowd-pleasing spectacle known as Christmas Tree Lane. The National Register of Historic Places recognized it in 1990.

Often described as one of the world's most graceful trees, the deodar cedar ornaments urban sites throughout England and Europe—including the Vatican Museum gardens—and the warmer American states. Usually, it will be found in pampered settings; after all, it belongs to a small aristocratic group of four species that botanists call genus *Cedrus,* or "true cedars."

Not that the 70 or so other species with "cedar" in their common names are impostors; most of these trees have the lightweight, enduring, and spice-scented wood that people have long associated with the word "cedar"—from *kedros,* a Greek word used for resinous trees. In botanical nomenclature, the terms "true," "false," "pseudo," or even "bastard" carry no value judgments, but have to do with sequence and consistency in naming.

Yet, there is an air of truth about the true cedars—the truth of their beauty and an eternal truth connected with their native sites and Biblical references. All four species come from forests roughly aligned between latitudes 30° and 40° N, a path of ancient civilization from northwest Africa to Nepal. But only patchy areas of forest remain from what might have been vast connected regions.

The deodars of the Himalayas grow far from the other three species and are physically distinctive. More closely related are the Atlas cedar of Algeria and Morocco, the Cyprian cedar of Cyprus, and the celebrated cedar-of-Lebanon of Turkey, Syria, and Lebanon. ("Command thou that they hew me cedar trees out of Lebanon," temple-building King Solomon asked of King Hiram of Tyre.)

CITY CEDARS

The surviving native cedar forests are mostly at elevated altitudes, where dry rocky soil and harsh weather make for wizened but long-lived trees. Perhaps in these rugged settings true cedars developed true grit for urban survival. They have traveled successfully across the continents, shrugging off local pests and diseases. Given sun, elbow room, and well-drained, gourmet soil, they can rise like gods in the lowly city air. Frigid temperatures and cold snaps, however, reveal their mortality.

While England loves its cedars-of-Lebanon (one duke planted 1,000 of them in 1761), the deodar seems to have won out as America's most commonly planted true cedar. It is neither the most storied nor the most picturesque of its clan, but, shooting up more than two feet a year when young, it soon develops its endearing "habit" or shape: a big layered pyramid of sweeping pendulous branches drooping gracefully toward the tips.

Like the other true cedars and the larches, the deodar bears most of its needlelike foliage in bunches sprouting out of stubby twigs (pegs or spurs). But the lovely larch drops its soft needles each year.

The evergreen needles of deodar (and other true) cedars sprout in bunches from spurs. Resin-oozing seed cones rise straight up.

True cedars are evergreens, replacing fallen needles fast enough to stay green year-round. They are the *only* evergreens to bunch their needles on spurs, which gives their shoots an attractive spidery texture. If you see such needle bunches in winter, the tree is a true cedar. It is a deodar cedar if the needles are stiff, very sharp, and one to two inches long, and the twigs are densely hairy.

Seed-bearing cones that look like little resin-oozing barrels often rise straight up from the higher branches of mature true cedars. The deodar's four- to five-inch cones turn from frosty blue-green to reddish brown as they ripen over two years. After they open their tightly wound scales to release winged seeds, they deteriorate. For allergy sufferers who thought the worst was over after summer, slim male cones on the lower branches spew their pollen as late as November.

From its U.S. debut in 1820, probably on Long Island, N.Y., the deodar has made its way into towns from coast to coast as an elite ornamental. Most of the plantings are in southeastern, Gulf, and Pacific Coast states, but cold-hardy cultivated varieties such as 'Kashmir' and 'Shalimar' have brought a taste of deodar to the nippier reaches. Specimens are found as high as Canada's eastern provinces, in Boston, and in British Columbia.

Warmer cities revel in the tree. The many deodars around the nation's capital include a colossal one behind the Custis-Lee mansion in Arlington Cemetery. The soil from which it draws its vigor is near-sacred ground, owned successively by the George Washington and Robert E. Lee families.

Garden writer Martha Tate cites dozens of stately deodars planted along Route I-85 near Cheshire Bridge Road in Atlanta and many more grayish or silver-green specimens around town. (Deodars also range from yellow-green to blue-green.) In Charleston, Savannah, and New Orleans, the tree is much in evidence. In Norfolk, Va., deodars were handed out for Arbor Day, 1998. Seattle and Sacramento boast massive specimens. Sunnyvale, Calif., places the deodar on its select list of "official" street trees, though street trees must be trimmed of their regal lower branches and given ample root space. The godly tree is known to heave up sidewalks if offended.

LEBANON CEDAR: THE "TANG OF SOLOMON'S TEMPLE"

In 1993, Irish writer Thomas Pakenham journeyed to Turkey's Taurus Mountains to see the reputedly oldest cedars-of-Lebanon. He had known the tree in England as one that sprang up huge and lush in the moist, rich soil—too huge and lush, exhausting its energy and dying within some 200 years. In the Turkish mountains, he found smaller and "less elegant" cedars, "gnarled and tormented," but up to 1,000 years old. "In the hot wind," Pakenham reported, "we could smell the resinous tang of Solomon's temple."

Not to slight Pakenham's impeccable nose, but the actual tang of Solomon's Temple might have belonged to a similar-smelling juniper rather than the cedars that grew on Mount Lebanon, north of today's Israel. Bible botany has little in common with modern classification, and no one can be sure which species were meant by the Bible's many references to "cedar."

Still, scholars believe that the Mount Lebanon cedars were well known and revered in the time of Solomon, and many a botanist has made a pilgrimage to the historic grove 6,200 feet up a 10,200-foot mountain. There they have found some 400 aged and aging trees, some believed as old as 2,500 years. True to their species, they are exotically beautiful, with fountaining multiple trunks and big branches of dark foliage held out in layers as flat as dinner plates—including the top layer. But new seedlings have been grazed by goats over the centuries, and unless recent conservation efforts prove successful, the grove could eventually die out.

ATLAS CEDAR

The Lebanon species is safe enough in cultivation, however. So is the similar Atlas cedar, native to North Africa's Atlas Mountains. Both trees are more cold-hardy than the deodar. With reasonable placement and care, they thrive in cool as well as warm cities. The Atlas is most frequently seen as the silvery-blue cultivated variety 'Glauca'. A popular 'Glauca Pendula' version weeps so heavily, says Seattle tree maven Arthur Lee Jacobson, it is "absolutely dripping." Normally, however, the Atlas is distinguished from the Lebanon by branches that rise slightly. (The standard mnemonic: A-Atlas, *ascending.* L-Lebanon, *level.* D-deodar, *drooping.*)

Older Lebanons and Atlases look like twins, but their cone sizes will aid the desperate differentiator. Lebanon cones are three to four inches; Atlas cones two to three inches. And if the tree in question sits in a parking lot or on a boulevard, as in Portland, Oregon, and San Diego, put your money on it being an Atlas. The cedar-of-Lebanon may be associated with Solomon the Wise, but streetwise it is not.

Arborvitae (*Thuja*)

Thuja occidentalis, T. orientalis (Platycladus orientalis), T. plicata

IMPORTANCE: Within the small *Thuja* group is one of America's most common yard trees and the first American tree known to be cultivated in Europe. Usually a reliable and unassuming spire of green in a dooryard, hedgerow, or border, but often a tall, striking specimen. More than 100 cultivated varieties. Well worth close-up observation.

FAMILY: Cupressaceae (Cypress). GENUS: *Thuja* (also *Thuya*) (thuja or thuya).

COMMON URBAN SPECIES: ❀ American arborvitae (*Thuja occidentalis*) or tree of life, arborvitae, northern white cedar, eastern white cedar. ❀ Oriental arborvitae (*T. orientalis*) or Chinese a. ❀ Western red cedar (*T. plicata*) or giant a.

TYPICAL CITY LOCATION: *Small to medium ornamentals:* Yards, driveways, foundation plantings, subdivision landscapes. *Larger trees:* Parks, cemeteries, property screens.

KEY FEATURES: Tree forms regular, compact, conical crown. Flattened twigs are covered with minute, scaly, evergreen leaves, about ⅛" long in overlapping ranks of 4: two folded outer leaves embrace 2 flat inner leaves (see figure below, page 347). Fronds of foliage start low on tree, resemble broad fans or fountain sprays. Fruit cones raisin-sized with 12 or fewer scales attached at base. Bark thin, fibrous, reddish brown, graying with age.

American arborvitae: Leaves yellow-green, apple scented when crushed, minute glassy dot (resin gland) appears on flat inner leaves. Foliage sprays mainly horizontal. Cones ½", erect, with 8–10 blunt-tipped scales.

Oriental arborvitae: Vertical sprays of foliage. Faintest resiny scent. Abundant, egg-shaped cones to 1" long, usually 6 pairs of scales with outward-curved spine at tips.

Western red cedar: Large tree. Dark green leaf, highly aromatic. Down-sweeping branches, drooping sprays of foliage. Cones erect, to ½", 10–12 scales, short spine just below scale tips.

AVERAGE MATURE SIZE IN CITY: Hedge trees and small ornamentals, 10–20' high. Large specimen or border trees, 30–60' high.

RECENT CHAMPION: *American:* 113' height, 42' spread, 18' circumf., Leelanau County, Mich. *Oriental:* 65' height, 24' spread, 6' circumf, Natural Bridge, Va. *Western red cedar:* 178' height, 54' spread, 61' circumf., Forks, Wash.

❧ TREE OF (EVERYDAY) LIFE

The munchkin-sized tree sold at a thousand malls in much of North America, the one growing by several million doorways, the evergreen with twigs that look ironed—this is likely to be the one and only tree of life, a species otherwise known as American arborvitae. If not this precise species, the shopping mall offering will be one of the tree's relatives in a small group of cypresses called *Thuja* (*thew-ya*).

The most common cultivated forms may be kitschy. And in winter, with brown foliage, the tree of life looks comatose. But consider its credentials: history, longevity, close-up beauty, and the genes of a robust forest tree.

The American arborvitae is native to the woodlands of northeastern North America, where it is known to loggers as northern or eastern white cedar (though no true cedars are native to North America). It grows to various sizes in swampy land, by water, or in rocky uplands. In its favorite soggy settings, it flourishes as a dense pyramidal conifer of some 40 to 60 feet or more, a fragrant haven for wildlife and one so resistant to decay that it endures for centuries and—in at least one case—a millennium.

Some writers attribute the name "tree of life" to the species' longevity. But the more likely story is that it earned its name in about 1536 in Canada's St. Lawrence region, where some of the men under French explorer Jacques Cartier had fallen ill with scurvy.

The men were near death when into their path came Domagaia, a local Native American who himself had been revived by a certain tree's medicines. The Native Americans had used aromatic northern white cedar oil as a treatment for every ailment from unconsciousness to possession by evil spirits. Domagaia told Cartier to boil the leaves and bark of this tree as a tea and salve. Thanks to the vitamin C in the decoction, Cartier could report that France's greatest physicians and "all the drugges of *Alexandria . . .* woulde not have done so muche in one yeare, as that tree dydde in five days."

When the story and the species itself reached the French king Francis I, he proclaimed the plant the tree of life—in Latin, *arbor vitae.* Its fame spread and the arborvitae became the first New World tree north of Mexico to be cultivated in Europe, as early as 1553. To this day, it is one of Europe's favorites, though usually in smaller cultivated forms.

New forms for cultivation happen to be a specialty of the *Thuja* genus. The six or so species in the group (each with arborvitae as part of their common English nomenclature) like to produce offbeat children—offspring with such variations from the parent as striking yellow foliage, weepy boughs, columnar form, or warm-weather tolerance.

Seeds, raisin-sized cones, and aromatic foliage of American arborvitae.

Such offspring can be selected and cultivated as "named" varieties (cultivars), and nurseries can offer them to suit the customer (see sidebar, page 349). Urban landscapers have well over 100 available models to select from for hardiness, novelty, or easy integration into new housing tracts.

In addition to northern white cedar, two species have given rise to many of the most popular varieties cultivated in North America:

■ The *Thuja* of the northwest forests goes by the common name of western red cedar or giant arborvitae, and a giant it can be: on the order of 200 feet high and 20 feet thick. Even in urban cultivation, the giant arborvitae usually merits its nickname.

■ Oriental or Chinese arborvitae, an introduced Asian species, completes the ruling triumvirate in North America. A lofty spire in its home landscapes, it wins hearts in North America as a small, heat-tolerant, often yellow-tinted ornamental that displays its fronds vertically.

LEAF OF LIFE

All three species have a leaf structure of uncommon geometric beauty, something they share with other members of the cypress family. Examine a branchlet, itself a lovely pattern of fernlike forkings and featherings—the Onondagas called the American arborvitae *oo-soo-ha-tah,* or feather-leaf. Look closer. The naked eye sees rows of minute, pearly green scales tight against most of the scaly brown twigs. Each of the green (sometimes yellow) scales is a leaf, with all the breathing and chlorophyll-making apparatus of a leaf. But an even closer look, ideally with a standard 8x magnifier, reveals interwoven and overlaid leaf scales in a museum-quality design.

There are two basic patterns, actually, one of them a quartet of elongated, lance-shaped leaves typically covering the central twigs or growing on vigorous new shoots. The more thematic pattern appears on the feathery end twigs, the exterior foliage that can be pinched off carefully for observation. These stubbier, spade-shaped leaves likewise come in quartets: two "keeled" or boatlike side leaves enfolding two flat leaves tight against the twig (see figure). Each quartet slightly overlaps the quartet above it. The overall effect is like braided jewelry.

American arborvitae close-up reveals individual leaves in sets of four, with resin dots.

Some species, such as the American arborvitae, add an exquisite, raised crystalline dot to the flat leaf. Though the dot is a resin gland, its appearance does not signal the amount of resin or fragrance the tree has in store. It rarely appears on the giant arborvitae's leaf, yet that tree is as fragrant as pine soap. The American arborvitae, too, is aromatic. Rub a green twig between your fingers and savor the crisp apple fragrance. If the scents seem to suggest something else familiar, little wonder. The arborvitae's essential oils are used in cleansers, disinfectants, hair preparations, insecticides, and room sprays.

The tree's essences—which used to be sold in country stores—now figure in the pharmacopoeia of alternative health care, with its revival of folk treatments and borrowings from Eastern medicine. Extracts of the resin are said to increase blood pressure and reduce fever. Formulas containing oriental arborvitae seeds, according to one supplier, nourish the blood, tranquilize the mind, moisten the intestines, and treat night sweating due to yin deficiency. A leaf extract was prescribed for baldness in China.

All this from a plant that lines the driveway.

ORIENTAL GOLD

Native to China and Korea, the oriental arborvitae is sometimes classed outside the *Thuja* genus, but the urban observer can still enjoy it as an

Fleshy cone of oriental arborvitae.

arborvitae with a twist—to the vertical. The shoots of foliage turn at right angles to the branches, so that the narrow edges of the sprays are as distinctively up and down as a karate shoulder chop.

Landscapers from the mid-Atlantic to the Gulf Coast, California, and the Northwest snap up the tree and its cultivars, especially compact varieties with tints of gold in the foliage. Forming a full-bottomed pyramid, the species matures at about 25 feet high, but can grow to some 40 feet. The leaves, usually devoid of gland dots, yield only the faintest scent when scratched and sniffed. But branches of them serve as good luck symbols in Chinese New Year celebrations.

The American and oriental arborvitaes can be distinguished also by their cones (in fall). The American's cone, about a half inch long, is like a leathery bud that opens its "petals" wide to disperse its two-winged seed. The oriental's cone is larger, fleshier, larvalike. Its scales end in an outward-pointing hook. The seed is wingless.

WESTERN RED CEDAR: "THE BEST ARBORVITAE"

Wherever you live in North America, you run into traces of what many consider the best arborvitae of the bunch—the western red cedar or giant arborvitae. You at least know it from its wood, the legendary decay-resistant, good-smelling, red-tinged lumber. Today it is the wood of choice for roof shingles and deck boards. Yesterday it was the wood of massive trunks hewn into canoes, indestructible craft to carry whole clans of West Coast Natives—as well as Lewis and Clark—down the great rivers. Western red cedar supplied the straight cylinders of wood that became the famous totem poles of the indigenous northwesterners.

Though it likes the West's cool rainfall and fog, the tree and its varieties are quick to adapt when cultivated elsewhere. They thrive in settings as diverse as North Carolina, Illinois, and Rhode Island. Europe adores the tree for itself and as an icon of the American West.

Rising more than 100 feet in forests from western Canada to mid-California, the giant arborvitae is treated as a big tree in landscaping, too, though in cities 30 to 60 feet is more the usual range. Here the trunks may not be 20 feet thick, but they still have the tough fibrous bark and big flared buttresses of the forest versions. More than size distinguishes the giant arborvitae from the other popular *Thuja*s. Its longer limbs extend their sprays of foliage in horizontal waves. Its leaves are lustrous dark green throughout the year. Few glands are visible, but white markings ornament the bottom side of the twigs. Cones no bigger than the half-inch fruits of the American arborvitaes carry the equipment needed to perpetuate this mighty race.

VARIETY, THE SPICE OF *VITAE*

From offbeat arborvitae offspring, cultivators breed varieties with attractive new features or advantages over the species. Those more than 10 feet tall and most likely to be seen in urban settings include:

American arborvitae cultivars: 'Smaragd' ('Emerald'), stays emerald green, hardy in heat or cold. 'Nigra', narrow, stays dark green. 'Techny' ('Mission'), broad-based, dark green year-round. 'Lutea', narrow form, dense golden foliage. 'Fastigiata', narrow pyramid, brownish in winter.

Oriental arborvitae cultivars: 'Pyramidalis', narrow, bright green. 'Bakeri', broad pyramid, light green, for hot, dry settings. 'Beverlyensis', narrow form, gold-tipped, fast-growing.

Western red cedar cultivars: 'Zebrina', vigorous broad pyramid, gold bands across foliage. 'Atrovirens', bright glossy foliage. 'Canadian Gold', broad form, green and gold foliage, fast-growing.

BAG OF WOES

The toughness of arborvitaes accounts for much of their urban success. They handle most city pollutants, if not road salt. Smaller branches sometimes break under accumulated snow, but can be trussed in advance. Various diseases and pests are usually held in check, though deer are a problem in the suburbs. Only one bug, the bagworm, could be considered the plant's nemesis—and a curious one to observe.

From June to late summer, a bagworm makes a bag, a cone some 1½ inches deep when finished, which it attaches to twigs. Females spend their whole life in the bag, there laying eggs and breeding bag-spinning, leaf-destroying larvae. Only males ever emerge, to mate with females in other bags. It seems a dull life here on the tree of life. But then who's to say whose bag is best?

Baldcypress (and Dawn Redwood)

Taxodium distichum (and *Metasequoia glyptostroboides*)

Youthful baldcypress.

IMPORTANCE: This long-lived swamp giant, widespread in prehistoric North America, has proved highly adaptable to urban sites. One of few conifers to drop all leaves each year. State tree of Louisiana. Related Montezuma baldcypress the national tree of Mexico.

(Dawn redwood, an ancient species rediscovered in China, is a similar-looking tree making its mark in urban settings.)

FAMILY: Taxodiaceae (Redwood). GENUS: *Taxodium* (baldcypress).

COMMON URBAN SPECIES: ❀ Baldcypress (*Taxodium distichum*) or common bald cypress, swamp cypress, Southern cypress, Gulf cypress, Tidewater red cypress, deciduous cypress. ✤ (Variety) Pondcypress (var. *nutans*).

CLOSE RELATIVES: ✤ Montezuma baldcypress (*T. mucronatum*) or Mexican cypress. ✤ Dawn redwood (*Metasequoia glyptostroboides*) or Chinese redwood. ✤ Giant sequoia (*Sequoiadendron giganteum*). ✤ Coast redwood (*Sequoia sempervirens*).

TYPICAL CITY LOCATION: Watery park settings, spacious grounds, public and residential gardens, street parkways.

KEY FEATURES: Until old age, tree forms an airy pyramid of horizontal branches. Straight trunk tapers from flared, sometimes fluted bottom. Trees can reach epic dimensions, but foliage is soft-looking, lacy. Older trees develop fat, buttressed trunk bottoms, lose lower branches, widen and flatten at top. Water-soaked roots often send up conical humps or bark-covered "knees" that protrude above water or ground surface near tree.

Twigs (branchlets) are of two types: persistent twigs stay on tree; deciduous twigs bear leaves and drop with them. Leaves needle-shaped, about ½″ long, soft and flexible, form feather pattern along two crowded rows (not exactly opposite); light yellow-green in spring, darker in summer, gold or rust in fall. Drop with twig.

Male flowers long, beady tassels, 4–6″, sway with wind in late winter and spring. One-tenth-inch female conelets become 1″ brown woody cones resembling miniature soccer balls.

Bark smooth gray-brown (young) to fibrous, peeling reddish brown.

(*Dawn redwood* similar to baldcypress in most features, with these main distinctions: Leaves and deciduous twigs in opposite pairs; 1″ leaves twice the size of baldcypress's; cavities or "armpits" appear beneath some branches; no root knees; tree retains pyramid form throughout life; cones on long stalks; bark is flaky and coppery.)

AVERAGE MATURE SIZE IN CITY: 50–80′ high, 20–30′ wide, 2–3′ thick.

RECENT CHAMPION: 83′ height, 85′ spread, 54′ circumf., Cat Island, La.

❧UP FROM THE SWAMPS

If you haven't run across a bald-cypress tree in your metro area, you owe it to yourself to seek one out. A good time to do so is between late spring and fall, when you can fondle its soft and feathery needles. In winter, this unusual conifer drops not only its needles but the delicate twigs that hold them. In this sense, it does indeed go bald; yet, with its pyramidal form and reddish fibrous bark revealed, it is bald and beautiful.

Often called swamp cypress, this native of American swamps and wetlands has a show for every season. Late winter features the male pollen flowers, which cluster into purplish, four- to six-inch tassels that dance in the wind. Spring foliage is a gauzy backdrop of bright yellow-green. Summer

Older baldcypress.

trees cast a dappled shade. And in autumn the evergreen-like conifer pulls its annual surprise: The needles turn gold, bronze, copper, or rust-colored and drop with their twigs. Also in fall (on mature trees), the fertilized female conelets become brown balls an inch wide, with woody cone scales fitted like segments of a soccer ball.

The good news is that this ancient swamp tree also thrives on dry land and in urban areas, where it tolerates various soils and performs all its seasonal acts. No longer does one have to paddle into the Oke-fenokee to find the species, though the baldcypress experience will be most authentic there and in such parks as the Corkscrew Swamp Sanctuary near Naples, Fla. Along a two-mile walkway, visitors to Corkscrew can view the state's largest stand of virgin baldcypress.

These baldcypress twigs and their feathery, half-inch needles will drop in fall. The cones are woody.

In such settings—which in the dinosaur age reached north into Canada—one beholds majestic giants much like their ancestors, the prehistoric baldcypresses. Some of today's giants were alive well before Columbus's voyages. Now as much as 130 feet tall and eight feet thick, these oldsters have lost their lower limbs and spread their tops into flat, irregular sprays. At the base of the straight, towering trunks are muscular fluted columns and buttresses that flare into the water. Below the water-line, shallow serpentine roots manage to support the massive trees in a bed of muck.

KNEES ON THE WATER

Eerie appendages seen on no other species rise from the underwater roots of many older trees (over 50 years old). These are known as cypress "knees," or "pneumatophores." Usually a few feet from the trunk, they break through the water (or saturated ground) like little volcanic islands. Sometimes these bark-covered knees grow three or four feet tall to stay above high-water level. Their spongy interior suggests that they exist to aerate the roots, but research seems to have sunk that theory. Others believe the knees contribute to the tree's stability in water. Their only verifiable function, however, is as tourist pleasers. For souvenirs, sliced-off pieces are sometimes fashioned into novelties. Apparently, knees can be pruned to water- or ground-level without harming the tree.

The natural range of baldcypress follows watery areas from Delaware down the coast to Florida, where the trees take on drapings of Spanish moss. As famously southern as Scarlett O'Hara, the species continues along the Gulf through the bayous to Texas, with a big hump—or knee—taking it up to southern Illinois.

Native baldcypress does not appear in the Far West, but two close and celebrated relatives do—giant sequoia (*Sequoiadendron giganteum*), the world's most massive tree, and coast redwood (*Sequoia sempervirens*), the world's tallest. Not many trees can make 130-foot, 700-year-old

Older baldcypress trees often sprout humpy "knees" from underwater roots. Base of trunk forms buttresses.

baldcypresses look like squirts, but these two cousins in the small Redwood family almost manage. Unlike their swamp kin, they are both evergreens; their bark, though the same shaggy reddish brown, is much thicker.

Remaining natural stands of baldcypress are now somewhat protected. Still, vast numbers of old-growth trees have been claimed by the southern lumber trade. The heartwood (core) of the mature baldcypress is so rot-resistant as to be nicknamed "the wood eternal," suited to products from boats and coffins to silos and stadium seats. Today's commercial groves supply the slow-to-decay cypress mulch beloved by gardeners.

BALDIES IN THE BIG CITIES

But the baldcypress rises again, thanks to its increasing popularity among urban landscapers. Planted baldcypresses stretch the tree's habitat as far as Nova Scotia, British Columbia, and southern California, skipping mainly the high altitudes and areas of alkaline soil. This spread almost recaptures the tree's territory of 100 million years ago, when North America was warmer and wetter. In fact, baldcypress fossils and prehistoric tree parts are being found in cities that have only recently welcomed the species to the landscape. Baltimore was digging for its new football stadium in 1997 when excavators found ancient baldcypress logs, roots, and stumps some 20 feet below street level. Philadelphia had a similar subterranean find 64 years earlier.

Europe, which cultivated the baldcypress as early as 1640, considers it one of the choicest American trees and plants it avidly. Numerous metro areas throughout North America—Washington, D.C., New York, Cleveland, Cincinnati, New Orleans, Seattle, and Ottawa among them—have embraced the tree as a specimen for parks or other large properties.

Also favored is a natural variety or subspecies known as pond cypress, smaller in size and with short bluish needles tightly overlapped on stringy twigs. The foliage looks like lengths of yarn, says one writer, and another, Kim Tripp, calls pond cypress "one of the most gracefully beautiful trees on the planet . . . a lost, silvered spirit of the mist ascending from the ground."

As a street tree, the baldcypress (along with its cultivated varieties) is getting rave recommendations and increasing use. The tree professionals of New Orleans rate it tops among street plantings—but, then, it *is* Louisiana's official tree. Charlotte, Tampa, and Dallas are among others that put it on the streets. Outside the South, urban-tree authorities such as Cornell's Nina Bassuk give it two big thumbs up.

Transplanting the taproots takes some know-how, but once established, the tree grows fast and tolerates hot and cold weather, windstorms, moderate salt, pollution, and even compacted and clayey soils. It is relatively free of damaging diseases and insects. Grass can grow in its shade. When its fine needles drop to the ground, they form a pretty rust-colored halo that needs no arduous cleanup.

The notion that baldcypresses must be in water is untrue. Though the seeds require wet, nonfreezing conditions to germinate, the tree itself is happy in nonmarshy soils. It will not produce its famous knees in such sites, however, so don't expect sidewalks and lawns to erupt with souvenir stalagmites.

MEXICO'S REVERED BALDCYPRESS

The legendary Tule tree stands in a churchyard two blocks from the industrial spread of Oaxaca City in southern Mexico. Called Montezuma baldcypress or Mexican cypress in English, its species (*mucronatum*) belongs to the same Taxodiaceae family as the baldcypress and California redwoods. Like those trees, it can achieve four-figure ages, growing all the while.

Tule tree of the city of Oaxaca, Mexico.

The Tule tree has been growing since the beginning of Christianity. In 1998, it measured some 139 feet around at its base—considered the largest bole in the world. At 132 feet tall, it dwarfs the Santa María de la Asunción church whose yard it occupies. Though threatened by local development, the Tule tree is a regional treasure and subject of such legends as the water fountain that gushed from one of its branches. The species (*ahuehuete* or *sabino* in Spanish) extends naturally into Texas. California has planted it since 1905, with fine specimens in Sacramento and Pasadena. A North Carolina specimen turns sandy gold and drops its foliage in December.

DAWN REDWOOD: A FOSSIL LIVES!

The baldcypress has more in common with its lovely look-alike cousin from China, the dawn redwood, than with its nearer California relations. Dawn redwood has the same type of feathery, needlelike foliage, which also drops off in winter with the deciduous twigs. The flared trunk bottoms are similar on the two trees. Both begin as fast-growing pyramids and can eventually top 100 feet. Both species date back some 100 million or more years to the Mesozoic Era. And both are finding their way into modern American urban life.

Size differences and certain other distinctions between the trees (see data summary) are subtle; but the paired leaves and twigs of dawn redwood are clearly opposite one another, and the tree—faster-growing than the baldcypress—seems to remain pyramidal to the end. Also, whatever the soil, dawn redwood never develops those telltale knees. Instead, it has its own anatomical feature, known bluntly as "armpits." Appearing on the trunk just beneath the branches, these dark cavities do suggest body parts in need of attention.

Dawn redwood was unknown to the modern world until two remarkable events of 1941: First, the study of an American fossil in Tokyo revealed the species. Later, by coincidence, living specimens were discovered in China's Szechwan region, where local people were using the tree for cattle feed. By 1948, excited botanists around the world were planting the tree, and today it ornaments North American urban gardens and parks from Ontario to southern California (but not the Southeast).

Tolerant of pollution, dawn redwood seems to be doing fine on the streets as well. Maplewood, N.J., near New York, is typical of a community that has "limbed up" the tree—trimmed its lower limbs—for planting along the avenues. Limbing up a dawn redwood risks baring armpits at eye level, but in this permissive age, how many will take offense?

PART III

PALM TREES

Palm: Desert, Mexican Fan, Cabbage, Canary Island, Royal, Queen, King, and Others

Washingtonia filifera, W. robusta, Sabal palmetto, Phoenix canariensis, Roystonea regia, Syagrus romanzoffiana, Archontophoenix alexandrae, and others

IMPORTANCE: Botanically estranged from "true" woody trees, the tree-sized palm plants help sustain life in the tropics and grace warm cities with their paradisiacal beauty. Cabbage palmetto is state tree of South Carolina and Georgia.

FAMILY: Palmae or Arecaceae (Palm). GENUS: Many (see below).

COMMON URBAN SPECIES: ❦ Desert palm (*Washingtonia filifera*) or California fan p., petticoat p., hula p. ❦ Mexican fan palm (*Washingtonia robusta*). ❦ Cabbage palmetto (*Sabal palmetto*) or cabbage p. ❦ Canary Island date palm (*Phoenix canariensis*) or pineapple p. ❦ Cuban royal palm (*Roystonea regia*). ❦ Florida royal palm (*Roystonea elata*). ❦ Queen palm (*Syagrus romanzoffiana*) or cocos p. ❦ King palm (*Archontophoenix alexandrae*). ❦ Coconut palm (*Cocos nucifera*). ❦ Chinese windmill palm (*Trachycarpus fortunei*).

TYPICAL CITY LOCATION: *In hot climates:* Streets, medians, parks, beaches, yards, campuses, hotels, courtyards, amusement centers, golf courses. *Cooler climates:* Indoors at megamalls and atrium lobbies.

KEY FEATURES (SEE TEXT FOR TERMINOLOGY AND ADDITIONAL DETAILS):

Coconut: Long feather leaves on bowed, often leaning trunk.

Desert: Huge, long shag of dead foliage over trunk, oddly angled fan leaves with threads at tips.

Mexican fan: Fan leaves and shag atop towering skinny trunk.

Cabbage: Twisted leathery fan leaves with stout midrib, wickerlike pattern of leaf bases on tall trunk.

Canary Island: Thick fountain of immense feather leaves on thick, pineapple-like trunk.

Royal palms: Soaring, smooth, powdery white trunks bulging at midsection or elsewhere above base; bright shiny green crownshaft atop trunk; tousled feather leaves.

Queen: "Feather-duster" foliage atop smooth trunk with alternating gray and white bands.

King: Shiny crownshaft, conspicuous rings on trunk.

Windmill: Trunk thinnest at base, covered with dark fibers. Fan foliage.

AVERAGE MATURE SIZE IN CITY: *Coconut:* 40–80' high, 1–1½' thick. *Desert:* 40–70' high, 2–3' thick. *Mexican fan:* 60–90' high, ¾–1' thick. *Cabbage:* 30–70' high, 1–2' thick. *Canary Island:* 30–50' high, 2–5' thick. *Royal:* 50–80' high, 1½–2' thick. *Queen:* 30–50' high, 1–2' thick. *King:* 40–70' high, ¾–1½' thick. *Windmill:* 20–30' high, ¾–1' thick.

RECENT CHAMPION: *Desert:* 101′ height, 22′ spread, 8′ circumf., San Diego, Calif. *Royal:* 99′ height, 18′ spread, 4′ circumf., Copeland, Fla.

❧ TOUCHES OF PARADISE

Of some 3,000 species of palm trees worldwide, just three urban street palms are native to the United States: the desert or California fan palm, cabbage palm, and Florida royal palm. But what classy palms they are. All three rise to impressive heights and flaunt their great green fan or feather leaves to say what palms say so distinctively: *Here is a place of warmth; here is a touch of paradise.*

Imagine the value of such trees to Shangri-las like Palm Springs, with its surrounding desert palms. To South Carolina and Georgia, each of which honors the cabbage palm as state tree. To communities like Florida's Palm Beach, whose royal palms uphold its name and reputation.

Palms make a statement. If the local palms aren't enough, urban landscapers seek other world-class palms to tropicalize their concrete jungles. Los Angeles has a mix of 50,000 palm trees on its streets. In the late 1990s, Las Vegas casino developers were paying $8,000 and up for each mature Canary Island date palm wrested from San Francisco in a bidding war for the trees. And New York's World Financial Center was installing rows of 35-foot Mexican fan palms in its glass-roofed, climate-controlled Winter Garden.

Millions of years ago, on a warmer, swampier planet, the palm species reached far into what we call the temperate zones. Today, they are "exotics," native mainly to the hot, moist tropics, with spillover into the desert oases and subtropical zones. Only a few hardy native palms of North America, China, and Chile can survive in frostier regions, provided they are insulated by steady warm coastal currents. With Chinese windmill palms in its northwest, even Scotland gets in touch with its tropical self.

Not all palms are trees; some are vines and shrubs. And those palms we consider trees are more like grasses or lilies in their botanical ways. Palms are different, just as the rich who frame their villas and estates with them are different. Some brief background on palms, offered below, will help observers appreciate their unique features and enrich the next stroll in a palmy paradise.

A PALM PRIMER

Palms distinguish themselves from other broadleaf trees even as they sprout from their seeds. Those other trees are dicotyledons, with tiny paired seed leaves breaking through the soil. Palms are monocotyledons (monocots), with one embryonic seed leaf; their stem grows more like a grass stem than a typical tree trunk. Developing slowly, the palm stem achieves its final width before rising very high, though some thickening may occur later from expansion of the original inner tissue.

A tough rind often covers the palm's fibrous wood, but there is no true bark. Unlike other trees, palms have no cambium layer producing successive layers of wood and bark; a cross section shows no annual growth rings. The rind cannot heal itself. Also, the monocot's conductive tubing (vascular structure) runs in straight parallel bundles, with no natural branchings off the stem, no networked leaf veins. Instead, you will see straight lines of parallel veins on the leaves.

Essentially, a palm tree is a tall, slow-growing stem with roots and a single growing tip or bud (*apical tip*) at its peak. From that tip and only that tip come the generations of leaves and new stem growth. Kill the tip and the tree dies. Bugs, animals, and people have been regular tip slayers, with a taste for the big cabbagelike bud. Some buds are harvested for the sake of hearts-of-palm salads. Luckily, thick foliage and spines and trunk spikes often discourage predators.

Unlike trees with rings of annual growth, a palm's only growth layers are in stacks: the layers of old foliage up the stem. The growing tip continues to rise, producing new leaves. How the dead foliage (the *shag*) clings to or falls from the trunk gives character to the palm. The shag may accumulate into a monstrously thick "hula skirt" or "petticoat," as on the California fan palm; or it might drop away and leave only its sheathed leaf bases or "boots" in a wickerlike geometric pattern, like that of the cabbage palm. Or, as on the royal palm, it may fall away cleanly to leave a stone-smooth trunk marked with horizontal rings of leaf scars. Almost every imaginable pattern is seen on one palm or another, including those shaped by prunings and trimmings to meet someone's aesthetic (or safety) standards.

Other stem features catch the eye: the King Kong–like hairiness of a windmill palm's trunk; the spindly, 90-foot rise of the Mexican fan palm; the prominent trunk rings of the king palm; or the curved, leaning stem of a coconut palm. But the enchantment of palms resides mainly in their leaves—spectacular, giant leaves in the case of most street palms, stirring romantic fantasies as they carry out the mission of all leaves: to make food for the plant via photosynthesis.

All palms are evergreens, but their leaf structure divides them into two basic types: palmate, as in fingers joined to one's palm (and thus the name of the tree); and pinnate, as in the barbs of a feather along a midrib.* The palmate-leaf trees are called *fan* palms, and the pinnate type *feather* palms. This is the first distinction to be made, and usually an obvious one, when observing or trying to identify a street palm. Does the leaf look like a big, rounded fan or a long, giant feather?

As in the accompanying diagram (page 366), the "fingers" or "barbs" of a palm leaf are called its leaflets or *segments.* Technically, the whole leaf (sometimes called a frond) consists of:

- a leafstalk or *petiole;*
- the broad *leaf base* where the petiole attaches to the tree;
- and the leafblade (all the segments together).

On feather palms, the extension of the petiole along the middle of the blade is called the *rachis.* All the feather segments grow off this

---

*Only one genus, the *Caryota* or fishtail palm, represents a third type: bipinnate, meaning leaflets growing off leaflets. From India and Malaya, the *mitis* species is popular in the United States for its jagged, wedge-shaped leaflets, which do resemble strings of fishtails.

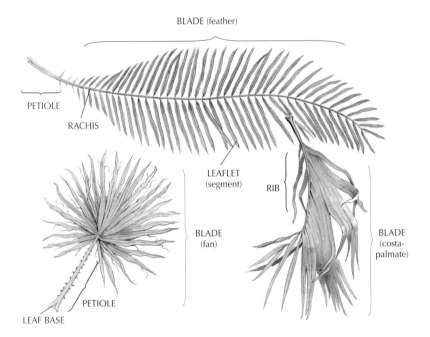

BLADE (feather)

PETIOLE

RACHIS

LEAFLET
(segment)

RIB

BLADE
(fan)

BLADE
(costa-
palmate)

PETIOLE

LEAF BASE

Types of palm leaves and their parts. Clockwise, from lower left: palmate or fan palm; pinnate or feather palm; costapalmate palm.

rachis. On fan palms, however, the petiole usually ends where the segments begin, as if it were just a handle. Where the petiole extends a bit into the segments, it is called simply a rib.

Speaking "palmese," then, one would say, "Pinnate segments grow off the rachis, and palmate segments off the petiole or rib." Further, "Palmate species with a significant rib extending into the segments are known as *costapalmate.*" An extremely costapalmate leaf such as that of the cabbage palm is really a mix of the two leaf types, with segments both fanning and feathering off its rib, curving and arching dramatically as if pulled in two directions.

Segments of a fan leaf relate to one another in varied and beautiful ways. Born of a single, accordion-folded leaf that splits as it opens and develops, the segments are usually joined partway to their tips, like webbed fingers. They may be stiletto-thin or wider; their tips pointed or split, firm or drooping. The sinuses, or spaces between the segments, may be deep or shallow; often they are lined with long fibrous threads.

In outline, the fan leaf makes a rounded shape anywhere from a semicircle (or less) to a full circle. Not every rounded fan leaf is suitable for fanning rajas and pharaohs, however. The leaves of the California fan palm, up to six feet broad, would be a bit unwieldy, not to mention the inconvenience of hooked spines along the three- to six-foot length of the petiole.

Palm leaves, all unfolding from the growth tip, form the crown of the tree, which can be airy or dense, compact or spreading, depending on leaf shape and profusion. One palm—the *Raphia ruffia* or raffia palm—grows leaves some 65 feet long. But among urban palms in the United States, the Canary Island date palm is probably leafiest, with up to 200 feather leaves, each looping out some 15 to 20 feet on mature trees.

Large sheaths commonly surround the leaf bases of the petioles. Clinging to the trunk or remaining after the leaves have fallen, the sheaths often contribute to the look of a species. Sometimes they form a cylindrical pack encircling the top of the trunk, overlapping and wrapped as tightly as a prosthetic bandage. Such a pack is known as a crownshaft, and in species such as the king, queen, and royal palms, it forms a notably glossy green pillar beneath the leafy crown.

Not to be outdone by other distinctive parts, the flowers of the palm tree are outlandish in their own way—even compared to such showy-blossomed hardwoods as chestnut and catalpa. Like the head of a wet mop on a fishing pole, they usually consist of a large, branching, droopy mass of small flowers held away from the tree by a fleshy, pliant flower stalk called a spadix. This stalk may originate among the leaves, or—unlike any other palm growth—from a point on the trunk beneath the leaves or crownshaft. Stalks on common urban palms range from about 3 to 12 feet in length. Just as the leafstalks are sheathed, the flower stalks usually have their own sheath or spathe, sometimes only a few inches at the base, sometimes as long and stiff as a sword.

A few palms repress their flowering and fruiting until late in life, then let it all go in one spectacular burst before they die. The talipot palm of Southeast Asia is said to raise a 25-foot-high spray of 60 million blossoms in its single inflorescence. But most palms flower repeatedly to bear fruit and the seeds of reproduction. Blossoms are usually yellow or cream; fragrance varies by species. Some trees carry only female flowers, others only male; some carry both sexes or bisexual flowers. One way or another, fertilization happens and strands of often colorful fruit develop. Size ranges from small berries to the freakish 40-pound, watermelon-sized fruit of the Seychelles Islands sea palm.

COCONUTS AND DATES

Of the edible palm fruits, the two most notable are coconuts and dates. Those coconut palms (*Cocos nucifera*) along Florida's beaches produce a palatable fruit, but several tropical varieties are said to yield better "meat." The heart of the coconut seed is what remains after the fibrous outer shell is removed, and the meat is the seed's endosperm or nutritive tissue. A symbol of prosperity in India, coconuts were stored in shrines and presented to aid conception.

The coconut tree, whose exact origins are unknown, has been well used for food, artifacts, and ornamental landscaping. On a bowed, flexible stem, it sways its 6- to 15-foot feather leaves to the beat of the waves. But as a street tree, it poses the inconvenience of leaf and fruit drop—some 40 to 80 feet to one's noggin.

The classic date fruit is that of the *Phoenix dactylifera,* the "true" date palm native to Africa and Asia, believed to be the Bible's oft-mentioned date palm. A staple crop of the ancient world and treasure of the Mediterranean, it is now cultivated widely (including in California and Arizona) for its matchless sugary dates. In America, it gets some ornamental use for its huge, ascending feather leaves. Old leaf bases pattern the tall trunk. But it is neither as hardy nor as lavishly leaved as its popular Canary Island cousin (see below).

DESERT (CALIFORNIA) AND MEXICAN FAN PALMS

The two great palm species native to southwestern North America honor easterner George Washington in their scientific names: *Washingtonia filifera,* the desert or California fan palm of southernmost California, and *W. robusta,* the Mexican fan palm, from over the border.

Latin for "thread bearing," *filifera* refers to the very thready, frayed segment tips on the desert palm's gray-green fan leaves. Some 50 or more segments make up these fans, which measure three to six feet across. Spiky stalks about six feet long hold the fans at erratic angles.

The enormous, trunk-length shag formed of dead leaves and flowers gives the tree two additional common names—hula or petticoat palm—as well as a place

Desert or California fan palm with thick shag of dead foliage.

in palm landscapes from Hawaii to South Carolina and Seville, Spain. It also has given the palm a reputation as fire hazard and habitat for rats, snakes, and scorpions, all of which do indeed love the shag and its supply of food and nesting material. Many cities either trim or remove the shag regularly, revealing a thick gray trunk up to 50 feet tall with vertical chinks or ridges. In its native desert canyons around Palm Springs, however, the shag becomes a mass up to eight feet thick, like a straw monster topped with unkempt green locks. Botanists knew little about the tree until the late nineteenth century, but indigenous peoples made good use of the tree parts, including its small black berries and their seeds.

The tall, slender Mexican fan palm.

The *W. robusta* is notably misnamed, being the less robust of the two species in cooler temperatures. Sometimes, however, it is the hardier along seacoasts and has survived some years in the San Francisco area. Fast-growing, the Mexican fan palm is said to be America's most common ornamental palm. It can be recognized as the palm that seems to grow too high—some 80 to 100 feet—for a trunk no thicker than a light pole and almost as straight. Few palms grow taller. Its "feather duster" cap of bright green fan leaves is smaller than the desert palm's crown. Dead leaves form a big shag, but landscapers often trim it to reveal a latticed pattern of leaf bases. The trunk is flared at the base and smooth gray-brown when the leaf bases drop off.

CABBAGE PALM

Under ideal tropical conditions, the cabbage palm native to Florida, Georgia, and the Carolinas can rise almost as high as the Mexican fan palm, to 90 feet. Some (in the southernmost range) actually do, but many others of this variable species top out at 30 to 50 feet. In fact, the name *palmetto* comes from the Spanish *palmito,* little palm, given by those who might have missed the taller specimens or judged by smaller varieties in Louisiana and Texas. The Seminoles boiled and ate the tasty apical bud, which would certainly have stopped the tree in its tracks. They also used its wood and twisty, leathery fan leaves for their houses and artifacts.

Those extremely costapalmate leaves—with a big rib extending well into the leafblade—can measure up to six feet long by eight feet wide. They form a bluish-green, globular array of 30 to 40 leaves on stalks four to seven feet long. The long, pointed leaf segments, split and thready at the ends, often turn up in dried bunches for Palm Sunday services. Foragers gobble the tree's shiny black autumn berries.

Big twisty fan leaves and wicker-like pattern of leaf bases on trunk characterize the cabbage palm.

The hardiest of New World palms, cabbage palms like the coasts but do well in almost any kind of soil. They stand among the street palms of Phoenix, Las Vegas, San Diego, and other western cities, their 1½-foot-thick trunks smooth or patterned with big crisscrossed leaf bases.

CANARY ISLAND DATE PALM

Beneath its spectacular crown of some 200 giant feather leaves, the Canary Island date palm puts on a sideshow with a trunk as thick as a

The Canary Island date palm, prized for its giant feather leaves and pineapple trunk pattern.

Greek column and as heavily patterned as a pineapple. "Pineapple palm" is one nickname for the tree, which can build its ornate trunk to a height of 40 feet over many years.

The trunk pattern is built of tough leaf bases that once supported 15- to 20-foot leaves. Air plants and ferns commonly piggyback on the thick growth. The palm is one that "suckers," or sends up new trees from its roots. These young leafy shoots may surround the trunk.

The big leaves often bear spinelike segments near the leaf base. Regular segments are distinguished by a V-fold down their length. This unusual, water-holding fold has the fancy name "induplicate."

The tree puts out bunches of orange dates on six-foot flower stalks, but the fruits are not for human consumption. They are part of its abundant beauty, a beauty that can be found from Charleston, S.C., down the coast and around Florida, as well as across the nation's southern edge into mid-California. But there is bad news: A fungus called fusarium wilt has so affected these palms of late that landscapers are being advised not to plant them.

While most urban palms hang tough within their climate range, they do fall victim to certain nasty diseases, fusarium wilt among them. The death of leaflets on one side of an older leaf is symptomatic of this fungus, which has no known remedy. A microbe known as lethal yellowing also attacks Canary Island palms, starting with yellowing foliage and blackened flowers and fruit.

ROYAL PALM

Among the royal palms towering above the Florida boulevards, the Cuban royal palms and native Florida royal palms dominate, sometimes indistinguishable from each other and possibly crossbreeding. Their regal features include tall, stately trunks, as smooth as sanded gray stone, bulging for some length between top and bottom and etched with horizontal rings. A tight green crownshaft glistens like a polished flask at the trunk's crest. Also distinctive are the three-foot flower stalks, sheathed in bright green spathes that stand erect at the base of the crownshaft like pointed baseball bats.

Atop the smooth bulging trunk of a royal palm are the upright flowerstalk sheaths and shiny crownshaft.

The dark green feather leaves of the royal palm extend 6 to 10 feet, with a stylishly unkempt look. The leaf segments coming off the rachis at four different angles give it that appearance. Not a chill-hardy palm, the royals flourish in the Miami–Palm Beach metro areas, where they get the royal treatment from landscapers.

A grotesque malady that threatens all palms, but especially those in the Southeast, has the fitting name "ganoderma butt rot." By the time the fungus shows up as small white lumps or larger woody "conks" protruding from a trunk, it is time to pull the rotted tree and get it to a landfill or incinerator.

QUEEN AND KING PALMS

The queen is from Brazil, the king from Australia, but the two smooth-trunked feather palms are linked in the minds of urban landscapers. Both (along with their varieties) thrive on the streets of southern California and Florida, both carry gracefully arching leaves atop a straight, conspicuously ringed trunk. Otherwise, they are proudly different.

The queen, also known as cocos palm, takes about 30 years to reach 40 feet, and can ultimately reach 50 feet with leaves up to 15 feet long. Growing in whorls around the rachis, the abundant 18-inch leaflets measure only an inch across and droop softly about halfway down their length, creating a light, weepy effect.

Leaf scars divide the queen's trunk into bands of light and dark gray. Flower stalks emerge from among the lower leaves and dangle five-foot masses of creamy flowers. By June, the masses are of green fruit, ripening to one-inch fleshy orange "dates"—colorful, but not for our palates.

The queen is not amused by chills or high winds, but resists lethal yellowing and will put up with smog, salt air, and some drought. On the

From left: Weepy segments of the queen palm leaf; the king palm's heavily ringed trunk, short-stalked flower, and jade-colored crownshaft; Chinese windmill palm, with hairy, inversely tapered trunk and stiff fan leaves.

California coast, Santa Barbara shows its high regard for the tree by maintaining some 1,500 queen palms among roughly 4,800 palms along its streets.

The king (*Archontophoenix alexandrae*) is named after a queen—Alexandra of Denmark, later queen dowager of Great Britain. But it does its best to distinguish itself from the queen palm. It grows taller, to 70 feet, on a slender, heavily ringed trunk and wears a glorious jade-colored crownshaft beneath its foliage. Though the leaves are just 5 to 10 feet long, the 2-inch-wide leaflets are twice as broad as the queen's, sword-shaped, and distinctively grayish white on their undersurface. Short, stout flower stalks emerge at the bottom of the crownshaft and dangle mops of whitish flowers yielding red berries. The smaller *A. cunninghamiana* king palm produces lavender flowers and chains of waxy berries as lavish as ceremonial jewelry.

WINDMILL PALM

The Chinese windmill palm may be no royal beauty, but it does lend palmosity to cooler climes where no other palms will grow. A shaggy-looking fan palm, it gives itself away with its dark coat of hairy fibers on a trunk that tapers in reverse, thinnest at the base. Pale yellow flowers yield bluish, kidney-shaped berries.

Just as Don Quixote saw windmills as giants, one can imagine the tree's stiff, round fan leaves to be blades of a windmill. But to this observer, the 20- to 35-foot palm looks more like some oversized emu standing tall and puffed out for romance. And, indeed, multitudes of gardeners and landscapers at the outermost rings of paradise have answered its love call.

But then it is easy to love any palm in the city, easy to stretch the definition of "tree" and "tree hugger" until palms fall within their embrace.

RESOURCES

Glossary: How to Speak "Tree"

The following terms are among those most frequently encountered in field guides and other resources on trees, trees as plants, and trees as urban plantings. Terms especially useful to the beginner are **boldfaced**. Words defined elsewhere within the glossary are *italicized* (except "leaf," "flower," and "fruit"). Several terms are illustrated pictorially in "Trees: A Briefing." For terms particular to conifers and palms, see the profiles "Austrian and Scots Pine" and "Palm."

ACHENE (AKENE). Small dry fruit with one seed; does not split open. See "Sycamore" profile.

ALTERNATE. Not in opposite pairs. Alternate is the most common arrangement of leaves on either side of a *twig* or *shoot*. See *opposite*.

ANGIOSPERM. A plant enclosing its seeds in a structure derived from an *ovary*, as do all *broadleaf* trees. See *gymnosperm*.

ANTHER. The *pollen*-bearing part of the male *stamen*, usually atop a stalk (*filament*).

APEX. The upper or outer end of a tree part, as the tip of a bud or leaf. Adjective: "apical."

ARBORETUM. Institution that collects, cultivates, studies, and exhibits trees.

ARBORICULTURE. The cultivation of trees (and shrubs).

ARBORIST. Practitioner of professional tree care.

AXIL. The upper angle where leaf joins *twig* or *shoot*. Site of an "axillary" bud.

BIPINNATE. A *compound leaf* structure consisting of a main stalk (*leafstalk*) that branches into secondary stalks, which in turn branch into stems that bear *leaflets*. See *pinnate*.

BLOOM. Waxy or powdery coating, as on leaf or twig, easily rubbed off.

BOLE. Lower, unbranched section of trunk.

BOULEVARD. Strip of planting area between sidewalk and curb. Also called *parkway* and "tree lawn."

BRACT. Leaf- or petal-like structure integrated into flower or fruit parts. See "Linden" or "Dogwood" profiles.

BRANCHLET. Subdivision of a branch, supporting *twigs* and *shoots* and their leaves. Sometimes used interchangeably with "twig."

BROADLEAFS (broad-leaved trees). Species whose leaves are not the needle like or tightly scaled leaves of the conifers, but comparatively broad. All are *angiosperms.*

BUD. Small protuberance containing the miniature beginnings of a *shoot,* flower and/or leaf, usually bundled within protective, leaflike bud *scales.*

BUNDLE SCARS. Patterns on a twig's *leafscar,* representing ducts ("vascular bundles") of the fallen *leafstalk.* Often used in tree identification.

BUR. Small spiny or prickly fruit.

CALYX. Collective term for flower parts that collar the petals, including the *sepals.* Usually green.

CAMBIUM. Thin layer of cells between inner bark (*phloem*) and wood (*xylem*) of a tree, manufacturing all the wood and inner bark. See "Trees: A Briefing" for discussion.

CANKER. Callus-ringed cluster of dead tissue on trunk or branch, caused by fungi or bacteria.

CANOPY. The umbrella of branches on an individual tree, or the average level of a forest's treetops. Also, the collective "tent" of trees in an urban setting. See *crown.*

CAPSULE. Dry fruit releasing two or more seeds when it splits open. See "Cottonwood" profile.

CARPEL. The flower's *pistil* or one of the *ovule*-bearing parts of a compound pistil. See "Crabapple" profile.

CATKIN. A floppy, tassel-like elongation consisting of many tiny flowers, as on oak trees. Usually of one sex.

CHLOROPHYLL. The green pigment needed for *photosynthesis* in specialized cells.

CHLOROPLASTS. The *chlorophyll*-containing parts within green plant cells.

CLONE. A plant reproduced from a single parent to be a genetic "twin" of that parent, accomplished by asexual reproduction or artificially by *grafting.* Cloning preserves parental traits. See "Crabapple" profile.

COMPLETE FLOWER. Flower containing male and female parts. See *perfect flower.*

COMPOUND LEAF. Leaf structure with main *leafstalk* branching into substalks bearing *leaflets.* See *pinnate, bipinnate,* and "Honeylocust" profile.

CONIFER. Tree whose fruits are woody or papery cones, such as pine or spruce cones, and with needlelike or tightly scaled leaves. Usually *evergreen.* All conifers are *gymnosperms.*

CORK CAMBIUM. Specialized cells of the inner bark (*phloem*), producing cells that become outer bark.

COROLLA. The ring of (often colored) petals on a flower.

COTYLEDONS (SEED LEAVES). Embryonic leaves within a fertilized seed, emerging as the plant's preliminary leaves. Palm seeds have just one, *angiosperms* two. *Conifers* have three or more.

CRENATE. Leaf having rounded or blunt teeth.

CROWN. A tree's mass of branches and foliage, above the clear trunk.

CULTIVAR. Referring to *cultivated variety.*

CULTIVATED VARIETY. A *species'* varying offshoot (*variety*) that has been selected, *cloned,* and nurtured to create a species subgroup with consistent, characteristic traits. Cultivated varieties or *cultivars* get an identifying (usually marketable) name in single quotes after the species name, as *Acer platanoides* 'Crimson King'.

DECIDUOUS. Plants whose branches are bare of foliage for some part of the year. See *evergreen.*

DENDROLOGY. The study of trees; a branch of botany.

DENTATE. Leaf having sharp teeth that are not angled forward. See *crenate* and *serrate.*

DIOECIOUS. Bearing male and female flowers on separate trees. See *monoecious.*

DOUBLY TOOTHED. On leaf edges, primary teeth bearing smaller teeth. See "Elm" profile.

DRIP-LINE. The water-dripping edges of the *crown,* key water source for roots.

DRUPE. Fruit with one seed surrounded by hard "stone" in turn surrounded by fleshy pulp, as with cherry or Russian-olive.

ELLIPTICAL. As leaf shape, an elongated oval—an ellipse. E.g., locust tree leaves.

ENTIRE. Describing smooth, unbroken leaf edges, no teeth or *lobes.*

ESTABLISHED. Said of a tree that has settled into a new site, with roots once again able to supply the tree's requirements from the soil. Critical for transplanted urban trees.

EVERGREEN. In foliage year-round, often through constant replacement of leaves. See *deciduous.*

EXFOLIATE. To peel in strips or flakes, as bark.

EXOTIC. As opposed to a *native* species. Many urban trees are exotics.

FAMILY. In botanical classification, a division that ties together groups of plants sharing certain (usually floral) characteristics, such as groups bearing seed *pods* (Legume family). The groups themselves are called *genera* (singular, *genus*).

FASTIGIATE. Narrow and erect, with branches angled close to the trunk. Also "columnar." See "Lombardy Poplar" profile.

FILAMENT. The *anther*-supporting stalk of the male flower part (*stamen*).

FLOWER. Reproductive organ of *angiosperm* trees. Compare with *strobili.* See "Trees: A Briefing" for discussion.

FOLIAGE. The leaves of a tree, collectively.

FORESTER. Professional maintaining and protecting trees within a jurisdiction. See *urban forester.*

FRUIT. The fertilized, mature, seed-bearing *ovary* of a plant. Takes many forms, sometimes encompassing other flower parts. (See *achene, capsule, drupe, pod, pome, samara.*) To various degrees, fruits nourish, protect, and disperse seeds. See "Trees: A Briefing" for discussion and illustrations.

GENUS (PLURAL, GENERA). In botanical classification, a group of plant types (*species*), such as oaks, with certain common traits that distinguish them from other groups. See also *family.*

GLABROUS. Hairless, as a glabrous leaf. Compare with *pubescent* and *tomentose.*

GLAND. Small secreting structure such as the dot gland on willow *leafstalk.*

GLAUCUS. With a bluish or whitish coating, or *bloom.*

GRAFTING. Technique of asexual *propagation,* commonly by bonding a bud of the parent plant to a compatible rooted plant (rootstock) to create a *clone* of the parent. See "Crabapple" profile.

GYMNOSPERM. Plant without flower ovaries, thus bearing "naked seeds." *Conifers* are gymnosperms. See *angiosperm.*

HABIT. The characteristic growth pattern of a tree, such as an elm's fountainlike spread of branches.

HARDINESS. Tolerance of temperature extremes in a particular climate.

HARDINESS ZONES. Bands of geographical areas mapped and rated according to average annual minimum temperatures. Tree *hardiness* is tied to zone, among other factors. In the United States, if a tree thrives from Minneapolis to Florida, it is said to be hardy in USDA Zones 3 (Minneapolis) to 10.

HEARTWOOD. The oldest wood of a tree, forming its core. Usually inactive and denser and darker than the *sapwood* that surrounds it.

HUSK. Heavy type of fruit covering, as nutshell or leathery chestnut husk.

HYBRID. Offspring of two different but genetically compatible tree types (*species*).

INTRODUCED. Non-*native* plant type purposely imported to grow in a region. Most *exotics* are introduced.

KEY. Nonfleshy, one-seeded winged fruit, usually flattened like paddle-shaped *samara* of ash tree. Maple "whirlybirds" are double keys.

LANCEOLATE. Shaped like the head of a pointed lance or spear, as ash or ailanthus *leaflets.*

LEAF. The food-making organ of a tree, having a *leafblade* that carries out *photosynthesis.* Joined directly to the woody *shoot* or *twig,* usually by a stalk (*petiole*). "Trees: A Briefing" illustrates leaf parts and arrangements.

LEAFBLADE. Expanded portion of a leaf or *leaflet,* beginning where the stalk, when present, ends.

LEAFLET. One of the "subleaves" of a branched or *compound leaf,* such as those of the honeylocust tree. Not joined directly to *twig* or *shoot.* See *leaf.*

LEAFSCAR. Scar on twig where *leafstalk* was attached, with a small *bud* above and distinct pattern of *bundle scars* within. Test of true leaf vs. *leaflet:* leafscar only under leaf.

LEAFSTALK (PETIOLE). Stalk connecting leaf to tree. Base usually swollen, snaps off twig.

LEGUME. Pod-type fruit characteristic of pea family. Usually splits at two sutures (seams) to release seeds.

LENTICELS. Breathing pores on bark, often clustered in visible bumps and horizontal patterns.

LOBES. The extended segments of *leafblades,* as rounded "fingers" of white oak leaves.

MARGIN. Edges or perimeter of *leafblade.* Margins can be smooth, toothed, wavy, etc.

MEDIAN STRIP. Planting area dividing lanes of a roadway.

MEDULLARY RAYS. Spokelike conduits (for liquids) emanating from tree core through wood and visible on cross section of trunk.

MIDRIB. The main central vein of a leaf or leaflet blade.

MONOECIOUS. Bearing separate male and female flowers on the same tree. See *dioecious.*

NAMED VARIETY. See *cultivated variety.*

NATIVE. Tree that has been growing wild or "naturally" in an area; indigenous.

NATURALIZED. A non-*native* tree growing wild (unplanted) in its adopted area.

OBLANCEOLATE. Reverse of *lanceolate,* broad end at the leaf tip.

OBOVATE. Reverse of egg-shaped, with the large end at the leaf tip.

OPPOSITE. Paired leaves exactly across from each other on twig, not *alternate.* See "Ash" or "Maple" profiles.

OVARY. Section of female flower that contains *ovules.* After fertilization becomes the part of fruit enclosing seeds.

OVATE. Egg-shaped, with small end at the leaf tip.

OVULE. Small structure in *ovary,* containing egg that becomes seed after fertilization. May be many ovules within ovary.

PALMATE. Shaped like fingers radiating from a palm, as horse-chestnut and sweetgum leaves.

PARKWAY. Planting strip between sidewalk and curb. Also *boulevard* and "tree lawn."

PEDUNCLE. Primary stalk of flower or flower cluster.

PENDULOUS. Hanging, pendant, as weeping willow branchlets.

PERFECT FLOWER. Flower containing male and female parts as well as *calyx* and *corolla* of petals. See *complete flower.*

PERSISTENT. Remaining attached to tree, as seed pods throughout winter.

PETIOLE. The *leafstalk.*

PH VALUE. Rating of acid–alkaline soil balance. High pH (above 7) is alkaline.

PHLOEM. Inner bark that conducts sugars from the leaves downward to nourish the tree. Compare with *xylem.*

PHOTOSYNTHESIS. Process by which leaves manufacture sugar from carbon dioxide and water, using *chlorophyll* and light energy. See also *stoma.*

PINNATE. Feather or fish-skeleton arrangement of *leaflets* on a *compound leaf,* the leaflets *opposite* or *alternate* along the sides of a central axis. See *bipinnate.*

PISTIL. The female reproductive complex within a flower, usually at center and consisting of an upright *style* topped by a pollen-gathering *stigma* and leading to the slightly swollen *ovary* below.

PISTILLATE. Flowers having one or more *pistils* but no functional *stamen.* Female flower. See *staminate.*

PITH. Core of a twig, varied in structure and sometimes useful in identification.

POD. Dryish *legume* fruit, splitting or otherwise opening to release seeds.

POLLEN. Grains or spores containing male sexual cells, borne on flower's *stamen* or, in conifers, on male *strobili.*

POLYGAMOUS. Species bearing separate male, female, and *perfect* (bisexual) flowers on the same tree. See *dioecious* and *monoecious.*

POME. Fruit with seed core surrounded by papery wall inside a fleshy mass, as apple and pear.

PROPAGATE. To generate new individuals by seeding, *grafting,* and other means.

PUBESCENT. Hair-covered, usually meaning small, fine hairs.

RACEME. Cluster of blossoms on individual stalks arranged along an elongated central stalk (axis). A further-branching raceme, like horse-chestnut flowers, is a "panicle."

RACHIS. Stalk (axis) bearing rows of *leaflets* on a *compound leaf.* Compare with *leafstalk.*

RECEPTACLE. The usually enlarged top of the stem that forms the base of flower parts. Often develops into exterior part of fruit.

SAMARA. A *key.*

SAPWOOD. A tree's younger wood or *xylem,* as compared to core *heartwood.* Located between heartwood and inner bark, it conducts water and nutrients upward.

SCALES. On *conifers,* the often woody, overlapping "flaps" of cones. Also, the tiny overlapping leaves of certain conifers (see "Arborvitae" profile), and the reduced modified leaves of *buds.*

SEPALS. Part of the calyx or flower collar surrounding the petals, usually green and leaflike.

SERRATE. Leaf having saw-toothed edges with teeth angled toward tip. See *crenate* and *dentate.*

SHOOT. The year's new growth at the end of a *twig* or from a branch, beginning when a shoot-containing *bud* opens.

SIDEWALK BASIN. The cutaway sidewalk area filled with soil to receive a tree.

SIMPLE LEAF. A leaf of just one blade on a *leafstalk,* not branched as is a *compound leaf.*

SINUS. The recess between two *lobes* of a leaf.

SPATULATE. Shaped like a spatula, as a leaf with broad, rounded tip and narrow base.

SPECIES (SINGULAR AND PLURAL). In botanical classification, the specific plant type, such as Norway maple or Colorado spruce. Individuals of a species are alike in traits and different from individuals of other species. They interbreed to produce similar individuals. See *genus* and *variety.* See "Trees: A Briefing" for discussion.

STAMEN. The male organ of a flower, usually consisting of a pollen-bearing *anther* on a *filament* stalk.

STAMINATE. Flower having *stamen,* but no *pistil.* A male flower. See *pistillate.*

STIGMA. Part of the *pistil* that receives *pollen,* often sits atop *style.*

STIPULES. Only on some species, the small leaflike appendages near base of *leafstalk.* See "Weeping Willow" profile.

STOMA (plural, STOMATA). One of thousands of breathing pores on the leaf surface (usually bottom), opened and closed by "guard cells." Allows entry of carbon dioxide for *photosynthesis* and release of oxygen and water.

STREET TREE. A *species, variety,* or *cultivated variety* chosen by a municipality for street use, based on such traits as easy transplantability, fast growth, *hardiness,* disease and pest resistance, compact *crown* and roots, safe branching habits, nonmessy fruits, reasonable life expectancy, and ornamental features. Species with undesirable traits may be banned by community ordinance.

STROBILI (singular, STROBILE or STROBILUS). Male and female reproductive structures of *conifers.* Conical, with overlapping *scales* or *bracts.*

STYLE. In the female flower, the stalk-like structure of the *pistil,* connecting the pollen-receiving *stigma* to the *ovary.*

SUCKERS. New ascending sprouts from the roots or lower trunk of a tree. An undesirable trait for street trees. Some species can reproduce *clones* of themselves by "suckering."

SURFACE ROOTS. Roots spreading through topsoil near ground surface. Often the greatest mass of a tree's roots.

TAPROOT. A tree's first root, driven straight down, later the strong central root.

TERMINAL BUD. Bud at the tip of a *twig* or *shoot,* where it can extend the tree's growth.

TOMENTOSE. Densely hairy, woolly.

TREE PIT. Planting pit for a street tree, often four feet by four feet or three feet by four feet, sometimes covered with a metal "tree grate." See also *sidewalk basin.*

TWIG. Generally, the last division of a branch, growing off a *branchlet.* Sometimes (but not in this guide) specified as only the current year's growth, or *shoot.*

URBAN FOREST. All the trees of an urban (or dense suburban) area, considered within the ecosystem that includes other vegetation and such environmental factors as urban structures, pollution, and people.

URBAN FORESTER. A professional steward of an urban forest, a forestry specialist, often serving in a municipal post.

VARIETY. Within a *species,* a group differing in consistent but minor ways from the rest of that species, and reproducing those differences in offspring. See also *cultivated variety.* "Trees: A Briefing" discusses species and variety, with examples.

VENATION. The pattern of leaf veins. Some patterns are named, as "arcuate" (following the curve of the leaf edges) and are helpful in identification.

WHORLED. An arrangement of three or more leaves grouped around the twig. Compare with *opposite* and *alternate* arrangements. See "Catalpa" profile.

WOOD. See *xylem* and, for discussion, "Trees: A Briefing."

X. Symbol used in scientific nomenclature for crossbreed or hybrid. *Magnolia denudata* x *Magnolia lilliflora* is a cross between two species, yielding *Magnolia* x *soulangiana* (saucer magnolia).

XYLEM. The tree's hard inner tissue or "wood" present from roots through twigs, produced by the *cambium* layer and consisting of cellulose-walled cells strengthened by the substance lignin. Old xylem is *heartwood,* newer xylem *sapwood,* which conducts water from the roots to the leaves.

ZONE. See *hardiness zones.*

Selected Sources and Further Reading

The following sources are among those consulted by the author. Items with an asterisk are recommended to new observers as well as more experienced ones. Many older, out-of-print books are still useful and can be found in library collections. Sources pertaining mainly to tree planting and care appear in the "Tree Wellness" section.

BOOKS

Encyclopedic Reference/History

*Collingwood, G. H., and Warren D. Brush. *Knowing Your Trees*. Rev. ed. Rev. and ed. Devereux Butcher. Washington, D.C.: American Forestry Association, 1984.

Edlin, Herbert, Maurice Nimmo, et al. *The Illustrated Encyclopedia of Trees: Timbers and Forests of the World*. London, New York: Salamander Books, published by Harmony Books, 1978.

Farb, Peter, et al. *The Forest*. Rev. ed. Life Nature Library. New York: Time-Life Books, 1967.

*Johnson, Hugh. *Hugh Johnson's Encyclopedia of Trees*. New York: W. H. Smith/Gallery Books, 1984.

Little, Charles E. *The Dying of the Trees*. New York: Viking, 1995.

Marshall Cavendish Illustrated Encyclopedia of Plants and Earth Sciences. 10 vols. Ed. David M. Moore. New York: Marshall Cavendish, 1988.

Padilla, Victoria. *Southern California Gardens: An Illustrated History*. Berkeley: University of California Press, 1961.

*Platt, Rutherford. *1001 Questions Answered About Trees*. New York: Dover, 1992.

Spongberg, Stephen A. *A Reunion of Trees: The Discovery of Exotic Plants and Their Introduction into North American and European Landscapes.* Cambridge, Mass.: Harvard University Press, 1990.

Lore/Natural History/Essays

America's Fascinating Indian Heritage. Ed. James A. Maxwell. Pleasantville, N.Y.: Reader's Digest, 1978.

Boulger, G. S. *Familiar Trees.* London: Cassell, 1907.

Corner, E. J. H. *The Life of Plants.* New York: New American Library, 1968.

Frazer, Sir James George. *The Golden Bough.* New York: Macmillan, 1935.

Garber, Steven D. *The Urban Naturalist.* Wiley Science Editions. New York: Wiley, 1987.

Heath, Francis George. *Tree Lore.* London: Charles H. Kelly, 1912.

*Heinrich, Bernard. *The Trees in My Forest.* Cliff Street/HarperCollins, 1997.

James, N. D. G. *A Book of Trees: An Anthology of Trees and Woodlands.* Tring (England), The Royal Forestry Society of England, Wales, and Northern Ireland, 1973.

Lembke, Janet. *Shake the 'Simmons Down and Other Adventures in the Lives of Trees.* New York: Lyons & Burford, 1996.

Mitchell, Henry. *One Man's Garden.* Boston: Houghton Mifflin, 1992.

Nardi, James B. *Once Upon a Tree: Life from Treetop to Root Tips.* Ames: Iowa State University Press, 1993.

*Pakenham, Thomas. *Meetings with Remarkable Trees.* New York: Random House, 1997.

*Peattie, Donald Culross. *A Natural History of Trees of Eastern and Central North America.* Illus. Paul Landacre. Boston: Houghton Mifflin, 1991 (1st ed., 1948).

*———. *A Natural History of Western Trees.* Illus. Paul Landacre. New York: Bonanza Books (Crown), 1953.

Phythian, J. Ernest. *Trees in Nature, Myth, and Art.* Philadelphia: Jacobs & Co., n.d.

*Platt, Rutherford. *Discover American Trees.* New York: Dodd, Mead, 1968.

Porteous, Alexander. *Forest Folklore, Mythology, and Romance.* London: Allen & Unwin, 1929.

Powell, Claire. *The Meaning of Flowers.* Boston: Shambhala, 1979.

Randall, Charles Edgar, and Henry Clepper. *Famous and Historic Trees.* Washington, D.C.: American Forestry Association, 1976.

Thoreau, Henry David. *Writings of Henry David Thoreau.* 20 vols. Boston: Houghton Mifflin, 1906.

*Vitale, Alice Thomas. *Leaves in Myth, Magic, and Medicine.* New York: Stewart, Tabori & Chang, 1997.

Wilson, Ernest H. *The Romance of Our Trees.* New York: Doubleday, 1920.

Identification/Description, Broad-based

*Brockman, Frank C. *Trees of North America.* Illus. Rebecca Merrilees. Golden Press/Western Publishing, 1979.

Canada. Department of Forestry. *Native Trees of Canada.* Bulletin 61, 6th ed. Ottawa: Roger Duhamel, 1963.

*Coombes, Allen J. *Trees.* Photog. Matthew Ward. Eyewitness Handbooks. Dorling Kindersley, 1992.

*Farrar, John Laird. *Trees of the Northern United States and Canada.* Iowa State University Press, 1995.

*Grimm, William Carey. *The Illustrated Book of Trees: The Comprehensive Guide to More Than 250 Trees of Eastern North America.* Stackpole, 1983.

*Harlow, William M. *Trees of the Eastern and Central United States and Canada.* Dover, 1957.

*Hough, Romeyn Beck. *The Trees of the Northern States and Canada East of the Rocky Mountains.* Lowville, N.Y.: published by the author, 1907.

*Little, Elbert L. *The Audubon Society Field Guide to North American Trees. Eastern Region.* New York: Knopf, 1980.

*———. *National Audubon Society Field Guide to North American Trees. Western Region.* New York: Knopf, 1980.

*Mitchell, Alan. *The Trees of North America.* Illus. David More. New York: Facts on File, 1987.

Nature Study Guild (Berkeley, Calif.). Pocket booklets for tree identification, including *Master Tree Finder,* May Theilgaard Watts, 1963, and *Rocky Mountain Tree Finder,* Tim Watts, 1972.

*Phillips, Roger. *The Random House Book of Trees of North America and Europe.* New York: Random House, 1978.

Polunin, Oleg. *Trees and Bushes of Europe.* London: Oxford University Press, 1976.

Rogers, Julia Ellen. *Trees.* The Nature Library. Garden City, N.Y.: Doubleday, Doran, 1926.

*Symonds, George W. D. *The Tree Identification Book: A New Method for* *the Practical Identification and Recognition of Trees.* New York: M. Barrows, 1958.

Viertel, Arthur. *Trees, Shrubs, and Vines: A Pictorial Guide to the Ornamental Woody Plants of the Northeastern United States, Exclusive of Conifers.* Syracuse, N.Y.: State University College of Forestry, 1959.

Regional/City Guides

Arizona Native Plant Society. Urban Landscape Committee. *Desert Trees.* Tucson: Arizona Native Plant Society, 1990.

*Choukas-Bradley, Melanie, and Polly Alexander. *City of Trees: The Complete Field Guide to the Trees of Washington, D.C.* Rev. ed. Baltimore: Johns Hopkins University Press, 1987.

Graves, Arthur Harmount. *Illustrated Guide to Trees and Shrubs: A Handbook of the Woody Plants of Northeastern United States and Adjacent Canada.* Rev. ed. New York: Dover, 1992.

*Green, Charlotte Hilton. *Trees of the South.* Chapel Hill: University of North Carolina, 1939.

*Jacobsen, Arthur Lee. *Trees of Seattle: The Complete Tree-finder's Guide to the City's 740 Varieties.* Seattle: Sasquatch Books, 1989.

Metcalf, Wodbridge. *Introduced Trees of California.* Berkeley: University of California Press, 1968.

Mohlenbrock, Robert H. *Forest Trees of Illinois.* 4th ed. Springfield, Ill.: Illinois Department of Conservation, 1983.

Muller, Katherine. *Trees of Santa Barbara.* Santa Barbara [Calif.] Botanic Garden, 1974.

*Petrides, George A. *A Field Guide to Western Trees: Western United States and Canada.* Illus. Olivia Petrides. Peterson Field Guides. Boston: Houghton Mifflin, 1992.

*Vines, Robert A. *Trees of East Texas.* Austin: University of Texas Press, 1977.

Specific Types/Uses

Callaway, Dorothy J. *The World of Magnolias.* Portland: Timber Press, 1994.

Coon, Nelson. *The Dictionary of Useful Plants.* Emmaus, Pa.: Rodale, 1974.

Egolf, Donald R., and Anne O. Andrick. *The Lagerstroemia Handbook/Checklist: A Guide to Crapemyrtle Cultivars.* Las Cruces, N.M.: American Association of Botanical Gardens and Arboreta, 1978.

Foster, Steven, and James A. Duke. *Eastern/Central Medicinal Plants.* Peterson Field Guides. Boston: Houghton Mifflin, 1990.

Handbook on Conifers. (Theme issue of *Plants and Gardens,* 25:2, Summer 1969.) Ed. Henry Teuscher. Brooklyn [N.Y.] Botanic Garden.

Kelly, Stan. *Forty Australian Eucalypts in Color.* "Drawn and described by Stan Kelly." Sydney, Australia: Dymock's Book Arcade, 1949.

*McCurrach, James C. *Palms of the World.* New York: Harper, 1960.

*Mirov, Nicholas T., and Jean Hasbrouck. *The Story of Pines.* Bloomington: Indiana University Press, 1976.

van Gelderen, D. M., P. C. de Jong, and J. J. Oterdoom. *Maples of the World.* Portland, Oreg.: Timber Press, 1994.

Gardening/Landscaping Guides

Bennett, Jennifer. *The Harrowsmith Book of Fruit Trees.* Charlotte, Vt.: Camden House, 1991.

Crockett, James Underwood. *Trees.* New York: Time-Life Books, 1972.

*Dirr, Michael A. *Dirr's Hardy Trees and Shrubs: An Illustrated Encyclopedia.* Portland, Oreg.: Timber Press, 1997.

———. *Manual of Woody Landscape Plants: Their Identification, Ornamental Characteristics, Culture, Propagation, and Uses.* 5th ed. Champaign, Ill.: Stipes, 1998.

Garden Club of America. Horticultural Committee. *Plants That Merit Attention: Trees.* Ed. Nancy Peterson Brewster. Portland, Oreg.: Timber Press, 1984.

The Hillier Gardener's Guide to Trees and Shrubs. Ed. John Kelly. Pleasantville, N.Y.: Reader's Digest, 1997.

*Jacobsen, Arthur Lee. *North American Landscape Trees.* Berkeley, Calif.: Ten Speed Press, 1996.

Shrubs and Trees. The Best of Fine Gardening. Newton, Conn.: Taunton, 1993.

Snyder, Leon. *Trees and Shrubs for Northern Gardens.* Minneapolis: University of Minnesota, 1980.

*Sternberg, Guy, and Jim Wilson. *Landscaping with Native Trees: The Northeast, Midwest, Midsouth, & Southeast Edition.* Shelburne, Vt.: Chapters, 1995.

Taylor, Norman. *Taylor's Guide to Trees.* Taylor's Guides to Gardening. Boston: Houghton Mifflin, 1988.

Tripp, Kim E., and J. C. Raulston. *The Year in Trees: Superb Woody Plants for Four-Season Gardens.* Portland, Oreg.: Timber Press, 1995.

Urban Tree Selection/Strategy

Arnold, Henry F. *Trees in Urban Design.* 2nd ed. New York: Van Nostrand Reinhold, 1992.

Bassuk, Nina L. *Recommended Urban Trees.* [Booklet, unbound.] Ithaca, N.Y.: Cornell University Urban Horticultural Institute, n.d.

Duerksen, Christopher J., with Suzanne Richman. *Tree Conservation Ordinances: Land-Use Regulations Go Green.* Chicago: American Planning Association and Scenic America, 1993.

*Friends of the Urban Forest. *Trees for San Francisco: A Guide to Street-Tree Planting and Care.* 2nd ed. San Francisco: Friends of the Urban Forest, 1995.

Koller, Gary L., and Michael A. Dirr. *Street Trees for Home and Municipal Landscapes.* Jamaica Plain, Mass. Reprint from *Arnoldia,* 39:3, May/June 1979.

Matheny, Nelda, and James R. Clark. *A Photographic Guide to the Evaluation of Hazard Trees in Urban Areas.* Urbana, Ill.: International Society of Arboriculture, 1991.

Moll, Gary, and Stanley Young. *Growing Greener Cities: A Tree-Planting Handbook.* Venice, Calif.: Living Planet Press, 1992.

Nature in Cities: The Natural Environment in the Design and Development of Urban Green Space. Ed. Ian C. Laurie. New York: Wiley, 1979.

Petit, Jack, Debra L. Bassert, and Cheryl Kollin. *Building Greener Neighborhoods: Trees as Part of the Plan.* Washington, D.C.: American Forests and National Association of Home Builders, 1995.

Phillips, Leonard E. *Urban Trees: A Guide for Selection, Maintenance, and Master Planning.* New York: McGraw-Hill, 1993.

*Street Tree Seminar, Inc. *Street Trees Recommended for Southern California.* Rev. ed. Anaheim, Calif.: Street Tree Seminar, Inc., n.d.

*TreePeople [Los Angeles]. *Smart Planting for the New Urban Forest: A Guide to Planting Trees Around Your Home.* Los Angeles Department of Water and Power/TreePeople, n.d.

*U.S. Department of Agriculture. Forest Service. Municipal Tree Restoration Program. *Street Tree Factsheets.* Henry D. Gerhold et al., eds. University Park, Pa.: USDA. Pennsylvania State University, 1993.

MAGAZINES/JOURNALS

American Forests. Bimonthly. Washington, D.C.: American Forests.

American Forests special issue: "National Register of Big Trees." (Yearly in spring issue, also issued separately.) Washington, D.C.: American Forests.

American Horticulturalist. Monthly. Alexandria, Va.: American Horticultural Society.

Arbor Age. Monthly. Van Nuys, Calif.: Arbor Age.

Arboricultural Journal. Quarterly. Hants (England): British Arboricultural Association.

Arnoldia. Quarterly. Jamaica Plain, Mass.: Arnold Arboretum.

Journal of Arboriculture. Monthly. Savoy, Ill.: International Society of Arboriculture.

Journal of Forestry. Monthly. Bethesda, Md.: Society of American Foresters.

Missouri Botanical Garden Bulletin. Frequency varies. St. Louis: Missouri Botanical Garden.

Morton Arboretum Quarterly. Lisle, Ill.: The Morton Arboretum.

Tree Care. Quarterly. Chicago: Illinois Arborists Association.

Trees Magazine. Bimonthly. Olmstead Falls, Ohio: Society of Municipal Arborists.

Urban Forests. Bimonthly. Washington, D.C.: American Forests.

COMPACT DISC

University of Florida and U.S. Department of Agriculture. *Southern Trees: An Expert System for Selecting Trees.* Edward F. Gilman et al., eds. USDA Forest Service, Southern Region, n.d.

INTERNET SITES

The Internet's World Wide Web offers an astounding number of tree-related sites, rich in images and updated information. Below is a selection of the sites researched for this guide. All are worth exploring, but items with an asterisk are especially good for new tree enthusiasts. Sites devoted mainly to tree care appear in the "Tree Wellness" section.

Site addresses usually require an **http://www** prefix. Internet addresses change often, but sites can usually be found by Web searches using keywords from the site's title or sponsor, e.g., "**Ohio State University Plants**." Addresses may also be truncated from the right until a host directory is reached, e.g., hcs.ohio-state.edu/~~plants/html~~

hcs.ohio-state.edu/plants/html
*Ohio State University. *Plants of Horticulture.* Excellent tree and tree-part images (some from Virginia Polytechnic Institute), many with detailed species descriptions.

floridata.com
*Floridata. *Plant Encyclopedia.* Leads to regional trees and palms, with photos.

bluehen.ags.udel.edu/udbg/trees
**University of Delaware Botanic Gardens.* Brief data, clear images for selected trees. Audio pronunciation of scientific names.

bcadventure.com/adventure/wilderness/forest/index.html
British Columbia Adventure Network. Includes illustrated descriptions of British Columbia's forest trees.

vg.com/
Virtual Garden. "Mother of all gardening sites." Includes *Time-Life Plant Encyclopedia* with tree descriptions and basic care advice. Links with garden forums and related sites.

orst.edu/dept/ldplants/index/htm#aehi226
Oregon State University, Horticulture, and Oregon Master Garden Association. Landscape Plants. Some 450 plants, mostly woody, with fine images. Compiled for a botany course.

uah.edu/admin/Fac/grounds/
University of Alabama/Huntsville. Campus Tree Section. Display of more than 275 campus trees. Good data, select images.

washington.edu/home/treetour/
University of Washington. Brockman Memorial Tree Tour. Notes and images for some 480 tree types on this lovely Seattle-area campus.

domtar.com/arbe/english/
Domtar and Comission Scholaire de la Seigneurie-des-Milles-Îles (Quebec). Trees in North America. Descriptions of trees and images of tree parts. Clickable North American map for regional trees. French or English.

galaxy.cs.berkeley.edu/photos/flora/
Calphotos. California Plants and Habitats. Searchable base of 20,000 native and naturalized California plants, including trees. Photos, basic data, distribution.

fs.fed.us/database/feis/plants/tree/
U.S. Department of Agriculture, Forest Service, Intermountain Research Station, Intermountain Fire Sciences Lab., Missoula, Mont. *The Fire Effects Information System* [database]. Abundant information on native and naturalized tree species from official source. Text only.

newton.dep.anl.gov/natbltn/natbltn.htm
Forest Preserve District of Cook County, Ill. *Nature Bulletins.* Charming, informative essays.

msue.msu.edu/msue/imp/modb1/masterb1.html
Michigan State University Extension. *Urban Forestry Bibliography.* Citations only. Massive.

greenindustry.com/search/aa.asp
Searchable archive of *Arbor Age* magazine. Excellent tree-of-the-month articles.

botanical.com
A Modern Herbal, by Mrs. M. Grieve. Text of the classic 1931 work including medicinal, culinary, cosmetic, commercial, cultural, and folkloric information on trees.

wisc.edu/botit/dendrology/
University of Wisconsin/Madison. *Woody Plant Collection.* Ambitious collection of images compiled for a course.

bbg.org/nymf/encyclopedia/
Brooklyn Botanic Garden. *Metropolitan Plant Encyclopedia.* Distribution maps, bibliography, other data on New York–area trees.

guiaverde.com/arboles/
José Manuel Sánchez de Lorenzo Cáceres. *Los Arboles en España. (The Trees in Spain.)* A fine Spanish site with such pictorial offerings as bark of 160 species.

aridzonetrees.com/
Arid Zone Trees. *Arid Zone Tree Gallery.* Photos and basic data on desert-region trees cultivated by AZT landscape architects. Acacia, mesquite, several others.

ag.uiuc.edu/~forestry/guide/
University of Illinois Department of Forestry. *Urban and Community Forestry Resource Material Guide.* Sources described include books, software, consultants, and education.

british-trees.com/
Links to a slew of exceptional tree sites in northern Europe, including the Royal Botanical Garden site.

ORGANIZATIONS/
INSTITUTIONS/
OPPORTUNITIES

Here we represent some of the many groups and institutions whose activities relate to urban trees and forestry.* Most offer materials or services for nonspecialists. See note in "Internet Sites" section on changes in Web addresses. For professional tree-care associations, see "Tree Wellness" section.

American Association of Botanical Gardens and Arboreta, Inc.
351 Longwood Road
Kennett Square, PA 19348
http://www.aabga.org
Membership organization serving North American public botanical gardens and arboreta. Publishes *The Public Garden* journal and a directory of internships and summer jobs at public gardens. Website links to institutional members.

American Forests
P.O. Box 2000
Washington, DC 20013
(202) 955-4500
http://www.amfor.org
Founded in 1875, a leading force in the protection, management, and enjoyment of urban and rural forest resources. Welcomes all tree enthusiasts. Sponsors National Register of Big Trees, Famous & Historic Trees (see sidebar on page 398), National Urban Forest Council (see below), and Global ReLeaf (see below). Publishes *American Forests* magazine.

*Several entries are based, with permission, on a broader compilation by Patrick Weicherding for the University of Illinois Department of Forestry ("Urban and Community Forestry Resource Materials Guide," posted on the Internet at **http://www.ag.uiuc.edu/~forestry/guide**)

Plant Your Own Historic Tree—for Peanuts!

For about the price of dinner downtown, anyone can own and perpetuate a tree descended from such ancestors as George Washington's tulip poplar, Johnny Appleseed's apples, and Elvis Presley's Graceland sycamores.

Under the auspices of American Forests, a Famous & Historic Trees Program offers dozens of species cloned or seeded from illustrious American trees and some foreign stock (e.g., Napoleon's graveside weeping willow). Planting kits ($35 in year 2000), contain the sapling tree, instructions, growing aids, and a certificate.

Tree profiles in this book note several of the historic scions. For a full and very engaging catalog, contact Famous & Historic Old Trees, 8701 Old Kings Road, Jacksonville, FL 32219. Tel.: (800) 320-8733; E-mail: historictr@aol.com.

American Horticultural Society
7931 East Boulevard Drive
Alexandria, VA 22308
(703) 768-5700
http://www.ahs.org/
Serves American gardeners through membership program. Gardening information hotline. Publishes *American Gardener* magazine.

Elm Research Institute
Elm Street
Westmoreland, NH 03467
(603) 358-6198
http://www.forelms.org/
Organized in 1967. Advises on elms and Dutch elm disease, funds research, supports broad plantings of American Liberty elms (*Ulmus americana libertas*). Publishes *The ERI News* newsletter.

Friends of Tree City USA
National Arbor Day Foundation (see below)
Organization of interested citizens. For nominal dues/donation, members get bulletins on community forestry topics.

Global ReLeaf 2000
American Forests (see above)
American Forests' national tree-planting campaign to restore and improve critical urban and rural forests. Plants millions of trees from modest donations. Offers curriculum/lessons guide for educators.

Awards competitive grants to ReLeaf groups nationwide.

International Palm Society
POB 1897
Lawrence, KS 66044
(785) 843-1274 (fax)
http://www.palms.org/
Membership group and resource center devoted to palms. Publishes the journal *Palms.*

Metropolitan Tree Improvement Alliance
c/o Thomas G. Ranney, Professor, Horticultural Science
Mountain Horticultural Crops Research & Extension Center
North Carolina State University
2016 Fanning Bridge Road
Fletcher, NC 28732
http://fletcher.ces.state.nc.us/
programs/nursery/metria
Professional organization dedicated to developing better trees for metropolitan and urban landscapes. Publishes *The Metrian* newsletter.

National Arbor Day Foundation
100 Arbor Avenue
Nebraska City, NE 68410
(402) 474-5655
http://www.arborday.org/
Educational organization dedicated to tree planting and conservation. Sponsors National Arbor Day (last Friday in April), promotes local Days. Also sponsors Tree City USA

(see below), Conservation Trees programs, and workshops. Publishes *Arbor Day News* booklets.

National Urban & Community Forestry Advisory Program
U.S. Department of Agriculture Forestry Service
20628 Diane Drive
Sonora, CA 95370
(209) 536-9201
http://www.treelink.org/connect/
orgs/nucfac/nfback.htm
Recommends policies that foster quality tree planting and maintenance, volunteer community programs, training, research, and business-citizen cooperation.

National Urban Forest Council
American Forests (see above)
Coalition of citizens and professionals for development and management of urban trees. Holds meetings in various U.S. cities. Publishes *Urban Forests* newsletter.

Society of American Foresters
5400 Grosvenor Lane
Bethesda, MD 20814
(301) 897-8720
http://www.safnet.org/index.html
Represents professional foresters. Publishes *Journal of Forestry* and *Forest Science.* Educational and research activities. Coordinates working groups, including one on urban forestry.

Tree Canada Foundation
220 Laurier Avenue West,
Suite 1550
Ottawa, Ontario, K1P 5Z9
(613) 567-5545
http://www.treecanada.ca/
Encourages Canadians to plant and
care for trees to improve urban and
rural environments. Education,
technical assistance, resources, and
financial support through working
partnerships.

Tree City USA
National Arbor Day Foundation (see
above)
For the honor of being an official
Tree City, a municipality must establish a Tree Board or Department,
enact a city tree ordinance, develop
an annual Community Forestry
Program, and decree an Arbor Day
observance. A program of National
Arbor Day Foundation (see above)
with U.S. Forest Service and National Association of State Foresters.
Applications from: National Arbor
Day Foundation or state foresters.
Tree City USA Bulletin newsletter
advises on urban tree programs.

COMMUNITY TREE GROUPS

Friends of the Urban Forest
Presidio of San Francisco,
Bldg. # 1007
POB 29456
San Francisco, CA 94129
(415) 543-5000
http://www.fuf.net/default.htm
San Francisco's urban forestry citizen's
group, founded in 1981. Financial,
technical, and practical assistance to
individuals and neighborhood groups
who want to plant and care for trees.
Participants have planted over 25
percent of the city's total street trees.

Friends of Trees
2831 NE Martin Luther King Boulevard
Portland, OR 97212
(503) 282-8846
**http://www.teleport.com/~fot/index
.shtml**
Builds partnerships to plant, care for,
and preserve urban trees. Coordinates
neighborhood street-tree projects,
school and natural-area plantings.
Educational programs. Distributes
trees and seedlings for yard plantings.

TreeFolks
POB 704
Austin, TX, 78767
(512) 443-LEAF
http://www.treefolks.org/
Helps renew Austin's urban forest
and ecosystem through public tree

plantings and education. Promotes cooperation between businesses, schools, government, citizen's groups, and individuals.

TreeKeepers
Openlands Project
25 E. Washington Street, Suite 160
Chicago, IL 60602
(312) 427-4256
Teaches nonprofessionals tree-care basics in seven-week course. Graduates are asked to give 36 hours during a year to community tree-care projects.

TreePeople
12601 Mulholland Drive
Beverly Hills, CA 90210
(818) 753-4600
http://www.treepeople.org/
Started in 1973 by 15-year-old Andy Lipkis, this is a model tree-action group inspiring the Los Angeles community to plant and maintain millions of trees. Strong on youth participation, welcomes all ages.

Trees New York
51 Chambers Street, Suite 1412A
New York, NY 10007
(212) 227-1887
http://www.treesny.com/index.html
Plants, preserves, and protects New York's street trees "as a grass roots, people-oriented organization dedicated to community self-help." Active in all five boroughs and surrounding region. Founded in the

seventies, carries out support services through education, training, publishing, advocacy.

ARBORETUMS AND BOTANICAL GARDENS

The Arboretum at Flagstaff
4001 W. Woody Road
Flagstaff, AZ 86001
(520) 774-1442
http://www.thearb.org/
Elevation 7,150 feet, encompasses 200 acres of ponderosa pine forest near Flagstaff. Educates visitors to plants and plant communities of the Colorado Plateau.

The Arboretum of Los Angeles County
301 N. Baldwin Avenue
Arcadia, CA 91007
(626) 821-3222
http://www.aabga.org/member-pages/losangeles/
Near Pasadena on 127 acres. Arranged primarily by world origins, includes such trees as acacia, eucalyptus, magnolia, and melaleuca. Also, tropical forest and palm sections, native Engelmann oak grove.

The Arnold Arboretum
c/o Harvard University
125 Arborway
Jamaica Plain, MA 02130
(617) 524-1718
http://www.arboretum.harvard.edu/

Boston's venerable tree-collecting, research, and educational institution founded in 1872, part of Harvard University. Manages collection of hardy trees, shrubs, and vines on 265 acres. Designed by first director, Charles Sprague Sargent, with landscape architect Frederick Law Olmsted. Publishes *Arnoldia* journal.

Brooklyn Botanic Garden
1000 Washington Avenue
Brooklyn, NY 11225
(718) 623-7200
http://www.bbg.org/
More than 12,000 kinds of plants on 52 acres. The long-range New York Metropolitan Flora Project is cataloging plant diversity of the New York–New Jersey–Connecticut area and studying effects of human settlement.

Dawes Arboretum
7770 Jacksontown Road SE
Newark, Ohio 43056
(740) 323-2355
http://www.dawesarb.org/
Founded in 1929 and located near Columbus, the Dawes Arboretum includes 1,149 acres of plant collections and natural areas offering educational experience year-round.

The Holden Arboretum
9500 Sperry Road
Kirtland, OH 44094
(440) 946-4400
http://www.holdenarb.org/

Largest U.S. arboretum, with more than 3,100 acres near Cleveland. Established 1931, focuses on woody plants of northeastern Ohio, which include a vast array. Education, research, and conservation activities.

Morris Arboretum of the University of Pennsylvania
9414 Meadowbrook Avenue
Philadelphia, PA 19118
(215) 247-5777
http://www.upenn.edu/morris/
Official arboretum of Pennsylvania. Its Living Collection, on 166 acres, contains some 9,000 labeled plants, primarily trees and shrubs, from wide range. Includes historic Asian plants collected in China by E. H. Wilson and some 42 record-size trees of the Delaware Valley.

The Morton Arboretum
Route 53
Lisle, IL 60532
(708) 968-0074
http://www.mortonarb.org/
One of the leading U.S. institutions devoted to the growth and nurture of woody plants and maintenance of a healthy environment. An education and research center where scientists study urban forestry, tree improvement, ecological restoration, and landscape management and conservation. Visitor mecca featuring 1,700 cultivated and natural acres near Chicago. Publishes *The Morton*

Arboretum Quarterly and *Seasons* newsletter.

The New York Botanical Garden
200th Street and Kazimiroff Boulevard
Bronx, NY 10458
(718) 817-8700
http://www.nybg.org
A National Historic Landmark, the 250-acre grounds feature dramatic landscapes and a 40-acre tract of the original forest that once covered New York City. Collections include flowering trees, conifers, and cherry trees. Largest publisher among botanical gardens.

Shaw Arboretum
Missouri Botanical Gardens
4344 Shaw Boulevard
St. Louis, MO 63110
(314) 577-9400
http://www.mobot.org/MOBOT/
arboretum/guide.html

An extension of the Missouri Botanical Gardens, Shaw Arboretum includes 2,500 acres of Ozark landscape and managed plant collections. Near St. Louis in Gray Summit, Mo. Education, research, public programs. Founded in 1925, when St. Louis coal smoke threatened garden plant collections.

United States National Arboretum
3501 New York Avenue, NE
Washington, DC 20002-1958
(202) 245-2726
http://www.ars-grin.gov/na/index.
html
Research, education, conservation, and display. The 444-acre campus in the capital contains an array of gardens, collections, and monuments set among native stands of eastern deciduous trees.

Tree Wellness:
Notes and Sources

Why touch on tree planting and care in a field guide? Because well-planted, well-tended specimens are not the only trees urban observers will see in their wanderings. They are likely to encounter at least as many casualties of neglect and abuse. Knowing why certain of these casualties happen, and how they might have been averted, gives insight into the urban forest and its future.

Observers will also come across planting and maintenance activities and will want some sense of what is going on. They may want to alert city foresters or local agricultural extension staff to serious-looking diseases and infestations.

For urbanites who would plant and raise their own trees, either on private property or in cooperation with community agencies, we highlight the major considerations here and point to information resources. Tree rearing is certainly accessible to amateurs—especially those who plant appropriate trees from good nursery stock and commit themselves to the "five years it takes to plant a tree" with follow-up. But difficult species, abnormalities, disease prevention and treatment, site alterations, and hazard trees quickly take on complexities calling for professional intervention—which is readily available.

According to many experts, the simplest advice to tree planters is this: Invest in a high-quality tree from a trusted nursery or garden center; follow the dealer's instructions for selection, planting, and maintenance of the tree; and for big problems or big trees, contact municipal, county, or state forestry agencies, cooperative extension agencies, botanical garden and arboretum clinics, or—not least of all—tree-care specialists certified by the International Society of Arboriculture (see below).

In *The Urban Tree Book* profiles, we point out many of the daunting ailments plaguing our trees. Often, we cite the best environmental conditions for a species. For highly cultivated trees, such as crabapples, we list some of the most promising commercial selections for planters. These beginnings, with the notes and sources below, could be your link from caring about, to helping care for, the trees around you.

TROUBLE IN RIVER CITY

The cultivation of forest trees for cities is one of those wonders that rarely make headlines. But think what it takes to keep forest blood flowing in the big towns.

Like Tarzan transplanted from the jungle (but with no Jane for company), most tree species are out of their element in the urban scene. Between pollutants, drought, compacted soil, poor drainage, salt spray, bugs, dogs, heat, construction, vibrations, vandalism, and opportunistic diseases, many trees simply give up the ghost.

Forest species have developed their genetic defense codes for survival in the forest, not downtown. In their natural habitats, tree types often grow in groups. They enjoy the group's protective mass and its systems as well as cooperative deals with other tree species and such organisms as certain fungi. Not that life in the forest is all peaches. There, many a tree is shut out from the sunlight, living as a runt in the lower canopy. Insect, bacterial, and destructive fungal attacks come wave after wave. Defense mechanisms can't always keep up.

But in the city a tree is usually on its own, without its naturally associated species, and genetically misdirected. It is lucky just to sit in soil with the acid-alkaline balance it needs. At worst, it quickly fries to death in such hot spots as parking lots. At best, it enjoys a partly sunny spot and finds the resources to manage urban stress, but usually not for its natural life span. Many species that can live more than a century in their forests average some 32 years in cities— and only 7 years in the heart of town. Out of every five trees planted, four fail to live out a happy city life.

Among the happier city trees are certain hardy regional natives, used to the local climate, soils, diseases, and pests. "Pioneer" trees such as aspens, first to repopulate burned or cleared forests, can handle the exposure of city streets but not always other stresses. Often a non-native species (such as Norway maple in the United States) is found to be as good as or even better than the local trees (such as sugar maple) for city life.

Crossbreeding between compatible species frequently strengthens the offspring's resistance to its attackers, an effect called "hybrid vigor." Like nature itself, tree cultivators have constantly tried out new crossbreeds, many of which have led to rugged trees for cities. The London planetree, saucer magnolia, and 'Prairifire' crabapple are such urban-tough hybrids.

TREE SELECTION

Urban tree wellness begins with selecting trees that fit the planters' goals *and* the conditions of the particular setting. According to the International Society of Arboriculture (ISA), planting the wrong tree for the setting is the number-one cause of tree death outside the forests, more fatal than all the insect and disease-related problems combined.

What does proper tree selection involve? Checklists galore enumerate the factors, including those given below. These are considerations to be discussed with nursery staff or borne in mind as one researches nursery catalogs, comparison charts of ornamental trees, species available from the city, and other selection sources. Spending time to find the right match between planter's needs, tree characteristics, and planting site can save years of later frustration. No one but a city forester would face all the following variables, but every planter must weigh several:

Purpose. Is the tree for shade? Summer shade only? Windbreak or sound barrier? Soil retention? Seasonal or year-round attractiveness? Public enjoyment? Bird attraction? Street use? To block a view? Frame a view?

Site. Private? Public? Spacious park? Open plaza? On a lawn? Paved patio or rooftop? By traffic? Near cement or asphalt? By children? Curbside? Under utility wires? Near sewer and water lines? Confined space? Exposed space? Along a foundation? Among competing plants?

Climatic and environmental conditions. USDA "hardiness-zone" rating? High and low temperature extremes? Summer and winter mean temperatures? Dryness? Amount and frequency of moisture? Ice and snow accumulations? Winds? Fog? Sun exposure? Limited light? Salt air or winter salt spray? Ozone and other types of known air pollution?

Soil. Fast-draining sand? Slow-draining clay? Well-drained nutritious loam? Compacted (as are most city soils) or crumbly enough to admit air and allow root growth? Slightly acidic (favored by most trees) or too acidic or alkaline as measured by pH rating? (Agricultural extension services and some nurseries will test soils for a reasonable fee.)

Size and shape desired. Small (15 to 25 feet high), medium (25 to 35 feet), or large (over 35 feet) at maturity? Narrow and upright ("columnar," "fastigiate")? Wide-spreading? Globular? Pyramidal? Fountain- or vase-shaped? Weeping? Layered foliage? Angular, irregular?

Ornamental features desired. Deciduous (with seasonal leaf drop) or evergreen? Broad-leaved or needle-leaved? Conifer? Palm? Dainty leaves? Big tropical leaves? Dark, light, or multitoned leaves? Ornamental bark, such as peeling, flaking, shaggy, platy, or white? Big showy flowers? Clusters of small bright flowers? Early-blooming, late-blooming, or repeat-blooming? Colors? Fragrance? Fruit type, color, and size? Persistence of fruit into winter?

Growth rate and longevity. Slow-growing (tends to grow strong, live longer)? Fast-growing (can be brittle, short-lived)? Long-range value, such as a monument? Short-range function, such as temporary landscaping while slower trees rise?

Tree characteristics that would be a problem. Disease-prone? Easily infested? Exposed surface roots? Aggressive water-seeking roots? Sends up root suckers? Brittle wood and weak branch structure? Difficult to transplant? Blows over? Heavy leaf, flower, or fruit litter? Dense shade blocks undergrowth? Thorns? Unpleasant aromas? Fruit makes for bird droppings? Vigor or weaknesses call for high maintenance?

Fit and diversity. Relation of tree to surrounding trees and plants? Character of neighborhood? Balance of native and exotic species? Of dense foliage and light? Of leafing-out and blossoming times?

Urban foresters now plant neighborhoods with varied species, not just one that can catch a disease and get wiped out—as happened with the American elm.

Though it might seem impossible to match a tree to all preferences and site conditions, planters can usually come close thanks to the thousands of hardy cultivated varieties available.

PLANTING

Are you itching to plant your first tree, or tell your neighbor how to do it? Here's an outline of advice usually given by nurseries and other experts, pertaining mainly to broadleaf trees in moist temperate zones and some needle-leaf conifers.

Best time to plant. Usually spring or fall, or, with a rigorous watering program, during the summer.

Preparation. You have selected a tree type that fits your purposes and environmental conditions. It comes as a small, bare rootstock or larger tree in a container or root ball wrapped in burlap. (Planting from seeds or seedlings is another story, often tricky, and not for this outline.) The planting site has been chosen based on your needs and the tree's, including soil requirements. You have tested the soil for drainage (a test hole one foot wide by a foot deep and filled with water should drain within six hours). The planting hole has been predug (see below) or digging tools are cleaned and ready to go. Clean clippers and watering devices are at hand. You have someone to help you.

The hole. Dig a circular hole two to five times the width of the roots, root ball, or container, depending on species and available space. Three times the width is common. Depth should be one or two inches *shallower* than the root cluster; root balls tend to settle slightly. The trunk's flare at the top of the roots must remain above ground level. Keep the base of the hole firm, to support the tree. Slope the sides like a bowl and rough them up.

Placement. Lift the tree by the root cluster, not the trunk, and place it in the hole. Balled and burlapped roots need to have their twine or wire removed and the burlap folded back about halfway down the ball. The top wires of a wire basket should be cut away and the roots inspected for damage or twisting. Work steadily and briskly, before exposure to light and air damages fine roots. For bare rootstock, cleanly clip off any damaged roots. Spread the tree's roots in the hole just before filling and watering. For container plants, tap the container and gently remove the root and soil bundle. Container plants have little or no root loss, but a few roots may have circled or twisted under pressure and need to be straightened or cut. Such roots can girdle other roots and strangle them. A badly twisting root cluster is cause to return the tree to the dealer.

Root balls should be flat on top, revealing the trunk flare, and about 10 to 12 times the diameter of the trunk (measured at six inches above the flare). A root ball represents only a fraction of the roots that the tree had grown in the field; it will need plenty of loose, rich soil, water, and time to reestablish in its new setting.

Fill. Straighten the tree in the hole (view from several angles) as you begin backfilling. Use the good soil you removed (or amended with up to 25 percent compost if clayey). Fill a third of the hole and tamp the soil with your foot— moderately, not with flamenco fury. Some guides suggest firming with water only. Fill the rest of the hole in small increments, watering and tamping out any root-drying air pockets. Fill to the base of the trunk flare, no higher. Cover any exposed roots, but not the top of the (burlapped) root ball. Most tipsters advise against adding fertilizer at planting. Some guides suggest berming the top-soil into moatlike basins to hold water: perhaps an inner, doughnut-shaped moat close to the tree to soak the root ball, and an outer moat at the hole's circumference to irrigate spreading roots.

Mulching. Everyone recommends mulching—usually with bark or wood chips—to suppress weeds, hold moisture, protect against temperature extremes, and keep mowers away. Mulch to a two- to four-inch depth, but be sure to leave at least one to two inches clearance around the trunk. The "volcano" mound around a trunk can rot it and lead to diseases.

Support. Some trees need stabilization, especially in high-wind settings. Use a single stake for small new trees, two parallel stakes for trees two to four inches thick, and three or more cable guys for trees over four inches. Supports are best attached with hose or flat, wide straps, never anything that cuts into the bark. Allow some flex so that the tree develops its own stability system. Check supports frequently and remove them as soon as the tree seems stable, usually six months to one year from planting.

Protection. Standard paper tree wrap can be wrapped (from bottom up) around thin-barked trunks from fall to spring, providing some protection against winter sun scald and bark-borers; remove it when the weather warms (wrap can be used to protect against summer sun in hot climates). Antirodent or antideer cages are an option in the suburbs.

Follow-up. Transplanted trees suffer enormous stress. Immediate watering and a program of deep-penetrating irrigation are critical. San Francisco planters insert a deep-reaching watering tube into the soil basin. Such subterranean devices and drip systems are best. Sprinklers won't do the job, and overwatering drowns the roots. One check for dryness is to extract some soil one or two inches down over the root ball. If wet enough, it should form a ball when squeezed. If it crumbles—more watering, please. The best general prescription is five gallons per inch of trunk diameter twice a week, but there are great variations by species and region. Many southwestern trees are adapted to dry summers and cannot handle a regular dousing. Elsewhere, during droughts, most street trees will welcome an extra drink. Few get it.

MAINTENANCE

The five-year "planting" cycle includes regular deep watering, weeding at the trunk base, pruning for healthy growth, checks for damage, and alerts to tree specialists when pests or diseases seem serious. Some fertilizing may be advisable after the first year. Washing leaves with a water-hose spray can be helpful.

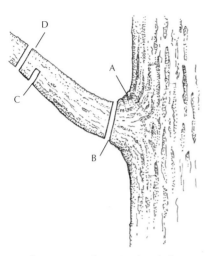

Correct pruning cut. The slight swelling (A) where branch meets trunk is called the "branch collar." Cutting just outside the collar at point (B) will allow specialized cells to form a liplike seal around the wound. If the collar is removed, as in a "flush" cut, the wound perimeter remains wide open to infection. Do not paint the cut. Do not leave a "stub" of branch beyond the collar. On large branches, before making cut (B), make an undercut (C) to prevent a tear, and then cut (D) to sever the branch.

Pruning. A well-selected, quality tree will usually have evenly spaced branches along the trunk and a clear, strong leader continuing up from the trunk. Junctures of branch and trunk should be strong, without seams or cracks, even if closely angled.

Pyramidal conifers do not like pruning, but new outer growth can be trimmed in spring. For other tree types, pruning is done to correct abnormalities, eliminate dead or diseased parts, thin a dense crown, and stave off structural problems. Trees are also shaped to allow for pedestrian or traffic clearance. Bad pruning is the cure that kills, opening the tree to infection.

Broken branches can be clipped off at planting. After a full season (but preferably not in fall), corrective pruning can eliminate crossing branches, "watershoots" that rise vertically from a branch, suckers from the trunk base, cramped branches, a competing leader shoot, and other problems. Thinning a dense crown can allow strong winds to pass through or help circulate light and air. Too much thinning can debilitate and eventually destroy the tree. One must know exactly what one is doing, for one's own safety and the tree's wellness. Would-be pruners need expert instruction, but even casual tree observers should know two pruning principles: (1) A tree should never be "topped"—sheared horizontally at the top of its crown—for any reason. If height or shape is a problem, nonmutilating trimming techniques are available. Another form of tree abuse is the shearing of a whole side, as unenlightened utility workers are wont to do. (2) Branches should be pruned just outside the "branch collar," not flush to the trunk. See the figure.

Fertilizing. Starting at least one season after planting, some trees may benefit from an annual fertilizing program. A local expert may be able to judge from leaf and soil samples what nutrients may be deficient. Requirements vary by species and site, but one rule is to *not* use fertilizer containing lawn herbicides. A mix that includes four parts nitrogen to one part each of phosphorus and potassium has been recommended for deciduous trees, and equal amounts of these three ingredients for needle-leaf evergreens. The idea is to distribute the fertilizer over the whole spread-out root system.

Disease and pest control. Here is perhaps the most difficult aspect of maintenance: diagnosis of disease and infestation problems, some of which are transient, some treatable, and some incurable. While certain species reliably get certain problems—cedar-hawthorn rust and bronze birch borer, for example— the range of possible ailments is staggering, and symptoms overlap. An amateur might try the most gentle remedies (soaps and oils, removal of dead and diseased wood) suggested by popular plant guides, and, these failing, call in the experts or bring them samples. Leaf diseases and leaf pests are usually the least catastrophic, except on needle-leaf evergreens. Most broad-leaved trees can survive an early defoliation in one year, but not repeated ones. (Late-summer defoliation, as with crabapples suffering apple scab, is less of a problem.) Diseases of the roots, stem, and conductive (vascular) systems are as grave as they are heartbreaking to see, because often by the time symptoms appear to the layperson, the problem is irreversible.

Urban tree growers who plant and maintain quality trees by the book, ideally in cooperation with a knowledgeable group, have a good chance of raising trees that hold their own over time. But when the situation merits professional intervention, the associations listed below stand ready to serve.

TREE-CARE PROFESSIONALS

Also, check the government pages of the local telephone directory under such headings as "Agriculture, Dept. of/Cooperative Extension Service," "Environment," "Forest," "Streets," and "Park," and the Yellow Pages under "Arborists" or "Tree Service" (look for "certified arborists" in the tree service listings). Other resources include local chapters of nurserymen associations (which do include women) and of landscape architect groups.

American Society of Consulting
Arborists
5130 W. 101st Circle
Westminster, CO 80030
(303) 466-2722
Referrals to practicing tree-care
professionals for diagnostic proce-
dures, tree inventories, tree evalua-
tions, general arboriculture, etc.
Publishes *Arboricultural Consultant*
newsletter.

International Society of
Arboriculture
POB 3129
Champaign, IL 61826
(217) 355-9411
isa-arbor.com
Affiliation of arborists "dedicated to
care and preservation of shade and
ornamental trees." Certifies
arborists. Publishes monthly *Journal
of Arboriculture* and various guides
and brochures for municipal
planters. Provides referrals to member arborists.

National Arborist Association
The Meeting Place Mall
Route 101, POB 1094
Amherst, NH 03031
(603) 673-3311
natlarb.com/
Trade association for management
needs of tree-service firms. Training
programs in arboriculture. Publishes *Treeworker, Tree Care Industry,* and *The Reporter.* Referrals to
member arborists. Resource for
videos and other materials.
natlarb.com/tips.htm
The association's online "Tree Care
Tips and Most Frequently Asked
Questions" (for consumers).

Society of Municipal Arborists
7000 Olive Boulevard
St. Louis, MO 63130
(314) 862-1711
urban-forestry.com/
Society of city arborists and landscapers. Publishes *City Trees* bimonthly newsletter. Provides
referrals to member arborists.

PUBLICATIONS

Gilerson, Linda, Pam Pierce, and Miranda Smith. *Rodale's Pest and Disease Problem Solver.* Rodale, 1996.

Gilman, Edward F. *An Illustrated Guide to Pruning.* Delmar, 1997.

Haller, John M. *Tree Care: A Comprehensive Guide to Planting, Nurturing, and Protecting Trees.* Macmillan, 1986.

Morton Arboretum. *Selecting and Planting Trees.* Booklet. Ed. Gary W. Watson. Lisle, Ill.: Morton Arboretum, 1990.

New Hampshire State Forester's Office. *Planting Trees for Communities: Checklists for Success.* Brochure. By Mary K. Reynolds. Concord, NH: New Hampshire Division of Forests and Lands, reprinted 1995.

Shigo, Alex L. *Modern Arboriculture.* Durham, N.H.: Shigo and Trees Associates, 1991.

Sinclair, Wayne A., Howard H. Lyon, and Warren T. Johnson. *Diseases of Trees and Shrubs.* Cornell University Press, 1987.

Tree City USA Bulletin. Bimonthly. (Topics ranging from tree care to municipal tree laws.) National Arbor Day Foundation, 100 Arbor Avenue, Nebraska City, NE 68410.

TreePeople [Los Angeles]. *The Simple Act of Planting a Tree: A Citizen Forester's Guide to Healing Your Neighborhood, Your City, and Your World.* "TreePeople with Andy and Katie Lipkis." Tarcher, 1990. (Text on Internet. See below. Print edition available from TreePeople—see page 401.)

Watson, Gary W., and E. B. Himelick. *Principles and Practice of Planting Trees and Shrubs.* International Society of Arboriculture, 1997.

INTERNET

(See notes on Internet site addresses under main "Internet Sites" section.)

ag.uiuc.edu/archives/phc/
International Society of Arboriculture. Launch point for the Arboriculture and Plant Health Care tree-discussion group archives. Lots of help from tree growers in the know.

arb.ncsu.edu/yearinTrees/yearinTrees.html
J. C. Raulston Arboretum, University of North Carolina. *The Year in Trees: Superb Woody Plants for Four-Season Gardens.* From a collection by Dr. Kim Tripp based on data from the J. C. Raulston Arboretum, Raleigh, N.C. Text only.

arborday.org/planting/planting.asp?event=#city_trees
National Arbor Day Foundation. *Nine Things You Should Know About Trees.* Nine quick illustrated tips on tree planting and care.

ci.chi.il.us/WorksMart/Environment/CityTrees/
Illinois Department of Natural Resources, Division of Forest Resources. *City Trees: The City of Chicago's Guide to Urban Tree Care.* Advice to citizens for selecting, planting, and caring for trees in the region.

crfg.org/pubs/frtfacts.html
California Rare Fruit Growers. *Fruit Facts.* Lively site for amateur growers of edible-fruit trees in warm zones. History, lore, and ample notes on care and cultivation.

deja.com/
Powerful index to online discussion. Search by specific tree species or tree topics. Much discussion pertaining to tree care (and bonsai).

floridaplants.com/trees.htm
Florida Plants Online. *Guide to Florida Plant Life.* Trees. Gathering of informative sites on Florida-region trees and their care.

gardenweb.com/forums/trees/#instruct
Gardenweb. *Garden Forum: Trees.* Online exchange on how to grow and care for trees, recommended selections, plant sources, etc.

greenindustry.com/search/aa.asp
Searchable archive of *Arbor Age* magazine. Tree-care articles by and for professional arborists.

mortonarb.org
Plant information from The Morton Arboretum.

msue.msu.edu/msue/imp/moduf/masteruf.html
Michigan State University Extension. *Urban Forestry.* Technical information from many sources on caring for urban trees. A prototype archive.

muextension.missouri.edu/xplor/agguides/hort/g06800.htm
University of Missouri Extension. *Selecting Landscape Plants: Shade Trees.* Advice on selection and care of several types of popular trees, large and small. Part of tree-advice series including "Understanding Tree and Shrub Problems."

ag.usask.ca/cofa/departments/hort/hortinfo/trees/index.html
University of Saskatchewan College of Agriculture. *Gardenline: Trees and Shrubs.* Items on general care (e.g., pruning) for such northern species as birch and spruce.

selectree.cagr.calpoly.edu/
SelectTree for California. Selection guide for pairing trees with suitable sites. Covers some 1,500 tree types with over 3,000 photos.

treefolks.org/guide/guide.html
TreeFolks. *Tree Planting Guide.* Experienced advice from the Austin, Tex., community tree group.

treelink.org/simpleact/index.htm
TreePeople [Los Angeles]. *The Simple Act of Planting a Tree: A Citizen Forester's Guide to Healing Your Neighborhood, Your City, and Your World.* Text of this classic community-organizing guide from Andy and Katie Lipkis, originally published by Jeremy P. Tarcher, 1990. Includes technical information on selection, planting, and maintenance.

vg.com/
Virtual Garden. "Mother of all gardening sites." Includes *Time-Life Plant Encyclopedia* with tree descriptions and basic care advice. Links with garden forums and related sites.

ACKNOWLEDGMENTS

The drawings animating this book are by Mary H. Phelan, Chicago artist, art educator, and illustrator whose clients include the Nature Conservancy, U.S. Fish and Wildlife Service—and me, her fortunate husband. She shares my passionate watch over the trees that grow in our city. During the last three years we have been happy to make trees the focus of our travels, weekends, and many an evening.

Christopher Dunn, director of research at The Morton Arboretum, generously answered a stranger's cry for help when *The Urban Tree Book* was a seedling in need of professional expertise. The Chicago-area arboretum, founded in 1922, is a 1,700-acre, not-for-profit botanical center with a breathtaking range of tree plantings and educational offerings. Its research programs are of world stature. *The Urban Tree Book* project fit the arboretum's goal—in part, "to encourage the planting and conservation of trees"—and Dr. Dunn opened the way for me to consult the institution's experts. His own reviews of every draft chapter, along with reviews contributed by staff members, have been an education and a salvation for this nonspecialist. His wit and good cheer, too, are deeply appreciated.

Gary W. Watson of the arboretum helped determine the trees to be included and reviewed the "Red oak" profile and "Tree Wellness" chapter. The arboretum's Kris Bachtell reviewed the "Crabapple" profile. These reviews, for which I am most grateful, prompted key revisions.

In compiling the tree profiles, I drew material from field observation and hundreds of printed and electronic sources, and although I have benefited immeasurably from the advice of the consultants, I alone am responsible for the accuracy of the final book.

I owe many thanks to Michael Stieber, administrator of the arboretum's Sterling Morton Library, and to his wise and service-oriented staff, including Rita Hassert and Peter Wang. The depth of the library's collections has been a distinct advantage for the book. Equally helpful were the Chicago Public Library staff, in particular Neal O'Shea of the CPL Sulzer Regional Library.

Rebecca Brown of the Takoma Park (Md.) Library was typical of reference librarians around the nation, who found time to help me track down a local tree story or fact.

Marya Morris of the American Planning Association was a godsend in leading me to urban forestry resources I would never have found otherwise.

City arborist Dan Condon of Santa Barbara, Calif., graciously helped me sort out the riches of California's urban trees. Master gardener Wesley Foster of Sunnyvale shared his savvy on Silicon Valley tree preferences. Mike Sullivan and Alma Hecht of San Francisco's Friends of the Urban Forest tipped me to the most common urban trees in their territory. Kevin Salamandra of Arid Zone Trees, Meza, Ariz., did the same for the Southwest region.

I thank the writers who have compiled enormous compendia of tree information essentially as labors of love, especially Arthur Lee Jacobson, Guy Sternberg, Jim Wilson, John Laird Farrar, Melanie Choukas-Bradley, and Hugh Johnson. Institutions, too, share amazing data-gathering efforts, largely on the Internet these days. Ohio State University is typical (see "Resources").

American Forests, of which I am a proud member, is an institution to inspire any tree enthusiast, urban or wilderness variety. I thank them for the millions of trees planted, and for permission to excerpt records from the American Forests *National Register of Big Trees 1998–99*.

Third-grade teacher Susan Gama of Wickford Elementary School (North Kingston, R.I.) helped me get student Felicia Hardy's permission to reprint her poem on the honeylocust. (See that profile.) Thanks, Felicia. Thanks, Sue.

Kind hosts and friends aiding our resource gathering include Robert and Sarah Hughes, Dave and Dawn Phelan, and Ann Hultgren. And all those I may have dizzily forgotten.

Finally, I thank my editor, Philip Turner, whose own love for trees was spawned in the well-forested environs of Cleveland, and my agent, Ed Knappman, who, should he ever get a chance to look up from a manuscript, could gaze upon some of New England's loveliest woodlands.

Index

Trees may be looked up by botanical or (selected) common names. Detailed indexing appears under the main common name used in this book, e.g., "box-elder." See Selected Sources, Internet Sites, and Organizations sections (not indexed) for additional resources. Terms are defined in the Glossary.

C

California planetree, 61
candle tree, 240
Caryota mitis, 365*n*
cassie, 225
Castanea dentata, 241
Catalpa (see also catalpa): 248–253;
 bignonioides, 249; *speciosa,* 249
catalpa *(see also* catalpa, northern; catalpa, southern):
 248–253; common, 249;
 flowers, 250; hardy, 249;
 infestation, 252; name, 253;
 pods, 250; 'Purpurea', 252;
 western, 249
catalpa, northern: 249; history in
 U.S., 253
catalpa, southern: 249, 251; 'Aurea',
 252; test for, 251
catalpaworm, 252
cawtawba tree, 249
cedar *(see also* cedar, deodar; cedar-
 of-Lebanon; cedar, atlas):
 336–342; African, 337; as city
 species, 339; Cyprian, 337;
 distinguishing the species, 342;
 Himalayan, 337; name, 338;
 true cedars, 338
cedar, atlas: 337, 341; 'Glauca', 342;
 'Glauca Pendula', 342
cedar, deodar: 336–340; cones, 340;
 habit, 339; in California, 338; in
 North America, 340; 'Kashmir',
 340; needles, 339; settings, 338;
 'Shalimar', 340
cedar, eastern or northern white. *See*
 arborvitae, American
cedar, western red. *See* arborvitae,
 giant
cedar-of-Lebanon: 337; ancient
 grove, Turkey, 341; and King
 Solomon's temple, 339, 341
Cedrus (see also cedar): 336–342;
 atlantica, 337; *brevifolia,* 337;
 deodara, 337; *libani,* 337
Celtis (see also hackberry): 185–190;
 laevigata, 185; *occidentalis,* 185;
 reticulata, 185
Chapman, John, 283
Charter Oak, 118

cherries *(see also* cherry): Japanese
 flowering, 254–261; Sato Zakura, 254, 256; celebrations of,
 258
cherry *(see also* cherry, 'Kwanzan';
 cherry, Yoshino): 254–261;
 apple blossom, 255; as street
 tree, 260; double Chinese, 255;
 festivals, 258; Higan weeping,
 261; Kanzan, 255; 'Okamé',
 261; Potomac, 255; propagation, 261; Sargent, 261;
 Sekiyama, 255; Somei-yoshino,
 255; white column, 255; wild
 sweet or mazzard, 261
cherry, cornelian. *See under* dogwood
cherry, 'Kwanzan': 254–259;
 'Amanogawa', 261; blossoms,
 257; foliage, 257; in Washington, D.C., 260
cherry, Yoshino: 255, 259; 'Akebono', 260; blossoms, 259; in
 Washington, D.C., 260
chestnut, American, 241; decline,
 244; edible nut, 245
Christopher Columbus White Oak,
 118
cigar tree, 249
Cocos nucifera, 362
Confederate pintree, 47, 52
conker, 243, 244
Cornaceae family, 268
cornel, white. *See* dogwood, flowering
Cornus (see also dogwood): 268–276;
 alternifolia, 268; *capitata,* 268;
 controversa, 268; *florida,* 268;
 kuosa, 268; *mas,* 268; *nuttallii,*
 268
cottontree, 78
cottonwood: 78–84; and kids, 82; as
 allergen, 83; bigleaf, 79; black,
 79; Carolina, 79; eastern, 78;
 eastern, oldest, 83; Fremont, 78;
 Great Plains, 78; liabilities, 81,
 82; mountain, 78; narrowleaf, 78;
 plains, 78; Rio Grande, 79, 81;
 'Siouxland', 84; swamp, 79;
 virtues, 80; western, 78; white, 79

Index to Illustrated Identification Features

ABOUT THE AUTHOR

ARTHUR PLOTNIK is an author and former American Library Association publishing executive who has lived among the urban forests of New York, Washington, D.C., Los Angeles, and (presently) Chicago. Among his previous works are two Book-of-the-Month Club selections on editing and expression and a prizewinning biography of Jacob Shallus, calligrapher of the Constitution, published by the National Archives. A devoted tree observer, he is a member of The Morton Arboretum and American Forests.

Illustrator MARY H. PHELAN is an award-winning artist and illustrator whose clients include the Nature Conservancy, U.S. Fish and Wildlife Service, and Chicago's Notebaert Nature Museum. She chairs the Life Drawing Department at the American Academy of Art in Chicago. A member of The Morton Arboretum, she shares a passion for urban-tree observation with her husband (the author).

THE MORTON ARBORETUM is located in Lisle, Illinois, 25 miles from downtown Chicago. It was begun in 1922 by Joy Morton, the founder of the Morton Salt Company.